W9-BED-659

Europe:
Restoring Hope

Deborah Meroff

© 2011 by Deborah Meroff

All rights reserved.
No part of this book may be reproduced in any form or by any means without permission in writing from the publisher, OM Books, Passaustr. 19, 4030 Linz, Austria.

Cover Design: Simon Specht, OM EAST (Austria)
Type and Layout by Heike Scharmann, Wetzlar (Germany)
Printed in the United States

Contents

Foreword vii

Preface ix

Section 1
Caring for the Marginalised 1

Section 2
Loving Muslims 55

Section 3
Empowering Kids and Youth 89

Section 4
Reaching Neighbours: Secular and Nominal Europeans 141

Section 5
Partnering with the Church 195

Appendix
Missions in Europe 249

Foreword

Many leaders would say that it's not enough to cast a compelling vision of the future without explaining why it is not possible and acceptable to stay where you are. Europe needs a God-given and holy discontent based on an accurate picture of its spiritual needs and challenges. This book should serve as a good guide for those who want to know more and become part of God's plan for the future of this continent.

Europe is very likely a battleground for the future of global Christianity. Although evangelical churches in other continents like South America and Africa or in countries like India or China have experienced exponential growth, Europe has gone through one hundred years of the most devastating de-Christianisation in its history. Although Europe played a crucial role in spreading and recovering the biblical gospel as a home of the Reformation and great missionary movements, today it's the greatest global exporter of secularism, atheism and ideologies hostile to Christianity and the Church. In fact, atheism and agnosticism comprise the fastest-growing religion in Europe, increasing from 1.7 million to 130 million people over the last century.

Europe needs the attention and support of the global Church. Until now, missionaries and church-planters from other continents haven't found easy answers as to how to break through to Europeans, and many are asking if trends here present a threat to Christianity worldwide. Europe is still perceived as a Christian continent by many outsiders, but growingly as post-Christian by its inhabitants. Very few would consider European people as being part of the 'unreached groups' who govern the agenda of foreign missions today. But due to the very low concentration of churches in Europe that reach out to their communities and the very few people who actively follow Jesus Christ, most of Europe is also out of reach of the true gospel, with Jesus Christ working through the lives of His followers. The current slow pace of church-planting also means that this situation is not likely to change under the status quo. Europe needs change. Europe is a region in need of mission.

Across Europe you can find two identifiable groups of Christians. Those who just see the giants in the Promised Land, who say that we can't do anything because we are too few, too weak, too small; and the soil is too hard. These are people who are paralysed by fear and resignation.—Christians with a 'grasshopper mentality' (Numbers 13:30). And then there is another group: the new 'Calebs' who see that we have in fact so many opportunities to share the gospel in Europe and so many doors open, that the only problem is not enough people ready to go and enter! The greatest battle is going on in our minds. Across my own region of Central and Eastern Europe you can find this type of younger, fearless leader; mainly among those born after the collapse of Communism or just before. They share much less of the ghetto mentality of previous Christian generations and are a dynamic force in youth ministry and more and more in church-planting and innovative Christian activities. If you are looking for this type of people, you will find many examples in this book. I am grateful to OM for gathering them.

This book is an attempt to attract appropriate attention to the actual needs of Europe and provides a more detailed picture of what is going on in various corners of this highly complex and diverse continent. As a whole it's a book of hope, with amazing stories; at the same time it is a sober and self-critical analysis.

Getting the right and balanced perception of spiritual reality in Europe is, indeed, incredibly important. Too many Christians here are victims of a 'theology of panic'—panicking about becoming a Muslim continent, panicking about losing our rights, being persecuted or discriminated against by secularists. We believers panic about losing the younger generation and the decline of church membership, and the massive influx of immigrants and being pushed out of our rightful space. We panic about homosexuality and euthanasia and losing our prominence and the church privileges we have been used to enjoying and imposing on others. But is our panic correct and our perception balanced? Has the gospel lost its power? Absolutely not.

We have become a minority, but we can learn to be a minority without an inferiority complex. We no longer live in Jerusalem where others follow our rules and laws. We live in a Babylon that needs a completely different mindset and approach. But there are many Daniels in Europe today and you are going to meet them. There is no need to panic. I hope that whoever reads the following pages will be encouraged and inspired to prayer and action. Although this is not an exhaustive analysis, it should be sufficient to allow all of us to become genuinely engaged.

Jiří Unger
President of the European Evangelical Alliance

Preface

Why a book about the needs of Europe?

That was the question I asked when Operation Mobilisation's European Area Leaders first approached me about co-ordinating this project. My job as a photo-journalist for over twenty-four years had exposed me to the needs of more than a hundred countries on five continents. Like many people, however, I tended to place Europe low on the priority list of either material or spiritual needs.

So I did a little research. Obviously there's no shortage of information about the continent, spanning every conceivable subject from wildflowers to political history. Only a comparative handful of books, however, target Europe's current spiritual status. These went some way towards raising awareness but did not serve as practical and specific guides for mobilising prayer and action.

My research began to uncover facts like these:

- 9 out of the 12 top atheist/agnostic countries in the world are in Europe.
- Of 731 million Europeans, less than 2% actively follow Jesus Christ. And at least 20 European nations have less than 1% of an evangelical presence.
- Europe's fastest-growing religion is Islam.
- The countries with the highest suicide rates in the world are in Europe: Belarus, Lithuania and Russia.
- European Union marriage rates have decreased from 6.3 marriages per 1,000 people in 1990 to 4.9 marriages per 1,000 in 2008; one-third of children in this 27-nation bloc have been born out of wedlock.
- The Netherlands became the first country in the world to legalise mercy killing in 2002, although it had actually been practiced since 1973. Doctors may now legally euthanise terminally ill, chronically ill, disabled and depressed people who ask for it. However, they also 'terminate without request or consent' 900 to 1,000 other patients each year, according to studies sponsored by the Dutch government. Belgium has also legalised euthanasia, and Swiss law permits 'private suicide facilitation,' resulting in the country becoming a destination for 'suicide tourists.'

I would hazard a guess that many Christians—even European Christians—are as unaware as I was of such disturbing truths. The proposition of the Area

Leaders to put this continent 'back on the missions map' suddenly made a great deal of sense.

Of course, tackling a project of such enormous proportions (particularly as an American, albeit one who has long resided in London) seemed highly presumptuous. I have therefore relied heavily on the information and advice of OM contacts throughout Europe. The five sections into which this book is divided are the ministry streams that the fields themselves have adopted. In order to give a broader picture of needs and solutions, however, I have deliberately invited a number of non-OM individuals and organisations to contribute to this work.

Most of the case studies and initiatives you will read about here are small, not affecting vast numbers of people; this should encourage us all as to what can be accomplished by a few. I apologise in advance for what many readers will feel are serious omissions or deficiencies. The book only represents a few of the thousands of worthy efforts being made by individuals, churches, missions and other agencies across the continent. The resource lists, as well, must be regarded only as a small selection of all that is available. I would highly recommend the use of *Operation World** as a country-by-country companion guide, containing more detailed facts and statistics about each nation's needs.

Please read these pages with an open heart.—And join me in my prayer that God will use them to jump-start further exploration and a surge of concerned action for this great continent. Europe has given so much to the world. For over 1000 years it was the heartland of Christianity. But the faith that was once central to everyday living has been pushed to the margins. I hope you will agree that the time has come to restore it to its rightful place.

Deborah Meroff

* Jason Mandryk, *Operation World,* 7th ed, (Biblica Europe), 2010.

Section 1
Caring for the Marginalised

Introduction

To the Weak, I Became Weak …

Lord, grow our compassion. I am not just talking about social engagement, but real compassion born from the Spirit living in us. Marginalised people are forgotten, uncared for, vulnerable, impaired, hurting, trafficked and enslaved. They are children of prisoners or parents with addictions; they are elderly or sick with no medical care, with diseases that cannot be healed; they are abandoned at home or dropped off at an institution. They have been hidden away because their impairment is shameful to the family. They have been forced into a life with no rights, no voice. They have been taken advantage of.

Are we interested in the fact that people like these are living right in our own communities? How can we ease their suffering, if we don't even know where they are? Let's search. Let's prepare by getting training. Let's pray. And let's make a difference in at least one life—or many.

Marginalised people are often forced to do things against their will and are often betrayed by those closest to them. Yet if we are courageous enough to go looking for these people, we will experience God's strength in new ways. We will see a hurting person smile. We will most certainly get angry with those who profit from another's pain. When we do not simply walk by but engage, the Father himself works through us.

On a winter's day in Kosovo I entered the doorway of a big old rundown terraced house and saw the woman with a patch over her eye we had seen months before. She started speaking in a rushed, local dialect.

'My daughter is now gone, she has married and her new family doesn't want me, so they've left me alone in this terrible place.'

We went on to meet another seven families and eight old people who were all alone. Some of the children were at school, while some had disabilities that kept them home. All the people were poor, many of them unhealthy. They were 'leftovers,' one person said, from the Kosovo war in 1999. Ten years later they still had no place of their own to stay; they were a liability to the state and outside every social net, but they were not being given any help by the city. They simply fought to survive.

Yes, they had permission to stay in the house, but what a house!—Drafty rooms, broken windows, revolting toilets. They explained that they gathered cold water and warmed it in their rooms to sponge bathe. We saw two rooms that had caught on fire from old, faulty electric installation.

This was our introduction to what we have since named 'the fire station house,' a house for the poor next to the city fire station. Eight kids were in school, six others sick and unable to attend. Everyone wore ragged clothing. The building had little or no lighting, and the stench of blocked sewage was everywhere. We made a mental checklist of what could be done. The next morning we asked contacts from the city water department to go and pump out the blocked sewage. We changed some pumps on the broken water system in the basement, and, together with the residents, we cleaned the bathrooms. An electrician friend was able to repair outlets and restore light to dark rooms and corridors. We fixed windows and the ladies distributed boxes of food and clothing; the children received school supplies, doctor visits and medicines.

One lady asked, 'Why do you help us? No one has cared for us since the war.'

Stela, a girl on our team, answered, 'Jesus told us to come here, and he can give you hope.'

Another lady wondered aloud, 'Who is Jesus?' and Stela smiled.

'He is a man who doesn't walk by when we cry for his help.'

I met a man who had recently been released from seven years in prison, after killing a person who held him under his unkind control. Enver had ultimately attacked the man in order to survive. He now lived in his own garbage pile and urine, broken and mentally unable to clean his room or live a normal life.

Later he told me, 'I want to do better, I just often can't.' We asked permission to clean his room and he agreed. Enver went for a long walk and we put on masks and gloves and buried his room with sawdust and lime calcium to disinfect it. By the end we had shoveled away ten big bags of garbage and filth towards a new start.

The next day I went back to his room and was amazed to see he had found a heater, a new blanket and a new coffee kettle, and had spread his old blanket on the floor as a carpet. Enver thanked us and promised he would try to do better. We prayed for him, gave him a big bag of clothes, shook his hand and left. Peter, a visiting German architect, said to me, 'He's a wounded child.' I couldn't help thinking that Enver was still being held prisoner in his spirit and needing to be freed.—*Lord, touch him!*

Hassan is an older gentleman in Kosovo who was once full of energy and strength. But an injury left him disabled, paralysed and fully reliant upon others for all his needs. Years have passed by as he lies in his bed. His sole visitors are a lady and her daughter from downstairs, also living in poverty, who cook for him and try to help in ways they can. We decided to literally pick Hassan up and carry him to the car, then drove him to our house and sat with him in the garden for a few hours. It was the first time he'd been outdoors in over two years. As Hassan smiled it seemed like Jesus, too, was smiling. *Do you see Jesus in people?*

Let me introduce you to a fifty-year-old lady named Natalia. A friend of mine, Nadya, met her for the first time in January this year. She had asked the city's Social Services Department in Montenegro who some of the poorest families were. Natalia's family was on the list so she and a friend went looking and found her in a small shack next to the railroad tracks. The woman was in bed, slowly dying of lung cancer. Her four children were with her, two boys and two girls between 9 and 16 years old. Her husband, an alcoholic, wasn't present. Since Natalia had fallen sick he came home more often but when he arrived she would find the strength to turn away from him in her bed, facing the wall.

The two women had brought gifts, food and supplies. My friend Nadya decided to give Natalia terminal care right there in her home. For the next days and weeks she visited regularly, singing songs and tending to her. The children learned the songs and the smallest boy, Boris, would then sing them to his mom. After sharing about Jesus a few times with Natalia, Nadya asked if she wanted to give her life to him. Natalia answered, yes. The next day when her husband visited again she did not turn away from him, but let him sit at her side and spoon-feed her. It was a clear act of forgiveness. Another day passed, and Nadya was there when Natalia died.

In the weeks following the OM team did some work on their small dwelling, putting in a new floor and painting the inside white. More jobs remain. The father is now at home, along with the grandmother, working and trying not to drink. The kids find it hard to go to school; they have a hard road ahead of them … *But who would have thought a little church in Montenegro would grow through a dying woman?* Natalia was one of the first three believers in this city; the three who formed the first church.—Just like the first three believers in Philippi: Lydia, a girl healed from an evil spirit, and the Philippian jailer.

It is not enough to just see a beggar and maybe give him a little food. In every town and city we need to be out in our neighbourhoods, identifying those who are marginalised. We need to find people who live alone and refugees. We need to go where homeless people live and inquire in places where children may be suffering. I have heard from Western Europeans in smaller towns who were shocked to realise that extremely poor or hurting people were living in their communities. They all exclaimed, *'I didn't think this could be happening here!'*

We should think of leaving our cars parked more often, to walk where marginalised men and women and children live and work. Only those who look for them will find them, and often, once you find one person, you will find many. As Mother Theresa said, 'Every town has its Calcutta.'

We need to find the individuals who God sees hurting. Then we need to discern which of them receive no help from others. We should contact our local police, schools and government officials to ask which people they know are most desperate and offer to help. They will often be surprised and encouraged by your interest.

Let's stop thinking that spirituality only evolves around our own lives. We should be like clean, flowing rivers, not stale marshes that just produce mosquitoes. A friend said to me last week, 'We will have heaven for hanging around with other Christians. Let's focus on those "outside" who have almost lost all hope!'

In the next pages we consider the situation of four groups of outsiders: the poor, Roma (gypsies); refugees or immigrants and trafficked persons; and HIV/AIDS-affected people. These are representative of many others who are pushed to the sidelines of European society, which we cannot unfortunately include here because of the space limitations of this book.

I don't know what picture you have of heaven, but one thing I imagine is the Lord's wedding feast with people who have suffered hurts, wounds and desperation. In appearance these men and women look as though they have been broken—like beggars, slaves, the lame and lonely—but they are now healed, complete; their eyes are shining with joy and thanks that they had been invited to the great gathering.

Paul writes, *'To the weak I became weak, to win the weak. I have become all things to all men, so that by all possible means I might save some.'*

—Dane Hanson, on behalf of OM Europe's
'Caring for the Marginalised' Stream

Immigrants and Refugees

Immigrants have changed the face of Europe.

An estimated 7 to 8 million African irregular migrants and 8.2 million Asians (27% of all migrants) now live and work on the continent, according to an independent think tank, the Migration Policy Institute.

Italy's total immigrant population now exceeds 5 million—about 8% of the whole population. It is estimated that by 2020, half of the population of France will have migrant roots (first to third-generation foreigners). In Norway, immigration in recent years has accounted for more than half of the population growth. From 1998 to 2008, non-western immigrant numbers increased 41 times more than the total population. Forty percent of pupils attending Oslo schools in 2010 were of immigrant background. And within London, England, where there are residents from all over the world, fifty nationalities have communities numbering over 10,000.

Since terms are often used wrongly or interchangeably, we ought to define them. A migrant is one who travels from one region or country to another, usually in search of work. Immigrants move from one nation to settle in another one where they are not citizens. An asylum seeker or refugee, according to the United Nations Convention's definition, is 'any person who, owing to a well-founded fear of being persecuted for reasons of Race, Religion, Nationality, Membership of a particular Social Group or Political opinion, is outside the country of his Nationality; and is unable to, or owing to such fear, is unwilling to avail himself/herself of the protection of that country.'

The asylum seeker becomes a refugee after their application to the government for asylum has been accepted.

Trafficking victims fall into yet another category, either transported against their will or going willingly after being deceived into thinking they will be given legitimate, well-paying jobs when they reach their destination. Most, instead, find themselves trapped in forced labour or prostitution.

It is thought the European Union now has as many as eight million illegal immigrants.—Around half a million more cross the borders every year.[1] And over 13,000 other men, women and children have tragically lost their lives since 1988, trying to reach a better life.[2]

While a great many who make it into Europe work hard to make a living and ultimately manage to succeed, others are frustrated, disappointed and exploited.

A recent British television documentary[3] revealed the shocking story of 'Britain's Secret Slaves,' some of the 15,000 domestic workers who are brought into the country each year (among a total of 3.5 million migrants). In hundreds of cases the passports of these maids and *au pairs* are confiscated by employers and they become virtual prisoners, forced to work eighteen or more hours per day and subjected to physical and emotional abuse.

As more and more newcomers make their way into Europe, both legally and illegally, the anti-foreign sentiment bubbling under the surface in many countries is erupting into acts of racism and xenophobia. Fear and hatred of Muslims—Islamophobia—is widespread, and attacks against Jews soared to the highest level in sixty five years in 2009, according to a study.

> When an alien lives with you in your land, do not mistreat him. The alien living with you must be treated as one of your native-born. Love him as yourself …—Leviticus 19:33, NIV

Neo-fascist and far-right political parties that openly oppose foreigners are gaining strength, and more politicians like Rome's Mayor Gianni Alemanno are being swept into power on a promise to get tough on immigrants. In September 2010 the Sweden Democrats, an anti-immigrant, far-right party with roots in the Nazi fringe, won seats in Sweden's parliament for the first time, allowing them to hold the balance of power.

Are we Christians permitting society's views to influence our thinking, or are we influencing society? If the Church does not recognise the remarkable opportunities offered by increased globalisation, it is a tragedy. Thousands of people previously unreachable with the gospel in their own countries are now on our doorsteps. God's Word admonishes us to go the extra mile in welcoming the strangers among us. If we fail to represent Jesus Christ to them, who will?

A World Apart

Most of the shoppers fingering jewels, furs and designer clothes along Zurich's elegant *Bahnhofstrasse* are blithely unaware of the trade going on just a few streets away. The majority of Swiss regard the sex and drug peddling on *Langstrasse* or 'Long Street' as an embarrassment. But the same stain darkens the streets of every city in the world.

OM's Global Action Zurich (GAZ) team was born a decade ago out of a desire to reach the troubled inner city for Christ. Increasing numbers of Swiss-owned homes in the centre were being occupied by refugees and immigrants as the former owners relocated to the suburbs. Close to one hundred nationalities now live within a few square miles. In some of the city's schools, 99% of the children have foreign backgrounds.

The Mafia had also moved in. For some years the epicentre of the drug scene was a park off Long Street, near the train station. 'Needle Park' drew dealers and users from all over Switzerland. The government finally shut it down, forcing the business to metastasise and spread to other parts of the red light area. Now officials do what they can to sanitise the image. Police cars maintain a visible presence along sex shop-lined streets. Cleaners are hired to pick up used syringes, obtainable from public vending machines for only a few francs. Card-carrying addicts are assigned places where they can get free needles and fixes, as well as showers and a place to wash their clothes. But although the situation looks controlled and most addicts appear to live normally, they are still imprisoned by their dependence on drugs.

Eventually a Methodist church near Long Street offered the use of a flat to the Global Action team and a stable network has been built. Observes a team leader, 'It's much more effective to work in a team, to be able to pray together, learn from and encourage each other. Without that we would have given up a long time ago. It's also important for the team to work alongside a church. It gives us credibility, and we can integrate our contacts into the church.'

19-year-old James from England joined GAZ because he wanted to do something worthwhile with his gap year. He spent most of his time working in a drop-in centre for drug addicts. University student Lizzie, also from England, was taking a year out to help run a club for children of mixed nationalities. Swiss team member Mario decided that when he finished he would like to plug his experience into helping youth in his home city of Bern. 'I've learned a lot,' he admitted, 'especially to be honest, and not just to play at being a Christian.'

GAZ now offers a training programme of six to twenty-four months. During the recruits' first eight weeks of orientation, experienced social workers ground them on different facets of inner city ministries such as working with children, teens, addicts and sex workers. After this trainees may decide where they want to focus their time.

Swiss nurse Andrea chose to volunteer at a Salvation Army drop-in centre in the red-light district. 'Sometimes you're tempted to think street people are less than you,' she admitted. 'But once you get to know them, you don't think that anymore. When I first met Angela she was always crying. She had lost her son and was very depressed. She wanted to kill herself. Someone told me I should visit her. I didn't want to but finally two of us went and asked if we could pray for her. A week later we saw Angela, and she was smiling! "When you prayed, something changed in me," she told us. God surprised me! I didn't really expect anything to happen. Sometimes a change takes months and years, sometimes it happens fast! We still visit and read the Bible with her.'

GAZ leaders stress, 'You don't have to have a big and expensive programme to help people, and you don't have to be specially gifted. You just have to be open to learn, to listen, to spend time with people and give them part of your life.'

Spending time may mean something as simple as dishing up food at a soup kitchen or at the church's weekly spaghetti luncheon. Practical service is a fundamental part of GAZ. Once the team even scrubbed the blood-spattered phone booths near a syringe-vending machine, where addicts customarily shoot drugs into their overstrained veins. Another time, in an exercise to help them see sex workers as real people, they personally handed each woman a rose.

One team member still remembers how deeply touched she was by the expression on those women's faces. 'In the past I was always very negative about missionaries,' she said. 'I always believed they went to places like the Congo and destroyed the culture. I never thought of being one myself! But where God uses me isn't so important, as how. My heart is for the underprivileged.'

The following true story of a Thai immigrant in Switzerland, written by Global Action Zurich team member Debora Grunenwald, is typical of many others who have moved to Western Europe. Let's pray that God's Church will be motivated to reach out to the refugees, the outcasts and poor on the back streets of cities all over the world.

No Longer Alone

Today Sompong's day had been spent as usual, sitting in a tiny booth at the entrance to a sex cinema on one of Zurich's sidestreets. It wasn't exactly comfortable in this cramped, windowless space. In front of her was a pane of glass with a semi-circular opening through which the mostly-male visitors to the cinema could dismissively thrust their entry fee. Others passed without paying her any attention. Only occasionally did anybody actually exchange a word or two with her.

The prospect was pretty dismal. Still, this was the only place in the cinema that offered anything close to a welcoming atmosphere; a slightly softer stool, a TV, and something to drink. Enough to survive on from one day to the next. Whenever she left the room, she was surrounded by images of naked women in various poses. All that awaited her outside was the gaudy goings-on of the red light district.

In truth, Sompong was thankful. At least here she had a fixed income. It wasn't much, but at least her boss paid her social security and insurance deductions. In this line of work that couldn't be taken for granted. Of course, she had to work hard to earn it. Every day she left her home early and returned after midnight. Often she worked in the home of the sex cinema's owner, taking care of the children, cooking or cleaning. She also had to go to the cinema at some point during the day and work until the early hours of the morning. Not exactly the job she'd dreamed of, but in the end she would have paid off her debts. Maybe then she would be able to improve her situation.

Back in Thailand where she had grown up, Sompong had trained as a police officer. She was an independent young woman, valued by her family who, though by no means well off, did not live in poverty. But then came the day that she had shot a man. The killing was in self-defence; nobody had charged her with a crime. But despite this fact the memory haunted her. Hadn't she been trained to protect human life, not take it? The knowledge that a man was dead because of her actions weighed increasingly on her conscience. When it became unbearable, she resigned from the police force. She hadn't known exactly what path her life should take next so it seemed a good choice to travel to her sister's home in Switzerland, a country she knew a little from previous visits. Perhaps a door would open for her there. As it did, when she met Hans.

Hans was the man of her dreams. By marrying him the door to stay in Switzerland was well and truly opened. Sompong was content to stay at home as his wife, taking care of his home. At the same time they built up a diamond-importing business together. Sompong took out the guarantees for the diamonds in her name, a very risky action as the gems were of inestimable value; but Sompong didn't care. With Hans at her side she felt safe and happy … right up until the day that he disappeared. It seemed that he'd run off to Thailand.—Of all places, Thailand! But that wasn't all. Hans hadn't travelled alone. With him was a young Thai lady, his new girlfriend, and he'd made off with all the diamonds for which Sompong had provided security. How could she pay off the mountain of debts she was now responsible for?

She'd had no choice but to accept whatever work she could get, in order to earn some money. But in Switzerland that was no simple matter. Hans had never encouraged her to learn German since they could understand each other perfectly well without it. But with no knowledge of German, it was practically impossible to get a well paid position. This was how she had finally landed in the job in which she now found herself.

Perhaps, she thought, somebody would stop by tonight and brighten her miserable evening. Her sister regularly popped by on her bicycle to chat, usually bringing Sompong something to eat. But there were also other people who came by from time to time; religious people who believed in God and Jesus. But they rarely mentioned their faith. Instead, the two women from the Salvation Army spent their time helping her to fill out forms and arranging for her to get to doctors. Others simply came to exchange a few words with her, or offered to pray for her. She let them do so. It couldn't hurt, could it? Most of all, however, she appreciated visits from Melanie, who had become a part of her family. Melanie regularly brought her pictures and used them to help her to learn German. Sompong worked very hard to memorise the new words and accompanying pictures every week. Every seven days she learnt eight to ten new words. In return, Melanie let her paint her nails for her. With Melanie she wasn't just someone in need, a burden; she could use her own hands to give something back. And her growing vocabulary helped her to live increasingly independently in this land and its culture.

The freedom this gave her was astonishing. She was sick of being treated as though she wasn't bright enough to go shopping by herself! Police on the street regarded her as a whore. Just because she worked in this district did not automatically mean that she prostituted herself! She decided it was time for a break and impulsively caught a bus that would take her out of the city. The nearby woods were the perfect place for her to stretch her legs and think things through.

As she got off the bus a short time later, however, her attention was drawn away from the woods. A group of people were standing nearby, radiating a sort of happiness. Somehow these people reminded her of Melanie. She followed them and soon saw them go into a large building. By the entrance was a noticeboard with a website, www.hoffnung.ch. 'Hoffnung,' she knew, was the German word for hope. Was there some kind of hope to be found inside this building? Why not just have a look, she thought? It wasn't as though she had anything to lose. She entered the building and found herself being greeted in a friendly manner. Someone else found her a headset which translated everything that was being said into Thai for her. It was a church, but she was so excited that she decided to bring her friend with her next time.

Months have passed, and Sompong continues to attend the church she happened upon. Her situation cannot in all honesty be said to have improved. In fact, if anything it has gotten worse because she has a different boss who wants to pay her less. But somehow she keeps going. There are people who are helping to guide her on this new way—and she wants to learn more about this God she has discovered! This *hope* for the future.

Ethnic Minorities

OM UK's Lifehope teams reach out to Polish, Chinese and other nationalities, particularly in the Birmingham area. The Chinese are now a substantial minority in many EU countries, particularly Belgium, France, Italy, the Netherlands and United Kingdom. Titus Koon shares below the opportunities that exist for reaching out to this large people group, and how Christians can be more effective in friendship evangelism.

Reaching Out to Chinese Immigrants

1.7 million migrants living in Europe are Chinese. The United Kingdom's National Census report of 2001 listed the Chinese population at 247,403 (approximately 0.5% of the overall population). Today the number is nearly 500,000. More than ninety percent of this growth was due to net migration.

The majority of Chinese immigrants have not traditionally integrated into mainstream society, either because of linguistic barriers or their intention not to remain in the country. A large number of Chinese students come to study each year (a million in all of Europe) and remain only a limited time. However, as the population has expanded, descendants of the original immigrants have begun to bridge the gap between Chinese and British cultures.

In 2002, my wife Bonnie and I arrived from Hong Kong to start the Chinese ministry at OM Lifehope. Our goal was to reach out to different Chinese communities in Britain, particularly in the midlands area. We linked up with existing Chinese churches, helping them with training and evangelism and mobilising them for world mission. We also began to conduct street evangelism, following up contacts with personal visits which then sometimes lead to Bible study groups. These activities give us opportunities to reach Chinese labourers and university students.

During the initial stage of the ministry we had a special experience. It started with a single gospel tract handed out along with hundreds of others on the streets by OM evangelist Stewart Smith. A couple from mainland China took the tract, read it, and wrote back to the reply address, giving their contact details. Seeing the Chinese name, Stewart passed on the details to us. We visited this couple for several months and studied the Bible with them. The wife had attended church but she was not very clear about what she believed. I was able to help her and she made a profession of faith. Her husband, however, was resistant. He was a deep-thinking, logical person and when I challenged him to make a commitment he refused.

One day this man called and asked us to visit. He told us that he and his wife were planning to move and, since they had just bought a second-hand car, they had decided a few days before to go for a drive and look for new accommodation. He was driving slowly, with his newly-pregnant wife in the passenger seat, but neglected to see a stop sign. Another car crashed into him, flew over the top of his car, rotated 360 degrees and skidded for thirty metres. The driver had to climb out of a window to escape from his wrecked vehicle.

Both cars were complete write-offs, but, incredibly, all three people walked away without an injury. This man could not believe what had happened, and realised that there really was a loving God who had not only protected his family, but the other driver. God had proven himself trustworthy! He explained that in the past he could not logically debate with me and could not convince himself to believe in God. After that accident, however, he knew that he had encountered God and was eager to make a complete surrender.

We were thrilled to learn how the Lord had brought this couple to himself. We continued to meet with them for Bible study and they settled down in a Chinese church, where they were later baptised.

However, the story does not end there. The family has experienced hard times since coming to Christ. The husband stands firm in faith but his wife, after having three young children, finds it harder to cope with life's situations in faith. She speaks very little English and hasn't made many friends. Attending the Chinese church is difficult because it's far from their home.

Recently the husband had a severe illness and has just recovered enough to do a half day's work. He is attending a local English-speaking church which is feeding him with the Word of God.

This is a common problem. The Chinese are scattered in the UK, and making the journey to a Chinese church is not always easy. Most are not able to settle into local English-speaking churches because of language and cultural differences.

So instead of inviting them to church, we often have to go and minister to them where they are. Not everyone has such dramatic experiences, of course, but all have their own stories. Each person needs care and support. With our very limited manpower we pray that God will send more loyal workers to reach the Chinese in this country, and lead them to become disciples of Christ. We also pray that local churches will do more to absorb this foreign community, particularly the younger second generation.

Our vision is to mobilise people for reaching Chinese, and at the same time mobilise Third Culture Chinese to get involved in world mission. OM embraces the world, providing many opportunities and a good network. Over the last few years some British-born Chinese we know have joined OM short-term mission trips to reach non-Chinese communities overseas.

Since 2006, our Chinese team has also been reaching Chinese beyond Britain through short-term outreaches. We have travelled to Paris, Sweden, Denmark, Finland and Italy. Most of these trips were co-organised with local Chinese churches. During OM's Transform 2010 initiative, an outreach team was arranged through missionaries in Prato, Italy, where one-fourth of the population is Chinese. The team was composed of Chinese believers from British Chinese churches and the Prato Chinese Church, members of OM Lifehope and other recruits. We were glad to see God using not only Chinese but four Westerners in Chinese ministry. A total of forty-one Chinese accepted Christ during this outreach!

Eight Basic Principles for Reaching Chinese and other Asians

1. Adopt a gentle and humble approach and keep a respectful attitude.
   Asian people like harmony and politeness, so using an aggressive manner in trying to convince them to accept your beliefs will not be acceptable.

2. Building relationships is essential.
   Learn to be a good listener and learner. Take time to really know and understand your new friends.

3. Practice hospitality!
    Inviting friends home for tea or coffee or a meal is a natural part of the
    Asian culture, and one of the best ways to build bridges.

4. Offer practical help.
    Moving house is a challenge for us all, but think of the difficulties of
    arriving in a foreign country. Newcomers will be grateful for advice in
    finding accommodation, schools, the best places to shop, to make re-
    pairs, receive medical care, and so forth. Some may also appreciate help
    in improving their new national language.

5. Be open to exchange opinions and compare cultures.
    A readiness to share about the strengths and weaknesses of your culture
    as well as genuine interest in listening to the differences in your friends'
    culture will go far. Try to talk about your thoughts concerning different
    matters without implying that your way is the only way.

6. When speaking about sins and spiritual needs, admit to your own fail-
    ures and struggles first of all.
    Instead of directly saying, 'You are a sinner,' say, 'I am a sinner. We are
    all sinners against God;' otherwise your listeners will think you are rude,
    and stop listening. The Asian culture is never confrontational.

7. Beware of nationalism.
    Avoid negative comments about the persecution of Christians and other
    policies in your friend's home country. We in the Western world are
    interested in these topics but our knowledge of the actual situation is
    in fact very limited. Touching upon sensitive areas could generate hard
    feelings.

8. Let new believers know they will need to count the cost of becoming a
    Christian.
    Many new Chinese believers rejoice to receive blessings from God, but
    when they face difficulty they easily lose their faith. Make sure they
    consider all that it means to be a disciple of Christ; that it won't exempt
    them from hard times, but they will be able to draw strength from God
    to overcome.

Human Trafficking*

- 12.3 million adults and children in today's world are slaves to forced labour, bonded labour, or prostitution.
- Officials estimate that more than 200,000 women and girls are smuggled out of Central and Eastern Europe and the former Soviet republics each year. The majority of them end up working as enslaved prostitutes. Almost half are transported to Western Europe. Roughly a fourth end up in the United States.
- 77% of trafficked persons are minors. 75% of trafficked women are from Eastern Europe. 75% have never before been sex workers.
- A woman purchased in Bulgaria for two or three thousand Euros can be sold to a bar owner in Macedonia where he can use her to make between ten to fifteen thousand Euros in one month.
- Between 200,000 and 400,000 women from Moldova have been sold into the sex trade since the collapse of the Soviet Union; up to 10% of its female population.
- A significant percentage of individuals engaged in prostitution in the Netherlands are, reportedly, trafficking victims—mostly young girls sold by Moroccan and Turkish pimps. The sex industry in the Netherlands is estimated to make almost $1 billion each year. It is a major Western European destination country for trafficked women, with 2,000 brothels and numerous escort services, using an estimated 30,000 women, 68–80% of whom are from other countries.
- Government figures suggest that approximately 80,000 individuals in the UK are involved in the sex industry. 4,000 more girls are forced into the trade every year; over 85% of brothel worker are of foreign origin. Each one is sold for around 36,000 Euros. Traffickers make 360 million Euros per year.
- 104 countries are without laws, policies or regulations to prevent victims' deportation.

* Sources: U. S. Department of State Trafficking in Persons Report, United Nations Office on Drugs and Crime (UNODC) Global Report on Trafficking in Persons. UK Channel 4 documentary, 'The Hunt for Britain's Sex Traffickers,' 31 Aug. 2010. Human Trafficking Search <http://www.humantraffickingsearch.net>.

> But this is a people plundered and looted, all of them trapped in
> pits or hidden away in prisons. They have become plunder, with
> no one to rescue them; they have been made loot, with no one
> to say, 'Send them back.'—Isaiah 42:22, NIV

Sex and the City

The illegal trade in human beings is a multi-billion dollar industry and the top human rights issue of the 21st Century. Adults and children are procured, transported and used against their will for sexual exploitation, forced labour or begging; even, most shockingly, for body parts. Athens was chosen as a representative study for this book because it is one of Europe's major hubs for immigration and trafficking.

Sex was a booming business in Greece's capital and main port even back in ancient days. The country has now legalised prostitution, and Athen's skin trade has increased tenfold during the last decade. Yet out of some twenty thousand full and part-time sex workers, only about one thousand are legal.

One in four Greek men regularly pay for sex. 24-hour-a-day brothels with white lights above their doorways are easy to find, even around the corner from the city's most glitzy hotels. Customers only pay fifteen Euros a visit; about half that amount actually goes to the girls. Other sex workers take their clients from streets or bars to cheap hotels. The great majority of women involved, however, are not Greek. According to estimates there are thirteen to fourteen thousand trafficking victims in the country at any given time, including a thousand between the ages of thirteen to fifteen. Most come from Eastern Europe—Russia, Moldova, Ukraine, Bulgaria, Romania, Albania—and Nigeria.

The EU's open borders have made it easy for traffickers to move girls around. And Nigeria has its own powerful—and highly lucrative—criminal ring. Although it may cost traffickers a thousand Euros to transport girls to their destination cities, they will force their victims to pay them up to eighty thousand Euros. And they are kept in line by the strong hold of voodoo oaths—and threats to their families.

Traffickers typically lure their victims to the city with false promises of jobs. Other girls are entrapped by 'lover boys,' pimps who talk convincingly of marriage and groom them before they're pushed into prostitution. Perhaps forty percent of sex workers are saddled with massive debts to repay. And then there are the women kept under lock and key, slaves controlled by violence. Some of them bear tattoos or other marks to indicate ownership. Without passports or identity papers, there is little chance of escape.

Joanna Bassham, who pioneered OM's work in Greece, met up with a fledgling New Life outreach ministry of International Teams about six years ago. The goal of New Life, or *Nea Zoi* in Greek, is to support and restore individuals involved in prostitution by addressing their physical, emotional and spiritual needs. Staff and volunteers offer their friendship along with practical help to develop exit strategies, cooperating with local officials and partnering with the local church.

When Joanna moved to Athens at the end of 2004 she began accompanying the team on some of their weekly late night outreaches; visiting brothels and street workers, distributing hot drinks and helpful literature in many languages.

'What we hope for is that girls will see their real value,' explains New Life team leader Emma Skjonsby-Manousaridis. She downplays their achievements, saying that it's only God who transforms. 'We care for the people He brings into our lives, but really we're just called to be faithful.—To show up! And sometimes we're witnesses to a miracle.'

Some girls who receive New Life cards keep them as long as a year or two before going for help. Volunteers speak a variety of East European languages. Young Bulgarian Dena tells of meeting a girl with an evangelical church background who had been trafficked to Athens. Dena was able to help her find a safe place and, eventually, a job.

But such happy endings are rare. When a Greek fifteen-year-old we'll call Lila was sexually abused by her aunt and uncle, she turned to her parents. They didn't believe her and threw her out. Lila met a man who gave her a baby and then left her. She met another man who put her in a brothel. Her earnings bought him a house and a motorcycle. But after getting infected with a sexually transmitted disease, Lila called Dena to ask for a way out.

Finding regular jobs for girls who have been involved in prostitution is difficult, but Dena managed to get her cleaning work. Failure to appear for a court hearing, however, landed Lila in jail for four months. Her boyfriend never visited, and Dena's attempts to see her failed. Lila cut her wrists twice after being abused by women inmates. When she got out she was bitter against God and man. By this time she was twenty-four. With no place to go Lila went back to work at a brothel.

'She told me it would only be temporary', sighed Dena. 'But that's what they all say.'

If women in prostitution are marginalised by society, transvestites and trans-sexuals on the streets are pushed to the very 'edge of the edge.' Joanna Bassham felt God's compassion stir within her when she realised how few people ever tried reaching out to them.

It took Joanna and the team several years of building relationships before she could start a Bible study for these men. Now a small group eagerly gathers around the Scriptures each week to ask questions.—And they are keen to bring their friends. 'They are really counting the cost,' Joanna observed, 'and some have even agreed to cut back on their working hours as a first step.' One of the group has acknowledged, 'If I did this God thing, there's a lot I'll have to give up.'

More Christian organisations and churches are beginning to tackle the plight of sex workers in Europe's major cities. In Vienna, another big trafficking centre, an inter-church team regularly ministers in the red light area. Prostitution is legal in Austria; in fact, brothel visits are sometimes advertised as part of a package for businessmen travelling to Vienna. And because the capital city borders other countries, many women travel there by train just to solicit customers overnight in the underground. Some are single mothers working to feed their families.

The irony is, explains a member of OM's Anti-Trafficking Network (ATN), Eastern Europeans can live in Germany and Austria, but they can't legally work there—except in prostitution. They can go on the streets because there's a special category that allows sex workers. So the system gives them few choices.

Police have advised the team to be on the watch for increasing numbers of boys being trafficked from the Czech Republic for the sex trade. And just as in Greece and other countries, large quantities of Nigerian girls are being exploited. Christian workers report meeting many with evangelical backgrounds. In fact, they have held Bible studies with them in a van before they go off to ply their trade!

'I've never given out so many Bibles in different languages in my life!' muses an ATN volunteer. She adds that some sex workers ask her to put the Book into their bag; they do not want to touch it themselves until they can go home and shower.

Emma of New Life believes the logical place to attack this ever-growing criminal industry is in the countries of origin, raising awareness and reaching out in those places to the abused and vulnerable, the children at risk, the poverty-stricken and minorities. Deal with problems at the root, she points out, and there would be no need to clear up the mess at the other end.

Education is certainly a critical factor. For instance, the issue of HIV/AIDS isn't much talked about in the 'shame' culture of Greece.—Many Greeks actually believe that only African people can contract the disease! But the fact that cities and even their officials sometimes profit from the sex business, and are therefore unwilling to act, makes it mandatory that people of integrity take up the challenge.

'We hear church people all the time exclaiming, "I could never do that!"' smiles Joanna Bassham. 'They can't imagine what to say to people on the streets. But when they try it, they realise they can do it.'

Perhaps a deeper question is whether churches are ready to open their doors to the marginalised—the homeless, alcoholics, druggies and sex workers. Joanna thinks that's a problem in every country. 'They expect people to change overnight when they get saved. But people who have struggles don't suddenly change. So how will they find Christ? And if they do find Him where can they go to grow as a Christian, if not the church?'

Christians cannot afford to sit on the sidelines. They must once again become God's hands, His feet, His voice.—Because they alone carry a message that can transform people both now and eternally.

A Shield of Faith and a Shield from Harm

Opposing the Evil of Sex Trade Trafficking

—By *Commissioner Helen Clifton, The Salvation Army World President of Women's Ministries*

Take up the shield of faith, with which you can extinguish all the flaming arrows of the evil one.—Ephesians 6:16

He is a shield to those that take refuge in him.—Proverbs 30:5

The 'shield' emblem of The Salvation Army's mission takes on a powerful and biblical significance when associated with opposing the twin evils of commercial sex exploitation and human trafficking.

The sex industry makes a cheap commodity of the most sacred and intimate of human relationships. Opposing this abuse is a core issue for The Salvation Army. In recent years, trade in vulnerable women has reached a scale that shocks the world. Still, modern culture accepts the existence of brothels, massage parlours, lap-dancing clubs, sex tourism and pornography available at the click of a button, all in the name of freedom and personal choice.

In fact, freedom is the last word which should be associated with these matters. Many women, girls, men and boys are trapped in an underworld of crime and fear, disguised by a veneer of glamour and easy money. The slave trade flourishes everywhere, bringing cheap labour across borders, enticing and coercing vulnerable people into working for minimal wages and keeping very young women in conditions of fear and exploitation.

Prevention, protection, prosecution—and prayer—are key elements in the battle. The Salvation Army, with its international networks and influence, joins others in the fight against an evil which touches nearly every country on earth. Prevention includes education, awareness-raising and empowerment. Those who are most poor are most vulnerable to being trafficked or having their children trafficked. Therefore, every programme which encourages independence, self-worth and freedom of choice is a plank in our strategy.

Prevention also means fighting the demand—and here we face the sad truth that many 'customers' who pay for sex acts are neither poor nor uneducated. However, their education falls short of teaching them that the women apparently available for their pleasure are hurting and trapped in an evil trade from which there is no easy exit. Pornography is often a factor, being addictive, presenting women as objects, destroying healthy relationships and creating the demand for more and more novelty and younger and younger girls. This culture leaves the door wide open for exploitation and crime.

Protection includes seeing trafficked individuals as victims or survivors, to be cared for and rehabilitated rather than left to fend for themselves and face probable retrafficking. Safe accommodation, with due attention to risk factors, is crucial and the Salvation Army has a professional record in this field. Support required for housing victims of trafficking includes access to legal advice, language facilities, health services, trauma counselling and activities which help recovery. Repatriation may be necessary and The Salvation Army's international or state-wide services come into play here.

Prosecution of perpetrators means advocating for laws and policies which enable and resource police to intervene and punish offenders, across national boundaries. Education also needs to be in place in prisons where men (and some women) involved in criminal networks have a chance to break the cycle of evil in which they are embroiled.

The Salvation Army is addressing these issues in more and more places, is fundraising for women and is ready to work day and night for the care of victims. It has a history of opposing sex slavery, particularly in the UK (1885) and Japan (1900). Today, protective programmes are in place in the USA, where the Army has been particularly active in advocacy at the heart of government, and where internet tools have been developed for training and reporting. In the UK, awareness-raising and fundraising have accompanied victim support and a dedicated safe house has been open for more than four years. In Africa, training and safe houses are being established, especially in Malawi and the Democratic Republic of Congo. The Philippines, Bangladesh, Sri Lanka and India are a few more countries where The Salvation Army is working in this vital area. The Army in Canada and Australia has also become active in seeking out opportunities to oppose human trafficking and to care for the victims and so has Switzerland. It is appropriate that combating trafficking for commercial sex exploitation should be one of the priorities for an Army whose shield remains a symbol of faith, spiritual warfare and protection of the weak (Ephesians 6:16 and Proverbs 30:5).

For a number of years the international leaders of The Salvation Army, General Shaw and Commissioner Helen Clifton, have called the worldwide Salvation Army to pray for the victims of sex trade trafficking. Some of the actions around the world prompted by this Call to Prayer have been:

- in Chicago, a Salvationist student made 800 copies of the prayer postcard and distributed them to fellow students at her university
- in London, a Salvationist took anti-trafficking campaign postcards into his place of work and spoke about them to colleagues
- Commissioner Nancy Roberts took postcards and a poster to the City of London Boys' School, which is across the way from International Headquarters
- in Sri Lanka, every person in the congregation at Colombo Central Corps lit a candle with the Bible verse 'Arise, Lord, lift up your hand! Do not forget the helpless!'
- in Nairobi, women leaders from 14 countries were attending a Salvation Army conference. Recognising the enormity of the catastrophe of human trafficking in Africa, they held a prayer meeting and came together in fervent prayer and heartfelt pleading with God for His guidance.

→ Check out the Salvation Army site and other organisation
websites below to learn how you, too, can be involved in
advocacy campaigns to change laws as well as awareness-raising,
prevention projects and shelters.

Resources—Human Trafficking

Also see resource list under 'Advocacy and Human Rights' in the 'Partnering
With the Church' section.

■ Websites

- Beyond the Streets (UK)   http://beyondthestreets.org.uk

- Captive Daughters   www.captivedaughters.org

- CHASTE   www.chaste.org.uk
  [Churches Alert to Sex Trafficking Across Europe]

- Coalition Against Trafficking in Women
                                       http://catwinternational.org

- ECPAT   www.ecpat.net
  [End Child Prostitution, Child Pornography and Trafficking of Children for
  Sexual Purposes]

- Faith Alliance Against Slavery & Trafficking (FAAST)
                                       www.faastinternational.org

- HumanTrafficking.org   http://humantrafficking.org

- Human Trafficking Search   www.humantraffickingsearch.net

- International Christian Alliance
  on Prostitution   www.icapglobal.org

- International Rescue Committee   www.theirc.org

- Project Rescue (Moldova)   www.projectrescue.com

- Shared Hope International   www.sharedhope.org

■ Stop the Traffik   www.stopthetraffik.com
  (website available in many languages)

■ Suggested Reading

2010 Trafficking in Persons Report, released by the office to Monitor and Combat Trafficking in Persons, 2010. www.state.gov/g/tip/rls/tiprpt/2010

Bales, Kevin. *Ending Slavery: How We Free Today's Slaves.* University of California Press, 2007.

Batstone, David. *Not for Sale: The Return of the Global Slave Trade—and How We Can Fight It.* HarperOne, 2007.

Carson, Dr. Marion and Ruth Robb. Working the Streets: A Guide for Christians Engaged in Outreach to Prostitutes. YWAM Publishing, 2003

Chalke, Steve. *STOP THE TRAFFIK: People Shouldn't Be Bought & Sold.* Lion, 2009.

De Stoop, Chris. They are so Sweet, Sir. Limitless Asia, 1994.

Ivison, Irene. *Fiona's Story.* Virago,1997.

Jewell, Dawn Herzog. *Escaping the Devil's Bedroom; Sex Trafficking, Global Prostitution, and the Gospel's Transforming Power.* Monarch, 2008. Lee, Maggy. *Human Trafficking.* Willan, 2007.

Malarek, Victor. The Natashas: Inside the New Global Sex Trade. Arcade Publishing, 2005.

Prostitution and Sex Trafficking, a free practical guide for churches with suggested action points; Signpost Series 3, the National Christian Alliance on Prostitution (NCAP) http://www.ncapuk.org/documents/Signpost_3.pdf

Waugh, Louisa. *Selling Olga: Stories of Human Trafficking and Resistance.* Phoenix, 2007.

Yankoski, Mike and Danae Yankoski. *Zealous Love: A Practical Guide to Social Justice.* Zondervan, 2009.

■ Other Resources

■ *'Demand'*   www.sharedhope.org/Media/
                                                VideoResources.aspx
16 minute (or shortened version) documentary video by Shared Hope
International about trafficking in several countries, available to view online in
English, German and Japanese.

■ *'Lilya 4-Ever'*
(PAL format DVD, 109 minutes, Russian with English subtitles) Harrowing
story about a Russian teenager abused and exploited. Tough watching but
recommended by CHASTE. Available from AMAZON or other outlet.

■ *'More Precious than Gold'*   www.unicef.org.uk/campaigns/robbie/
                                                video.asp
Short DVD about child trafficking distributed by UNICEF, available to view
online.

■ *'Wanted'*   www.youtube.com/watch?v=uTf4b_
                                                bckew&feature=channel_page
Compelling short film by Marie Vermeiron featuring 5 survivors of
prostitution, produced by the European Women's Lobby and Coalition Against
Trafficking in Women.

■ *'How You Can Stop the Traffik'*   www.stopthetraffik.org/resources
Films, quiz, song, Bible study, banner and other resources.

■ Salvation Army   www.salvationarmy.org, www.iast.net
Resources on site. An email service with news and information concerning sex
trafficking, commercial sexual exploitation of women, hyper-sexualisation of
culture, and human rights abuses against women is also available. This has a
U.S. emphasis but they do frequently distribute international news. To join
people should email their request to: anti_sextrafficking@usn.salvationarmy.
org. The Army also encourages an Anti-trafficking Day of Prayer on the last
Sunday of September each year. See their website for further information.

Resources—Immigrants and Refugees

Also see resource list at the end of the 'Loving Muslims' section of this book, especially regarding the multi-language media that is available.

■ Suggested Reading

Billy Graham Evangelistic Association. *Friendship Evangelism: Reaching Others for Christ Through Involvement in Operation Andrew.* Downloadable PDF from www.billygraham.org website.

Boyd, David. *You Don't Have to Cross the Ocean to Reach the World: The Power of Local Cross-Cultural Ministry.* Chosen, 2008.

Glaser, Ida and Shaylesh Rajah. *Sharing the Salt: Making Friends with Sikhs, Muslims and Hindus.* Scripture Union, 1999.

Lane, Patty. *A Beginner's Guide to Crossing Cultures.* IVP, 2002.

Phillips, Tom and Bob Norsworthy. *The World at Your Door.* Bethany House, 1997.

Thomas, Donna. *Faces in the Crowd: Reaching Your International Neighbor for Christ.* New Hope, 2008.

Wretlind, Norm and others. *When God is the Life of the Party: Reaching Neighbours Through Creative Hospitality.* Navpress, 2003.

Xuede, Fan. *Reaching out to Mainland Chinese.* Overseas Campus Magazine and Great Commission Center, 2005. Downloadable: www.oc.org/eng_txt/ReachingOutToMainlandChinese-English.pdf

■ Other Resources

▪Chinese Christians in Europe (magazine)   http://ccineurope.org

▪Churches' Commission for Migrants in Europe
                                                  www.ccme.be

▪Ethnic Harvest   www.ethnicharvest.org
  Resources for multicultural ministry.

▪Mission Training International   www.mti.org
  Offers videos and games that further cross-cultural understanding.

▪Neighbours Worldwide (UK)   www.wec-int.org.uk/index.
                                              php?option=com_content&view=article
                                              &id=1185&Itemid=422

WEC International outreach to unreached minority ethnic groups living in UK.

▪OMF International   www.omf.org/omf/uk/omf_at_work/
                                              omf_at_work_in_the_uk

OMF Diaspora Teams in Europe reach out to several million East Asians
(Mainland Chinese, Japanese, Thai, Vietnamese and Filipinos) in the UK,
Germany, Netherlands, and Switzerland. See their national website for the
valuable resources and training days they offer to equip you and your church for
effective outreach, or email eudmdir@omf.org.uk.

The Roma (Gypsies)

They are the most hated minority in Europe. For centuries they were seized
and imprisoned without courts even bothering to record their names. In 1530
the Diet of Augsburg ruled that Christians could legally kill them. Scores were
deported and enslaved on southern plantations in America. Under Communism
their culture was repressed, their language outlawed. In Nazi Germany they were
targeted as subhumans, along with Jews and mental patients. An estimated half
million men, women and children died in gas chambers or experiments.

We call them gypsies, a name invented by Europeans who mistakenly believed they came from Egypt. In reality the Roma people, as they prefer to be
called, originated in India. '*Rom*' means 'men' and is derived from the Indian word
'*Dom*,' meaning 'a man of low caste who gains his livelihood by singing and dancing.' Worldwide, Roma number approximately twenty million. An estimated sev-
en to fifteen million live in Europe, with the largest concentration in the Balkan
peninsula. Numbers are difficult to determine because they are often not counted
in official census statistics. However, Roma people make up between five and ten
percent of the population of many European countries. Although they used to be
known as travellers, most have now settled in one place. Only about five percent
of European Roma still live as nomads.

The Roma people represent many diverse cultures but all seem to have one
thing in common. They are almost universally despised and marginalised by soci-

ety. France admitted to deporting ten thousand Roma to Eastern Europe during 2009, and a new wave of deportations began in 2010 in spite of opposition from the European Union, Vatican and United Nations. But France is not alone. Italy, Belgium, Austria, Denmark, Sweden and Italy have also been expelling Roma immigrants. Germany has signed an agreement with Kosovo to repatriatriate 14,000 refugees, 10,000 of which are Roma.

The educational plight of many Roma children in Europe is little short of disastrous. According to a UNESCO report, as many as 50% fail to complete primary education. Over 85% of Roma children in various countries are segregated in special schools which prevents them accessing higher education and entering the labour market.[4] Very often Roma also suffer heavy discrimination when it comes to employment, health care and social services. Whole communities have been uprooted and relocated to substandard housing near garbage dumps, sewage treatment plants or industrial sites on the outskirts of cities. Up to 1990, Roma women were systematically sterilised in Czechoslovakia, and cases continued in Slovakia into more recent years. Thousands of Roma women and children today are trafficked to other countries for sex slavery or forced labour.

A 2009 European Union survey[5] revealed widespread discrimination against Roma, with officially recorded incidents only the 'tip of the iceberg' of what was actually taking place. While one in five Roma was a victim of a racially motivated crime, 79% of those questioned did not report their experiences of assault, threat or serious harassment, mostly because they didn't think it would do any good. Others did not know how to report incidents and still others feared retribution by the perpetrators. Few knew of an organisation they could turn to for support.

An OM worker described the plight of Roma in Albania: 'The kids are dirty. They wear old clothes, and many have bare feet. Their houses are mostly one-room shacks made from mud or concrete blocks. There is no indoor plumbing or water and when it rains the roofs leak. Most families have four or five children. They all live, sleep and eat in the same room. They heat and cook with wood stoves and wash all their clothes by hand. Most of the kids aren't in school and most of the parents can't read or write. When they get hurt, they rarely cry. But if you show them a little love, they'll love you back with all their hearts.'

In this country, which has 84,000 Roma, OM has helped to build a half dozen simple houses for the most destitute and a centre for street kids, 70% of whom are gypsies. Related one person, 'Some of the children were sold to child traffickers for sexual exploitation, but they ran away to try to make a living on the street. It's believed that others have had some of their organs cut out for sale on the black market, to organ clinics in Italy. The system provides an easy way for the parents to get their hands on money. Some of the girls are sold into prostitution.'

Western Ukraine near the Hungarian border has the second largest Roma community in Europe. OM's summer camps there led to a gypsy church being built. A team has also crossed into Romania to show Jesus' love to some of the 3,500 Turkish Roma living in the city of Babadag.

'I was shocked at the really low level of life for gypsies there,' observed Ukrainian Anya Matkovska. 'Some kids do not have any shoes and many of them never eat properly. Even a piece of bread is great food for them and they enjoy each little crumb. We washed them, cut their hair and cleaned the wounds on their feet. We visited poor families to give them food and played with the children. The gypsies are nominal Muslims, so I was amazed how the youth love God and want to follow him!'

The good news is that an estimated 500,000 to one million Roma people in Europe are followers of Jesus. A quarter of Roma living in France are Christians, and they now form the largest evangelical segment of the country's population. Life & Light, a branch of the Assemblies of God that majors in ministry among the Roma, claims that Spain (with the largest Roma population in Western Europe) has at least five hundred gypsy churches, and that 8% of gypsies in England, or twenty-five thousand out of three hundred thousand, are born again. So are at least 10% in Finland—one thousand out of ten thousand. And within Eastern Europe are 2,000 Arli Roma Christians.—One church alone has 700 members who meet in a tent!

Yet the supply of Bibles and other Christian literature in Romani languages is extremely limited. OM EAST has produced *My First Bible* in Bayashi for those living in Croatia and Serbia. Only sixty percent of Bayashi children ever go to school, and of those, ninety percent drop out by age eleven. The team believes that *My First Bible* could have a profound impact on this barely literate people group. However, many more resources are urgently needed.

If transformation is to become a reality in Europe, the apartheid that exists against the Roma population—even, sometimes within the Church—must be resisted and dealt with. The next section gives a glimpse into Roma life and ministry in several different countries.

Greece: 'Rejected Like Us'

The rain is falling down as we approach the camp. The amount of rubbish increases, so we must be close. Fortunately, the rain also keeps the flies away.

We pass by the big rubbish dump, amazed to see many blankets hanging over the fence separating the street from the dump. Just thirty meters lower, the camp starts. Fifty-one families are living here, approximately 300 people.

Their shelters are creatively built with plastic and wood, old doors and windows. These are the winter houses of this nomadic Roma tribe. The people are originally from Albania, but they have already lived more than fifteen years in Greece. A worse combination is hard to imagine. Being both Albanian and gypsy means belonging to the most rejected level of society. It doesn't make any difference whether family roots are Greek or not. They seem to be a group without rights, without any legal status. No running water, no electricity. Access to schooling is denied, so the 150-plus children have no hope of advancing themselves. Together with their parents they do seasonal work, sometimes pruning vines and at other times picking olives from the thousands of trees that surround the camp. If there is no work they gather old iron which they can sell for five cents a kilo.

I look up and see a beautiful Greek village on the other side of the camp. Close, yet far away. The Roma people are not welcome there.

Vasilis, the leader of this small community, is waiting for us and we are welcomed into his tiny home. The wood stove gives some heat but rainwater drips in. The family doesn't seem to notice anymore. Several grandchildren are sitting in the room. We listen to their stories and our hearts ache for these people.

Suddenly our pastor's wife, Dhespina, takes the initiative. These people might not be able to read or write but they can listen and enjoy the pictures in her book while she tells the Christmas story. Everybody gives their full attention. And then the story comes to the point where there was no house for Mary to give birth. No bed to lie on, and no cradle for the baby Jesus.

'Worse than us,' Vasilis nods. 'Rejected like us.' He is clearly moved by the story.

As we leave the camp that day we hand over fifty-four bags of clothing. Included in each bag are three pairs of new good children's shoes which we were able to buy. It's not much, yet so important. Nobody before has ever come to their camp from outside. But God wanted his church to share His love with these people.

As we drive away, full of impressions, we start to dream. Could we somehow help these people to read and write Greek? And at the same time, could we teach them more about the God who became man—"Immanuel"—God with us?

Oh Lord, bring your peace on earth, good well to all men … including those who live behind the rubbish dump …!

—Kees den Toom, OM Greece

Czech Republic: Seeing Through Jesus' Eyes

In 2005 our family felt God wanted us to move from Holland to the Czech Republic. We needed two years to learn the basics of the Czech language and to find a more or less final place to live. It was a frustrating and very difficult time in a culture which is very different from the Dutch culture we knew. We used this time to rethink what we believe, and why. All our beliefs regarding the church and what a Christian is and how he should function were tested.

Shortly after arrival I met my first Roma. The man was working outside and I stopped the car to ask him where I could find something we needed at the time. He understood that I was a foreigner and said I would be welcome at his house to drink some coffee. One or two weeks later I decided to make that visit. It was a bit uncomfortable in the beginning, but I soon found out the family didn't have much money. We had chickens that laid more eggs than we needed, so I started dropping off some eggs each week. It was a slow process of getting to know each other. The man, who was family head, told me about the racism and fascism that existed in the Czech Republic against the Roma. It hurt me to hear this, and I decided to try to love this family in the way they needed.

As time progressed, we started to speak about the gospel of Jesus. I am not a missionary but work as a computer programmer. Still, what is inside your heart will automatically come out, though it is difficult to express it in a foreign language. You need to be careful that it is a proper expression of your thoughts and that the other person not only understands the facts you express but also the context; for instance, your motivation.

At a certain moment during a conversation with this family, I 'lost it' emotionally. Although we had spoken a lot, they still continued honouring another god: money. It hurt me that I could not give them the desire to open their hearts to

God, let alone the Lordship of Jesus. The family was shocked at my outburst and evident sadness. But it was a turning point. A few months later the family head expressed a desire to become a follower of Jesus, and this was the beginning of a spiritual awakening in his household. A few months later the man was baptised. He is currently learning about Jesus' teachings and how to practice what he learns.

Another Dutchman once said something interesting about evangelising: 'If you have never wept over the fate of the people you want to reach, you are not a good worker ... You should stop doing what you do and learn to see people through Jesus' eyes, so you can become compassionate about them (Matthew 20:34). Only then will you have the attitude you need, for you will love them as Jesus loves them.'

Through this Roma man and through other ways I later came into contact with more Roma families. The poverty, the relational problems, the ignorance about vital issues, the consequences of their sin, all disturbed me. The need for repentance becomes more and more clear in this sort of an environment, and so does the sharp contrast between sin and obedience to God.

Beginners' mistakes are unavoidable. We Westerners usually learn by reading. The Roma, however, do not. I soon discovered they like telling stories and parables as a way to gain a better understanding. Since I had thought they should read Scripture I provided Bibles, not taking into account that some read badly and try to camouflage their inability to read. After finding that out, we started a project of recording the Old Testament so people could listen to it.

A Bible society had already recorded the New Testament but it was dramatised and, I feel, reads like a fairy tale, so we will probably need to record that, too. However, I was truly amazed by the way people responded to the words of God that were read to them on CD and DVD-audio. The recording turned out to be a true blessing. Roma people are currently playing this material again and again in order to memorise the words of God. And it works! Faith comes by hearing ...

At this point in time we see new life springing up. We want to use the right strategy and are preparing to initiate a so-called 'church planting movement' where indigenous house churches will reproduce in the fast way of a movement. I am developing structured lessons for Roma people who will teach others about the foundations of faith. The lessons will be available both online and offline for reading and listening.

Roma understand the metaphors of the 'body of Christ' and 'family of God on planet earth' better than most of us.—I think they can become living examples for believers.

The Kingdom of God consists of relationships. Whereas Westerners commonly think of organisation and knowledge, the Roma focus on relationships.

Roma in the Czech Republic do not need more people to come do projects among them and then leave. What they need are believers who are dedicated to loving the Lord their God with all their heart, soul, mind and strength (Mark 12:30); so they will be able to love with the intensity that obviously comes from Him.—Workers who accept no higher authority than Jesus. The Roma need men and women who want to invest their lives into long-term relationships.

> —Written by an independent Roma worker in the Czech Republic, identity withheld by request.

Poland: Born Into God's Family through Family Camps

Our family left the U.S. and arrived in Krakow, Poland, in 2003. Within twenty-fours hours we met with a Polish couple that had been working with Roma children for several years. This couple had a 'person of peace' contact in three villages. As we went to meet these Roma people and share with them that we were there because of Jesus, we too were blessed with their friendship.

The children's meetings were good.—The moms were glad we spent time with their children. But the parents would never participate or really listen to what we said. They would walk away or totally avoid us; they were not interested in the gospel message. Sometimes they asked for food or clothes or money.

After visiting the three villages for seven months I really started getting discouraged. Most Roma are illiterate, so tracts and Bibles did not help them. We gave them the New Testament on cassette and I encouraged them to listen to the Word of God. But I kept seeking the Lord for answers to the unresponsiveness of the people. God had clearly told us to go to Poland and share what Jesus had done in our lives, and I knew He wanted the Roma people to clearly understand the gospel.

God spoke to my heart then, and told me to take them out of their villages and away from the distractions around them. South Poland is very mountainous and there are many ski resorts and pensions (hotel bed & breakfast-type ski lodges). These are usually empty during the summer months, however, and I felt led to rent an entire building to fill with Roma families for five days.

Some pension owners were prejudiced against the Roma. Others did not like Protestants. But most owners I talked to were willing to rent us the whole pension. Gifts from Christian brothers and sisters in America who wanted to participate in the 'Roma Family Camp' plan allowed me to rent a pension which could hold eighty people.

I had previously made many contacts with those I invited to the camp, telling them up front what it would be like and what I expected from them. The three rules they had to agree to were: No alcohol.—Alcohol would cause them to break rule number two, which was no fighting. And I required attendance at every organised function and worship each evening. If any rules were broken the person or persons would be asked to leave and leave at their own expense.

Buses picked up each group of people from five different villages. Some saw other Roma they hadn't seen in a long time, including rival groups who were not friendly towards each other.

Each day we had Bible studies and worship each evening. The week's schedule also allowed plenty of free time and organised recreation and crafts. The family camps were an opportunity of a lifetime for many of these people. Quite a few had never had indoor plumbing—or even three meals a day. And all of this was at no cost to them. As the days of camp went on, we could see the Roma people open up. They saw Christians each day living their faith, and the difference Jesus made in their lives. The Spirit of God was clearly felt and seen each day. Relationships and trust were being built. The seed–the Word of God—was being planted.

That first family camp was awesome. Although not one Roma person gave their life to Jesus that week, it opened homes in five villages where we could teach the Bible and pray. And it was because of that first camp during a Bible study in a Roma home that a 44-year-old man stood up and surrendered his life to Jesus, in November 2004.

We had just read John 1:12–13 and I had asked the group, 'Who are God's children?' They looked at each other, spoke in some Romani language and then said in Polish to me, 'We are all children of God.'

I asked them to read the verses again. I saw a huge man named Andrzej turn and start talking to the man beside him, looking as though something was really wrong. I thought at first, *This is going to get ugly!* But then Andrzej stood up. He folded his hands in front of him and said, 'Only the people who believe in Jesus can be God's children.' Then he declared, with tears welling up in his eyes, 'I want to be a child of God!'

Andrzej prayed to ask Jesus for forgiveness for his sins that evening, and became

God's child. During the following years he has grown in faith and become a strong man for the Lord, often travelling with me to share his faith with other Roma people. Since then we have baptised thirty-five Roma people; another twenty-three have been saved and baptised by churches near their villages. We have held several more family camps with funds donated by Lifeway-Fuge. The camps take place in demographic areas that are ideal for the Roma to start new churches and groups.

We have Roma believers from two of the four known Roma dialects in Poland, and ministry is growing as the believers grow. With their knowledge of the language and culture and the respect of their peers, they are leading other Roma and Polish people to a saving faith in Jesus! They now have two church plants and hold home Bible study and prayer meetings every day. Two of our family camps have actually been led by Roma nationals. Because of their obedience to the Word of God and to the leading of His spirit, the Lord is bringing Roma people into his Kingdom!

—Jerry and Brenda Goss, *International Mission Board.* [http://teamromapoland.com]

Bulgaria: The Children

'The children in our Sunday schools, orphanage and soup kitchen are from homes where there is drunkenness, women and child trafficking, selling of children for body parts, fortune telling, placing of curses, fear of evil spirits, wife beating, absent fathers, ill health, unemployment and poverty. A significant number of the children are illiterate so we are considering starting a literacy class. The soup kitchen for thirty of the poorest children, after running for six months at a cost of 15 Euros per week, has closed this month due to lack of funds.'

—Excerpted report from a worker among Roma in Bulgaria, 2010, name and mission agency withheld by request

He was part of a group that was referred to as 'they.' They are lazy, they are dirty, they are always drunk, they need to get jobs, they can't be trusted with a job. The cycle was endless and there was no way that dignity could ever be allowed to exist in their own thinking about themselves.—Excerpt from *The Roma Chronicles*, by Bob Hitching

Resources

■ Literature and Jesus film in Romani language dialects

See resource list following 'Partnering with the Church' section of this book.

■ Useful Websites

Also see Appendix, 'Missions in Europe—Roma (Gypsies)'

- Association of Gypsies/Roma International
  www.christusrex.org/www2/gypsies.net

- European Network Against Racism   www.enar-eu.org

- European Roma Information Office   http://erionet.org/site

- European Roma Rights Centre   www.errc.org
  Many useful links to other sites about Roma culture, issues and advocacy

- International Mission Board (IMB)   http://romaministries.com

- Light and Life Gypsy Church Site   www.lightandlifegypsychurch.com
  Roma churches in UK (Light & Life also work among Roma in other parts of Western Europe.)

- Conservative Baptist Fellowship   www.gypsyministries.com
  (Key workers in Eastern Europe)

- Roma Bible Union   www.romabible.com

- Rroma   www.rroma.org
  Site devoted to Roma culture, history, traditions and current issues.

■ Selected Reading

Crowe, David and John Kolsti, editors. *The Gypsies of Eastern Europe.* M. E. Sharp, 1991.

Fonseca, Isabel. *Bury Me Standing; The Gypsies and Their Journey.* Vintage, 1996.

Hancock, Ian F. *We Are the Romani People.* Univ. of Hertfordshire Press, 2002.

Hancock, Ian F. *The Pariah Syndrome: An Account of Gypsy Slavery and Persecution.* Web version: http://reocities.com/Paris/5121/pariah-contents.htm

Hitching, Bob. *The Roma Chronicles.* Spear Books & Media, 2009.

Lazell, David. *Gipsy Smith, from the Forest I Came.* North American ed. Moody Press, 1973. British ed. published 1970.

Leigeois, Jean-Pierre. *Gypsies: An Illustrated History.* Saqi, 2005.

■ Videos

A number of good documentaries about Roma/Gypsies are available on YouTube and Vimeo.

■ 'Colorful But Color Blind: Roma Beyond Stereotypes.'
                                                        http://roma.glocalstories.org
Website with excellent videos about Roma in various countries.

→ April 8th is the International Day of the Roma. Why not consider a special focus in your church or other group?

Children, you show love for others by truly helping them, and not merely by talking about it.—I John 3:18, Contemporary English Version

People Affected by HIV/AIDS

While the rate of HIV/AIDS infection in Europe is not on the same scale as Africa and Asia, it is nonetheless significant. According to UNAIDS estimates, around 2.5 million people are living with HIV in Europe. Many of us know at least one person who is infected and without any known cure the spread is unlikely to be contained.—Especially when one considers facts like these:

- The rate of HIV infection in Europe has nearly doubled since 2000, and tripled in Eastern Europe. The highest rates of new infections were found in Estonia, Ukraine, Portugal and the Republic of Moldova.
- Young people aged 15–29 account for 26% of new infections in Western Europe and 40% in Eastern Europe, and these figures are growing daily.
- In all of Eastern Europe, injection drug use is the chief route of HIV transmission.
- In Russia, women and their infants are increasingly being affected. Latest figures show 22,000 babies have been born to HIV-positive women. Many of these infants are abandoned by their mothers into the care of the state.
- Public education and understanding of how HIV is spread is dangerously deficient in many European countries.
- The World Health Organization points out that 'no country knows exactly how many infected people it has within its borders, making it difficult for the health system to offer appropriate scale of medical services.' [6]

Lesley's Story*

Four years ago I was admitted to hospital because of recurring stomach infections. The possibility of HIV never entered my mind, and the doctors didn't think of testing me for it either, for some time, because I'm not in the risk group. But then one day a young doctor came to where I was lying in the mixed ward, drew the curtains round my bed and said, 'I'm sorry to tell you that you have

---

* Lesley's name has been changed to protect her identity. Her story was provided with her permission by Alison Bourne, Support Services Coordinator of Blue Sky Trust, a Christian agency that provides HIV training and support in the UK.

tested HIV positive.' He then drew back the curtains and walked away, leaving the rest of the ward staring at me. I cried. The other people in the ward were very comforting, but I knew nothing about HIV except that it led to AIDS, and you die from it.

I was single at that time, living with my sister-in-law and her two teenage children. I told my sister-in-law the diagnosis and she said she wouldn't tell anyone. But within a week it was all round the small housing estate we lived on.

Later, whenever my niece started rowing with me or if I told her off about something, she would shove the fact that I was HIV positive in my face, saying I was a dirty little slut and I shouldn't sleep around. I said that I wasn't a slut, I don't sleep around.—I'm not that kind of person. It just made me feel awful, because I was still trying to come to terms with being positive.

Once I went into a shop and when I bought something, the woman (clerk) made it obvious that she didn't want to touch me when she returned my change. She actually did the same with my sister-in-law and is still doing it, which is silly because you can't catch the disease that way. It's just childish. I didn't know a lot about HIV myself. There's a lot to learn about and I'm still learning. But I feel as if I want to grab people around me and say, hey, come on, learn a bit more about this and you'll find that I'm a nice person! I feel hatred for them because they don't know anything about it, so how can they judge me like that? When they look at you or when a clerk avoids touching you, you think, oh God, do I look that diseased, do I look so bad? But actually I look quite healthy. If people didn't know what I had they wouldn't notice any difference, really. It's not on the outside, it's on the inside.

If you tell some people that you are HIV positive their attitude is, 'Oh, you're a slut.' That's not the case. I've never used drugs, I very rarely even drink. I've never slept around. I had one partner and I thought we were going to last forever. That's why I didn't use condoms, really. I was given the choice but I felt that I trusted him. He didn't even know himself that he was HIV positive until I was diagnosed. Now he supports me, and we try to support each other.

Eventually I had to move out of my housing estate and out of the area. My life became too difficult with everyone knowing my diagnosis. People would throw eggs at my window and shout things at me. My own family turned away from me. I felt I needed a new start.

My attitude on life now has totally changed ... I think now that every day is another day and just take things day by day, really. I do make a plan for the future, but it's a daily plan. You can get down. Your immune system's down so you sit there and cry and feel sorry for yourself. But then you've got to perk yourself up, because if you don't help yourself no one will. I'd rather just think, well, I'm still a normal person, and just carry on as normal.

Now I'm much happier. I've decided not to tell people around me about my diagnosis.—It seems better that way, but it also makes me feel very lonely at times. I've got one friend who's absolutely brilliant. She understands what HIV is and supports me in every way possible. She treats me as 'a normal person.' That's what I value most.

> The bottom line is that the people we support don't see the church as relevant, or even feel the church would reject them.
> —HIV/AIDS Support Services Coordinator Alison Bourne, Blue Sky Trust, UK

HIV/AIDS in Europe: A Real and Present Danger

—by Rosemary Hack, AIDSLink International

About 33.4 million people in our world today are infected with HIV. Since AIDS emerged in the 1980s, almost sixty million people have been infected, and twenty-five million have died of AIDS-related causes.

The human immunodeficiency virus (HIV) that causes AIDS is transmitted three ways: through sexual contact, blood (the use of needles and syringes), and through a mother to her child during pregnancy, birth and breast feeding. *There is no cure.*

Almost thirty years into the pandemic, HIV is on the rise in Europe. Between 2000 and 2007 the rate of newly reported cases of HIV infection in Europe nearly doubled. The HIV and AIDS epidemic here has changed significantly since AIDS was first discovered. However, Europe is a vast and varied continent and as such the situation differs greatly between different countries and regions.

The problem of stigma and discrimination against those living with HIV, however, is widespread. This was clearly demonstrated when it came time for an expatriate Christian worker in Moldova to get his visa renewed. The authorities told Airton he needed to get medical clearance so he went to the clinic and gave blood for an HIV test. A few days later the police showed up at his door and told

Airton he was HIV-positive and had twenty-four hours to leave the country. They further informed the worker—who realised he must have gotten infected before following Christ, and was still in shock—that he was a danger to Moldova, and proceeded to escort him to jail. Only at the intervention of a local pastor was he allowed to stay under 'house arrest' before being deported.

Russia, Cyprus and Armenia also deport foreigners who have HIV and want to stay longer than thirty days. Hungary may expel foreigners who do not take treatment. And, in Bavaria, Germany, foreigners wanting to stay for more than three months may be required to undergo an HIV test if there is suspicion of HIV infection.

The treatment Airton and others receive clearly goes against international standards of informed consent and pre- and post-test counselling concerning HIV. It is also a blatant abuse of human rights, showing a deep misunderstanding of HIV.

Eastern Europe

According to the UN, HIV in Eastern Europe is escalating at an alarming pace, fueled by drug use, risky sex and severe social stigma that stops people asking for help. 80% of those infected are under thirty years of age.

HIV is now spreading faster in Eastern Europe and Central Asia than anywhere else. Russia now has the fastest-growing epidemic in the world. HIV prevalence in this area has risen 66% since 2001, bringing the number of people living with HIV in 2008 to 1.5 million. *Each week, another 3,500 people in this region will be infected with HIV.*

UNICEF has reported increases in HIV prevalence of up to 700% (since 2006) in parts of Russia. In Ukraine the infection rate of 1.6% is the highest in Europe.

Why Is HIV Spreading so Fast in this Region?

About 25% of the world's drug users live here. Some young people start injecting drugs as young as twelve years old. The sharing of needles is one of the reasons for such a dramatic increase in the disease. A third of the new infections are amongst teenagers and young adults, aged between fifteen and twenty-four. Sexual transmission is also a major cause of HIV's spread. Some eighty percent of sex workers in Eastern Europe and Central Asia are young people. Many of them are selling sex to support their drug habit, creating a vicious cycle of risk and infection.

Social, economic and political changes have also made many vulnerable to being trafficked into the sex industry, both at home and in other countries. These people turn to survival-sex work as a means of income. The number of sex workers has risen dramatically. HIV knowledge among Russian sex workers is low, with just thirty-six percent rejecting popular misconceptions and correctly identifying how sexual transmission can be prevented. In Ukraine, HIV prevalence among sex workers ranges from 13.6% to 31%.

Street Children[7]

An estimated one million young people live on the streets in Russia. 31,000 street children are picked up by the police each year in Ukraine.

Recent reports say that as many as 40% of young people living on the streets in some areas of Eastern Europe are infected with HIV.* Many street children find it difficult to access health and other services because of their position in society, a situation further exacerbated if they are also HIV-positive. Many do not seek treatment because of the stigma associated with HIV. Or they fear being harassed by the authorities and facing criminal prosecution.

Those most at risk are young, marginalised, often uncared-for by their families or living on the streets. Russia's and Ukraine's health systems have poor or non-existent harm reduction and rehabilitation programmes. This has left a gap into which the Church is stepping, and most success in rehabilitation programmes in Russia is due to Christian interventions. But there is still a huge gap to be filled.

The situation for adults living with HIV, especially marginalised adults, is equally dire. Again, many fear the social stigma of seeking treatment for HIV more than they fear the disease. This is driving HIV and AIDS further underground, and also making it more likely that HIV is passed on to a woman's unborn children.

Western and Central Europe

In Western Europe much progress has been made with regards to antiretroviral treatment and preventing transmission among certain groups. Mother-to-child transmission has been virtually eliminated due to HIV testing and prevention services available to pregnant women.

Widespread access to antiretroviral therapy in high-income countries has reduced the number of AIDS-related deaths. In Switzerland, AIDS-related deaths dropped from more than 600 in 1995 to less than 50 in 2008. However, there is a danger that progress has led to complacency.

A high number of new HIV diagnoses still occur each year, and a significant proportion of them are diagnosed at a late stage of infection. *In the European Union it is estimated that around a third of those living with HIV are unaware of their infection.* In the UK just over a quarter of people with HIV do not know their status, and in Poland estimates are as high as fifty percent. People with heterosexually-acquired HIV infection are most likely to be diagnosed late. *A great many (though not all) of those at risk of HIV in Europe come from marginalised groups.*

Immigrants

According to a study done in Italy, approximately 43% of HIV cases occurred in people coming from countries with a generalised epidemic (e.g. sub-Saharan Africa). However, about 20% of those diagnosed with HIV probably became infected *after* they arrived in Italy, which points to their vulnerability in situations that increase their risk of HIV. This includes survival sex, abuse and human trafficking.

Injecting Drug Use

There has been a steady decline in new HIV infections among injecting drug users (IDUs), which could be explained by the increasing availability of interventions such as needle and syringe exchange programmes.

In Western and Central Europe, injecting drug users represent 8% and 13%, respectively, of new HIV diagnoses. Numbers have gone down, but they are still too high for those they represent. Also, not all European countries are witnessing a decline. IDU is still an important transmission mode in several countries, including Italy, Portugal, Spain and Poland.

Men Who Have Sex with Men

Around 35% of HIV diagnoses in Western Europe are a result of sex between men. In Central Europe this figure is slightly less, at around 27%. In the United Kingdom, HIV among men in this category rose by 74% between 2000 and 2007. In Europe overall, the number rose by 39% between 2003 and 2007.

Heterosexual Transmission

Heterosexual transmission is still the main mode of passing on HIV, accounting for 42% of newly diagnosed cases in Western Europe, and 53% of new diagnoses in Central Europe. And it doesn't look like things are getting better.

Among British teenagers, sexually-transmitted infections, which are an indicator of sexually risky behaviour, have doubled in ten years. More than a thousand girls aged fourteen and under had abortions in 2009, up 8% on the previous year.

First sex is often the riskiest sex, in part because of lack of knowledge, lack of access to contraception, lack of skills and having relations while drunk or drugged. And the risk of being excluded from the 'in-group' or of looking un-cool is often a more immediate and pressing threat to teens than a possible future health risk.

What Can You and Your Church Do?

- *Be intolerant*: of stigma and discrimination against people living with HIV, of homophobia, of judging sex workers because of their profession and thinking that drug users should just pull themselves together. Rather try to understand them. Put yourself in their shoes.
- *Pray:* on your own, with friends, with the marginalised.
- *Talk:* in church, in Sunday school, in your homes. Discuss the facts and possible consequences of sexual activity. *Ignorance is not bliss!*
- *Research:* what is already being done, what the gaps are and how you can help fill them.
- *Learn:* from others who are already involved. Dealing with HIV/AIDS can be complicated and they've probably already made a lot of mistakes. You don't need to repeat them!
- *Volunteer:* at a shelter, group home or rehabilitation centre. Get involved with groups reaching out to people infected or affected.

- *Form:* an Action Team with others who are interested.
- *Give resources:* (money or time) to groups or agencies who are effectively helping those with HIV or people at risk.
- *Use special events:* such as International Womens' Day (8ᵗʰ March) and World AIDS Day (1ˢᵗ December) each year, to raise awareness. Take positive action, like going in small groups to a red light area to distribute flowers or chocolates along with practical health leaflets. This can be followed up by forming a team which goes out weekly with thermos flasks of hot coffee and prayer to build relationships.
- *Be warned:* This is not something that you can dabble in for a few weeks. If you want to really bring change, it will mean a long-term commitment.

Resources

■ Christian Organisations with an HIV/AIDS Focus in Europe

■ ACET International Alliance   www.acet-international.org
AIDS Care, Education and Training. International network of independent organisations committed to developing a Christian response to AIDS. Many resources offered.

■ Christian HIV/AIDS Alliance   www.chaa.info
'Exists to facilitate a compassionate, strategic Christian response to the HIV/AIDS pandemic' by engaging the church, raising awareness, caring for the affected and encouraging advocacy. Supplies links to member organisations.

■ Judah Trust   www.judahtrust.org
A global ministry engaged in intercession, teaching, training, evangelism and caring for those affected by the HIV/AIDS pandemic. Offers powerpoints, film clips, handouts, newsletter and a training team.

■ Mildmay   www.mildmay.org
International HIV/AIDS charity with work in Eastern Europe as well as other parts of the world. Provides treatment and training of health care workers.

▪ Other Recommended Websites

▪ AIDSLink International   www.aidslinkinternational.org
Resources include free downloadable videos *'Hope Positive'* and *'What Can I Do?'*

▪ Global AIDS Partnership (GAP)   www.globalaidspartnership.org

▪ STOP AIDS Campaign (UK)   www.stopaidscampaign.org.uk

▪ UNAIDS   www.unaids.org

▪ World AIDS Day   www.worldaidsday.org

▪ World Vision   www.worldvision.org
Experience AIDS. Take a few minutes to walk in the shoes of those affected: http://media.worldvision.org/getinvolved/aids_experience/index.html?Open&lid=AIDS_Exp&lpos=day_img_Exp_image.
Caregiver Kits and Resources:
http://www.worldvision.org/content.nsf/getinvolved/cg-resources

▪ Recommended Reading

Bourke, Dale Hanson. *The Skeptic's Guide to the Global AIDS Crisis; Tough Questions, Direct Answers.* Authentic Media, 2004.

Cimperman, Maria. *When God's People Have HIV/Aids: An Approach to Ethics.* Orbis, 2005.

Dixon, Dr. Patrick. *AIDS Action.* ACET International Alliance & Operation Mobilisation, 2010.

Dixon, Dr. Patrick. *The Truth About AIDS.* ACET International Alliance & Operation Mobilisation, 2004.

Dortzbach, Deborah and Meredith Long. *The AIDS Crisis: What We Can Do.* Inter-varsity Press, 2006

McMickle, Marvin A. *A Time to Speak: How Black Pastors Can Respond to the HIV/AIDS Pandemic.* Pilgrim Press, 2008.

Shelp, Earl. *AIDS & the Church: The Second Decade.* John Knox Press, 1992.

Thomas, Joy and Ray. *I'm Not At Risk, Am I?* Judah Trust & Operation Mobilisation, 2005.

The Poor and Homeless

An OM worker in Siberia met 40-year old Vitali while handing out tea and sandwiches to people on the streets.

'Vitali was proud to tell me that he had studied medicine in Poland,' she remembers, 'and he went on to set up one of the first fitness clubs in Novosibirsk in the early 90s. How, I wondered, had this educated, intelligent man been reduced to sleeping on the floor with no job or prospect of ever having one again?

'With tears running down his cheeks Vitali told me how he had gradually lost his wife, his job and his children, and how he had ended up homeless. Recently he had entertained serious thoughts of hanging himself.

'The man could still be re-issued a passport and documents to work and rent a room, but he had lost the will to live and make decisions for himself. Tears came to my eyes. How could I begin to share the love of God with people like Vitali, and help them re-gain their lives? How could I integrate them into the church? How could I make a difference in a city full of need?'

The so-called 'Third World' is a familiar term to most of us, but what about the hidden 'Fourth World': the vast sea of poor people who struggle to live without even basic necessities, within our borders?

Few would think of placing Europeans into that category. So consider these surprising statistics:

- More than 165 million people in Europe live below the poverty line. In eighteen countries of Central and Eastern Europe and the newly independent states for which data now exist, eight have 50% or higher of their population living below the poverty line. Some 2% of the population of the European Region lives in absolute poverty. [WHO]
- More children are living in poverty in Eastern Europe and the former Soviet Union *today* than when the Berlin Wall fell in 1989. 18 million children in this region are living on less than two Euros a day. [UNICEF]
- The number of homeless people in Western Europe is at its highest level in 50 years, with homelessness levels not seen since the end of World War II. [UN-HABITAT]
- 3 million people in the European Union have no home, another 15 million live in poor or substandard homes. [UN-HABITAT]
- The UK has the highest number of avoidable deaths due to winter cold in Western Europe, because of householders unable to pay fuel costs. [BBC

News] Nationally, there are 187 day centres serving an estimated 10,000 people per day who sleep rough. [www.homelessorg.org.uk]

'Absolute poverty' means lacking the basic necessities for survival. This level of need can be found in almost every European country, especially among Roma (gypsies), immigrants, ex-prisoners, the homeless and some disabled or elderly people living in institutions.

'Relative poverty' is much more widespread. According to the European Commission, this situation occurs when a person's way of life and income is so much worse than the general standard of living in the country or region in which they live that they struggle to live a normal life, participating in ordinary economic, social and cultural activities. Those with less than 60% of the median income are classified as poor. This 'poverty line' is the agreed international measure used throughout the European Union.

Philip O'Connor, Chairperson of the European Anti-Poverty Network Ireland has noted, 'The voice of the poor and the marginalised has been largely silenced in the current recession as–unlike most other groups in society—they have no powerful interest groups to represent them.'

But aren't Christians called upon to represent the poor? The Bible contains more than 2,000 verses that speak of God's deep concern for poor people. Perhaps we need to do an attitude check. Do we tend to judge someone as either deserving of our help or undeserving—-poor because it's their own fault? Do we regard poverty simply as an 'issue' or do see real men, women and children behind the numbers?

The medieval walled town of Cittadella, forty miles from Venice, Italy, made the news a few years ago when the mayor passed a law forbidding residence to any who are poor, homeless or unemployed. Although the government denounced the ordinance as discriminatory, forty other towns in the area soon adopted the law.

Most of us would react to something like this with indignation. Yet we are also sometimes guilty of a fortress mentality, unconsciously building walls around our small, safe worlds and not allowing anyone in who makes us uncomfortable.

Missions and NGOs in the Balkans and other parts of Europe are doing what they can to alleviate the grim consequences of inadequate food, housing and medical care they see every day. But to make an impact, more individuals and churches must first become aware of this situation, and then concerned enough to get involved.

The answer to knowing how to share God's love with poor and homeless people starts with sharing their tears. We must let our hearts be broken with the things that break the heart of God.

If you're not yet convinced of the need take a walk, below, with Lee Saville of Networks [www.networks.org.ro]; an international, inter-denominational Christian mission working towards spiritual and physical transformation amongst some of the poorest of the poor in North-West Romania.

Come With Me …

In a world of ergonomic furniture, triple glazing and click flooring; a world where central heating is simply normal and where we never really have to go hungry; a world where the first signs of snow bring not despair but thoughts of recreation; how do you explain poverty in a country like Romania …?

I am beginning to believe that you have to see it, to smell it, to experience it, to begin to touch the horror and the hopelessness of it. Poverty is bad enough anywhere but in a country where the temperature can fall to −35 degrees Celsius in winter, it is difficult for us to comprehend.

Groups of people (both adults and children) try to get enough money to feed their families digging by the ground to gather rusty scrap metal. On cold days the ground is too hard to dig.

It is a late winter afternoon and the light is fading. A young boy picks his way through the deep soft mud that makes up the road, a huge bag of scrap textiles on his back. He leans forward to balance the weight of it. This will be the fuel that will keep his brothers and sisters warm tonight. They cannot afford food so they cannot afford fire wood which costs nearly twenty-five Euros for one cubic meter and which would keep the house warm for just under a week.

In the distance a little girl struggles to carry five litres of water home from the water pump. She takes a few steps and stops and then another few and then stops again, setting the container down in the mud each time she stops. The closest water supply is five hundred metres from her home.

I move carefully along the mud road, past tiny houses made of mud brick and old planking. I have to lower my head to duck under the rusty tin sheets that make up the roof of the house I am visiting. A small, dirty face smiles at me through the cracked glass as I approach the broken wooden door and the little girl struggles excitedly to twist the bent nail that holds it (nearly) closed, to let me in.

Small. It is a small space for so many people to live. The floor is mud and turns to sludge when it rains. A small tin stove in the corner gives out heat and fumes. Old shoes found in the rubbish are burning to provide some heat.

Mum smiles at me, a tired smile as she holds the hand of her husband, paralysed and unable to move or speak, as a result of a stroke over one year ago. Five children crowd around her, a twelve-month old baby is cradled in one arm.

There is no running water—the closest water pump is around five hundred metres away. Every drop of water has to be carried for drinking, cooking, cleaning and washing clothes. There are no toilets, and there's no drainage in this area. The woman cannot work because she needs to care for her family, but even if she wanted to find work she couldn't since she has no identity card and little chance of getting one. With no ID card she can get no benefits from the state, and even if she could they would be insufficient to meet their needs.

Since being released from hospital over a year ago, her husband has needed constant attention. Medication and nappies are required every day, but there is no money for them. They cannot even obtain the vital prescriptions that they need for the medication since they cannot register with a local doctor without an ID. So night after night as her husband struggles with the pain of his condition she gets neighbours to call the overworked ambulance service who come and administer pain relief, but who are more and more reluctant to do so. From time to time they provide a prescription for medication, but the family cannot even afford bread or baby milk. There is no money for medication.

It is impossible to keep anything clean here. Step outside and you are in the mud. Just keeping pace with the laundry for her children is an impossible task alongside everything else. To carry the water means an approximately one kilometre round trip, and clothing for the family of eight must be washed by hand in cold water, since there is no wood to heat it. And how to find the money for washing powder when there is not enough money for food to keep hunger from your children?

The neighbour is a woman around seventy years old. For four years she and her daughter and grandson lived in a structure measuring 2.5 metres by 2 metres. The walls of this 'home' were made of two ranch-style fences covered with plastic sheeting erected between the back of another house and a neighbour's garden fence, which was the fourth wall. No birth certificate and no ID mean that such people receive no help from the state. Each day this old lady climbs into garbage skips behind apartment blocks to find food for her family.

How do you ever begin to help other people understand poverty?

I have lived in Romania for ten years and have witnessed huge changes here. With the help of many public and private foreign agencies, humanitarian aid projects have developed and flourished. A whole system of social services has emerged and continues to grow. Foreign business investment has brought in new employment. Basic infrastructure continues to be put in place, like the repair and building of road systems.

The years since the revolution of December 1989 have seen real change for many. If you travel down the main street of many of Romania's cities today you could be in any city in Europe. Street cafes hug the edge of tree-lined boulevards where people sit and drink latte in the late afternoon. The shops are filled with appliances, plasma TVs and the latest mobile phones. There are now Mercedes garages and Volkswagen has opened a large outlet. Much continues to change for the better. But this progress has been a double-edged sword.

We in the West heard a lot about Romania just after the revolution: the awful conditions in state orphanages; the impossible struggle of thousands of street children living in terrible conditions through freezing winters; the day-to-day battle of families to feed and clothe their children.

Western Europe responded in an awesome way. Trucks full of aid, funding, volunteers, and all manner of help poured over the border. Visitors and media began to see the beginning of change and so the cry went out that all was now well. The fickle media, keen to maintain its audiences, soon turned its attention to other horrors and disasters around the world, and the real and present needs in Romania began to fade in the minds of many.

More recently, with Romania's acceptance into the EU, media attention has again swung around. We are learning that there are still communities living in incredible poverty, and whilst the government does all it can to alleviate the problems there is still an urgent need to help and support humanitarian aid agencies: Children with no shoes; families with no income; whole areas without fresh water or drainage. People unable to resolve papers and identity cards, which means they cannot work or access social benefits or medical care. It also means that their children cannot attend school. No food, no heating … no hope.

> Speak up for those who cannot speak for themselves, for the
> rights of all who are destitute. Speak up and judge fairly; defend
> the rights of the poor and needy.—Proverbs 31:8–9, NIV

> … and if you spend yourselves in behalf of the hungry and satisfy
> the needs of the oppressed, then your light will rise in the
> darkness, and your night will become like the noonday. The Lord
> will guide you always …—Isaiah 58:10–11, NIV

Resources

▪ Recommended Reading

Andrews, Dave. *Can You Hear the Heartbeat?* Hodder and Stoughton, 1989.

Andrews, Dave. *Compassionate Community Work.* Piquant Editions Ltd., 2006.

Buckley, Christian and Ryan Dobson. *Humanitarian Jesus: Social Justice and the Cross.* Moody Publications, 2010.

Corbett, Steve and Brian Fikkert. *When Helping Hurts: How to Alleviate Poverty Without Hurting the Poor … and Yourself.* Moody Press, 2009.

Linthicum, Robert C. *Empowering the Poor: Community Organizing Among the City's 'Rag, Tag, and Bobtail.'* MARC, 1991.

Linthicum, Robert C. *Transforming Power: Biblical Strategies for Making A Difference in Your Community.* Intervarsity Press, 2003.

Myers, Bryant L. *Walking with the Poor: Principles and Practices of Transformational Development.* Orbis Books, 2000.

Myers, Bryant L. *Working with the Poor: New Insights and Learnings from Development Practitioners.* Authentic, 2008.

Sider, Ronald J. *Churches That Make a Difference: Reaching Your Community With Good News and Good Works.* Baker Books, 2002.

Sider, Ronald J. *Rich Christians in an Age of Hunger: Moving from Affluence to Generosity.* Word, 2005.

▪ Websites

▪Action Week (UK)   www.actionweek.org.uk
Poverty and Homelessness Action Week runs every year from the last Saturday in January to the first Sunday in February. Includes 'Homelessness Sunday' and 'Poverty Action Sunday.' This site offers downloadable resources.

▪Baptist Global Response   www.baptistglobalresponse.com/new

▪Besom (UK)   www.besom.com

▪Christian Aid   www.christianaid.org.uk/

▪European Anti-Poverty Network   www.eapn.org/

- Fight Poverty   www.fightpoverty.mmbrico.com/
                                         index2.html/

- Integral Alliance   www.integralalliance.org
  Global alliance of 14 Christian relief and development agencies to respond to
  world poverty.

- Micah Challenge   www.micahchallenge.org/
  Global movement to encourage a deeper Christian commitment to the poor.

- Present Foundation (Netherlands)   www.stichtingpresent.nl

- Salvation Army   www.salvationarmy.org

→   Pray for hope: 12.12, Annual Global Day of Prayer for the Poor
    and Suffering. www.prayforhope.com/12-12-global-day-of-
    prayer

Section 2

Loving Muslims

Introduction

Islam in Europe: A Threat or an Opportunity?

The assassination of Dutch film producer Theo van Gogh for his film, *Submission*; the suicide bombings in the London underground and the trains in Madrid; the riots in several cities throughout France; the wars in the Balkans between Christian Serbs and Muslim Albanians; and the growing influence of extreme right-wing parties in several European countries all seem to indicate that Islam (the second-largest religion in sixteen of thirty-seven European countries) is a threat to the stability and well-being of this continent. On the other hand, never before have there been more opportunities for Christians to share the gospel with Muslims, and never before have so many Muslims in Europe converted to Christianity. So in that light, the presence of around fifty million Muslims on European soil provides unlimited opportunities for the gospel.

History of Islam in Europe

Islam is no newcomer to Europe. It has been part of this continent ever since the seventh century: first, the state of Andalusia (756–1492) on the Iberian Peninsula, and later with the Crusades (1095–1291). In the Eastern part of Europe, Islam became part of the society due to the centuries-long control of the Ottoman Empire over substantial parts of the Balkans.

After World War II, Islam became more visible again in Europe as more and more Muslim immigrants from North Africa and the Middle East were invited in by European governments, to compensate for the shortage in the labour force.

During the last three decades, Islam has emerged as Europe's second largest religion after Christianity, as the ranks of Muslim communities have swelled in all major countries of Western Europe. Meanwhile, following the collapse of the Soviet empire, parts of South-Eastern Europe with long-established Muslim communities have rejoined the continent politically.

Thus, while constituting a small percentage (6%) of Europe's total population, Muslims have become a permanent fixture in the continent's religious landscape. In many European cities and towns this landscape now includes mosques and Islamic centres alongside churches and synagogues. In fact, major Muslim cities of the world today include not only Cairo, Damascus, Islamabad and Kuala Lumpur, but also London, Paris, Marseille, Amsterdam, Rome, Frankfurt and Barcelona.

Characteristics of Islam in Europe

We can identify the following general characteristics of Muslims in Europe:

They are a diverse people. There is no 'Islam' in Europe but rather 'Islams.' Muslims may be broadly divided into the following categories:

1) The old Muslim communities of Europe, found mainly in Eastern Europe and the Balkans.

2) Muslims who came to Europe in the colonial or postcolonial contexts. Many of these Muslims cooperated closely with colonial authorities like soldiers, officials or traders.

3) Muslims who came as labourers. More than 75 % of Muslim communities in Europe are essentially the result of the labour migrations of the 1960s and 1970s, and their families following them.

4) Muslims who came as refugees. Amongst this number were many Muslim intellectuals who had been persecuted in their homeland for their religious beliefs or political convictions; included were prominent spokesmen of opposition Islamist movements, as well as scholars, artists and writers with outspoken liberal views.

5) European converts to Islam. These make up less than 1 % of all Muslims in Europe. Although their numbers are relatively small, they are highly visible in the media.

Europe's Muslim population is also ethnically diverse. The largest group consists of Arabs, especially North Africans. The second-largest group is Turks, although some of these so-called Turks are ethnic Kurds originating from Turkey. The third-largest group of Muslims in Europe is those originating in the Indian subcontinent, especially Pakistan.

The Muslim community in Europe is also theologically diverse, varying from extreme fundamentalists to liberal and nominal followers of Islam.

A great number are young. Today, approximately 50 % of Muslims in Western Europe were born here. The Muslim birth rate in Europe is currently more than three times that of non-Muslims. As a result, Islamic communities in Europe

are significantly younger than the non-Muslim population, and Europe's 'Generation X' and 'Millennium Generation' include considerably more Muslims than
does the continent's population as a whole. 30% of the Muslims in Germany and
France are under the age of eighteen; 30% of the Muslims in the United Kingdom
and Belgium are under the age of fifteen; 25% of the population of Brussels under the age of twenty-five is Muslim. In 2002 Mohammed was the most popular
boys' name in Amsterdam; in 2010 it became the most popular name for newborn
males in the UK.

They are urban. Geographically, most Muslims are located in low-rent housing in the suburbs on the peripheries of major urban European centres. 40%t of
Muslims in the UK reside in the greater London area; one-third of those in France
live in or around Paris; and one-third of those in Germany are concentrated in the
Ruhr industrial area. Muslims now constitute more than 25% of the population
of Marseille, France; 20% of Malmö, Sweden; 15% of Brussels and Birmingham
and 10% or more of London, Amsterdam, Rotterdam, The Hague, Oslo and Co-
penhagen.

They are unreached. European Christians who for centuries ignored the
world of Islam in their missionary efforts now find themselves living in the same
cities, or even the same streets, as Muslims who used to live in so-called 'closed'
countries.

Unfortunately, research shows that, as was the case with Jews and Samaritans
in Jesus' time, Christians and Muslims often do not associate with each other.
Throughout Europe we find Christian communities and Muslim communities
living in close proximity to each other; individuals passing each other in the
streets, standing next to each other waiting for a bus, or sharing apartment buildings, classrooms and business canteens; but essentially strangers to each other.

What hinders Christians from sharing their lives with Muslims? People don't
have to fly across the world to meet Muslims, they just have to cross the street.
What keeps them from doing so? Is it lack of information about Islam? That does
not seem to be the answer. There are plenty of good books available and at many
schools, churches and seminaries across Europe one can learn about Islam. But
somehow this doesn't seem to result in more friendships between Christians and
Muslims.

I believe that fear is the single biggest factor preventing Christians from relating to followers of Islam. Christians seem to share some of the so-called 'Islamophobia' (referring to a fear and accompanying hostility towards the religion of
Islam and its adherents), that is prevalent across Europe.

This lack of desire to share one's life with Muslims means that those who want to know about the true meaning of the Christian faith may only see the outward forms of Christianity, instead of faith lived out on a daily basis in the lives of Jesus' disciples. They see the Christianity represented by beautiful cathedrals and decide this religion is something from the past that has lost its relevance for the Europe of today.

Many young immigrants born in Muslim families are not religious. Influenced by their weak social situation and experiences of discrimination, however, they may choose Islam as a means of finding an identity.

Wouldn't it be great if those searching for identity would turn to Jesus Christ, the Saviour of the world? But how can they, when His representatives keep their distance? It is my prayer that each of the fifty million Muslims in Europe will find at least one Christian friend: a friend who loves them enough to share their life with them, who is genuinely interested in their welfare and willing to treat them as a person rather than a potential terrorist. The kind of friend who shows them what Christ is able to do in lives that are submitted to Him.

Will you be such a friend? Will you pray that Christians in Europe will become such friends to Muslims in Europe? I believe that this will result in thousands, if not millions of Muslims, becoming followers of Jesus. God is ready. Are you?

Bert de Ruiter
European Muslim Ministries, OM

→   Bert de Ruiter has developed a "Sharing Lives" course to help
    Christians deal with their fear of Islam and/or Muslims and how
    to gracefully share their lives so that they, too, might discover
    the truth of the gospel. Already available in English, Dutch and
    German, the course is now being translated into French, Spanish,
    Italian, Russian, Bosnian, Portuguese and Swedish. Bert is also
    working on a version for Muslims that will help them get a
    different perspective on Christianity and build friendships with
    Christians. To find out more check the website:
    www.sharinglives.eu

Muslims in Europe, October 2009

Bert de Ruiter

	Country	Population	Muslims	%	ethnicity (% of Muslims)
1	Albania	3,600,000	2,500,000	70	Albanian
2	Andorra	84,500	700	< 1	Moroccans
3	Austria	8,300,000	350,000	4,2	Turkey (50), Bosnia (25), Kosovo (10)
4	Belarus	9,600,000	19,000	< 1	Tartarrs
5	Belgium	10,700,000	350,000	3	Morocco (55), Turkey (33)
6	Bosnia-Herzegovina	3,800,000	1,500,000	40	Bosnian
7	Bulgaria	7,600,500	1,000,000	13	Turkish (75), Pomak (20), Tatar
8	Croatia	4,500,000	50,000	< 1	Bosniaks
9	Cyprus	790,000	200,000	25	Turkish Cypriot/Turkey
10	Czech Rep	10,300,000	15,000	< 1	Bosnia, Middle East
11	Denmark	5,500,000	200,000	3,6	Turkey (27), Yugoslav (20), Iraq (17), Iran (11) 2), Lebanon (11), Pakistan (10)
12	Estonia	1,340,000	4,000	< 1	Tatar
13	Finland	5,300,000	19,500	< 1	Somalia (23), Yugoslav (20), Iraq (17), Iran (11)
14	France	64,300,000	4,500,000	7	Algeria (30), Morocco (20), Turkey (10)
15	Georgia	4,600,000	440,000	9,5	Ethnic Georgian, Azerbijani
16	Germany	82,200,000	3,600,000	4,3	Turkey (68), Yugoslav
17	Greece	11,100,000	300,000	2,7	Turkish (50), Pomak (25), Romani (15)
18	Hungary	9,950,000	30,000	< 1	Middle East
19	Iceland	319,000	1,000	< 1	Kosovo, Middle East
20	Ireland	4,300,000	33,000	< 1	Asia, Africa, Arab
21	Italy	60,000,000	1,000,000	1,6	Morocco (34), Albania (27), Tunisia (10)
22	Kosovo	1,800,000	1,550,000	86	Albanian
23	Latvia	2,200,000	2,000	< 1	Tartar, Turkic
24	Liechtenstein	35,000	1,600	4,5	Turks
25	Lithuania	3,300,000	3,000	< 1	Tatar

	Country	Population	Muslims	%	ethnicity (% of Muslims)
26	Luxembourg	480,000	10,000	2	Montenegro (25)
27	Macedonia	2,042,000	650,000	32	Albanian
28	Malta	412,000	2,500	< 1	North Africans
29	Moldova	4,100,000	17,000	< 1	indigenous, Tartar, Middle East
30	Monaco	33,000	136	< 1	North Africans
31	Montenegro	630,000	112,000	17,7	Albania
32	Netherlands	16,400,000	850,000	5	Turkey (40), Morocco (34)
33	Norway	4,800,000	80,000	1,6	Pakistan (31), Bosnia (17), Turkey (13), Iraq (11), Iran (11), Somalia (11)
34	Poland	38,100,000	31,000	< 1	Tatar
35	Portugal	10,600,000	15,000	< 1	Mozambique, Guinea
36	Romania	21,550,000	70,000	< 1	Turkish, Tatar
37	Russia	141,900,000	20,000,000	14	Tartar, Turkic
38	Serbia	7,500,000	240,000	3,2	Albanian, Bosnian
39	Slovakia	5,300,000	5,000	< 1	Middle East
40	Slovenia	2,028,000	48,000	2,3	Bosnian
41	Spain	46,600,000	700,000	1,5	Morocco
42	Sweden	9,200,000	360,000	4	Yugoslav (25), Iran (14), Iraq (14), Turkey (13), Bosnia (13)
43	Switzerland	7,700,000	330,000	4,2	Turkey (43), Yugoslav (36)
44	UK	60,900,000	1,600,000	2,6	Pakistan (45), India (19), Bangladesh (13–16)
45	Ukraine	46,300,000	456,000	1	Tartar
	Total	735,454,000	43,245,436	6	

Population statistics from US Department of State, accessed October 2009.

Pew Forum on Religion and Public Life/Mapping the Global Muslim Population; www.pewforum.org, October 2009.

Europa-Archiv des Zentralinstituts Islam-Archiv Deutschland, Soest, November 2006.

Meeting European Muslims

A great many people in the West have never had a personal relationship or in-depth conversation with a Muslim. The stories in this section, contributed by workers in different countries, may help to lift the veil of our thinking and allow us to see the majority of Muslim people as ordinary men and women, with hopes and dreams common to us all. Personal names have been changed for security reasons.

Netherlands: A Place of Rest

It was a wet and grey Monday afternoon in February. I met her in our neighbourhood, this Muslim lady whom I'll name Hagar. We knew each other from church. She had been coming for the last few months, together with her four-year-old son. I had just heard that Sunday that they had been kicked out of their little room. They no longer had a bed to sleep in, no place to rest. Hagar had been in our country illegally for some years, her attempts to gain asylum so far rejected. I asked her if she would allow me to go with her to some help organisations; maybe the people there would know about a temporary shelter. This was by no means an ideal solution, but preferable to sleeping outside.

That afternoon we got to know each other better. Hagar was angry because nobody helped her, lonely because hardly any Dutch person spoke her language. She was restless as a result of the uncertainty in her life and taken hostage by choices she had made in the past. She was also frightened to be homeless with a child, and proud of her son. That was the point where we connected! We were both mothers. Mothers who love their children, and seek the best for them.

In the months following that Monday afternoon, Hagar and her son 'Ishmael' came often to our home. They came for a cup of tea, a chat, and sometimes for a bed to sleep in. Our kids, both four years old, played together at church on Sunday, and during the week at our place. They excitedly greeted each other in the street. 'Mom, look, there is Ishmael. He is also from our church!'

Hagar isn't a woman who is easy to get along with. But slowly we saw her hardness melt away. We noticed that she felt loved by us and by others in our church who took an interest in her. She allowed us to share about the God who is always faithful, even when our circumstances are uncertain. How beautiful it was to see that she wanted to know more and more about this God we knew! As time went on Hagar would stay seated at church during the sermon, instead of popping in and out. And we saw that she was hungry to learn more from the Bible. We were able to do some Bible studies with her in our home, in her own language. There, at the Lord's feet, she eventually found a place to rest.

It was a difficult period, with several highlights even among the deep dips. But what a blessing it was when Hagar was ready to be baptised just after the summer! Looking back at the time before her baptism, we can honestly say, 'Lord, it was worth it all. You have given us a new sister!'

Hagar and Ishmael now live at an asylum-seekers' camp over two hours away from us. They are waiting for the answer to their latest application for asylum. When we looked them up recently to bring them their last things from Amsterdam, it was moving to hear Hagar say that we are truly like a brother and sister to her. *Thank you, Lord!*

—By members of OM Netherland's Global Action Amsterdam Noord (GAAN), a one year training programme for those wanting to learn more about understanding and building relations with Muslims.

→ **Fact**: Germany has 3.6 million Muslim residents from 40-plus nations, although the majority are of Turkish origin. Germany has at least 2,200 mosques and prayer houses, France over 1,600 and the UK at least 1,700.

Germany: Secret Believer

One of the young couples who visit our drop-in café is from Central Asia. They are in their early twenties, and both have completed their studies. The wife, Ana, is pregnant. For the past four months they have been residents in Germany, having crossed the border illegally between cardboard boxes stacked tightly in a lorry. When Ana saw an Arabic Bible at the café, she exclaimed, 'I had such a Bible at home!' She revealed that she had met secretly with another lady to read the Bible, and in the anonymity of the city where she had studied, she had attended church, too. Religion was not important to her, but she wanted a place to pray. Yet the fear of being discovered had been great.

'In my heart and home I am a Christian,' she confided. 'But I can't tell anyone.'

Her husband tolerates Ana's faith. What he seeks in Germany is security. Members of his family were kidnapped at home and then set free for a ransom; others were murdered when the payment was delayed. Fear and mistrust is part of their lives. Pray that this family will one day know the freedom and safety that can only be found in God.

—OM Germany

Greece: 'The Injil Makes Me Cry'

We are seeing unprecedented interest from the women here in Athens. A few weekends ago, one of the women on the team had a day off and was asked by some Muslim refugees to give a Bible study. She went to the study planning for thirty to forty minutes, and finally forced an ending after *seven hours* of women asking question after question.

Another team member reported, 'Thursday was Farsi day and we had a full tea house … One of the refugee women was talking about how we had read in the Bible about God releasing Peter from prison. She said that we prayed for her son who was in jail, and the next day he was released. Another woman then said she wanted to read this for herself. We got her a Farsi Bible and she sat for the rest of the time pouring over the Word. Afterward, she told us she thought it was very beautiful and she wanted to read more.

'Another young woman who I met on Monday and speaks a little English also took a Farsi Bible and some other literature. She said she liked what she heard that day, and wanted to learn more. I noticed several other people around the room reading Bibles and in the middle of the day we put out more copies because the ones we had put out in the morning were gone.'

'Last week at our Farsi lunch event,' reported another staff member, 'we had a lady at the lunch table try to tell the other ladies that Christians are "bad people" and that they should not be listening to the message that was given earlier.—They were only nice because they wanted them to become Christians.

'She picked the wrong table! The first lady exclaimed, "These Christians prayed to Jesus for my son to be released from prison and the next day he was released!" The next lady said, "I've read the injil (New Testament). It makes me cry. The Quran has never affected me that way." The next woman told her, "These Christians found me a place to live when my family was living in the park. They give us showers and clothes and food. They love our children even though we are

Muslim and not Christian. You cannot call them 'bad people,' they are good!" Those of us sitting there did not even have to open our mouth to defend ourselves.'

She added, 'Almost all of the women that come to the shower ministry [Helping Hands provides shower facilities a few times a week, since many immigrants live in cramped conditions with no bathing facilities] are very close to making decisions to follow Jesus. One lady described herself this week like this: "Below my waist all of me is Christian, and my left side, above my waist is Christian. My heart and right side is still Muslim because I am afraid." Pray that God will take away "Z"'s fear. What she is afraid of will likely happen, but what she doesn't understand yet is that with Jesus in her heart, she won't face it alone and He will be enough to see her through the difficult days.'

The team leader shared the story of an Afghan woman who came to the ministry centre two weeks previously, for the first time. 'After taking in the environment, she pulled one of our Farsi-speaking teammates to the side and, in a whisper, shared with her that she had seen Jesus in a vision seven years before. This Afghan woman was intrigued by the vision, but never had an opportunity to learn more. Now, with both excitement and fear, she is asking questions and seeking to know this Jesus who has been pursuing her for so long. Praise God for His continued work!'

—Stories from International Teams and Helping Hands,
partnering to share the gospel with refugees in Athens, Greece

→   **Fact**: Each year tens of thousands of Afghans, Iranians, Iraqis, Turks and other Muslims make their way legally and illegally to the EU gateway city of Athens, hoping to start new lives in the West.

Italy: A Place to Begin Again

In the streets of Turin we encountered a young Muslim who had recently lost everything he owned: his house, income, money and even his girlfriend. When some of our team began to speak with Hadi he admitted he was contemplating suicide.—He had even been advised to take his life by some of his friends! The team members prayed with him and tried to find out how they could help with his physical needs. They referred him to the local social services, and God worked on his behalf to provide for a room for him to stay that night. The social service worker even arranged for a job interview.

When the young man was asked, 'Who referred you to our agency?' Hadi didn't actually know, so he simply replied, 'I went to the place where I received hope and prayer.'

This young man did not know our names, denominations or organisation. He only knew that God had met his needs through us. Hadi represents many thousands of other newcomers to Italy who feel lost and alone. Pray that they find the true source of hope, in Christ.

—OM Italy

→ **Fact**: About 600,000 Muslims live in Italy legally, but many more are illegal residents and the total population is estimated to be close to 1.5 million. Islam is the second largest faith after Catholicism.

France: Entering the Circle

When we explained the gospel to Hannah, she fell on her knees. She explained that she actually knew Jesus, although she didn't know who He was. She had seen Him in a dream many years before. Now she wept as she accepted the Lord Jesus Christ as her Saviour.

Hannah is totally illiterate and only speaks Arabic, which makes it very hard to communicate. Her life is not easy. She has a husband who treats her very badly, and she is childless. She lives far from our meeting place; we have to visit her only when her husband is absent. Since she cannot read and there's a high risk in leaving any Christian literature, we just try to encourage Hannah and share the Word with her. She watches Christian TV in her language when her husband is away.

Fatima also comes from North Africa. She lost her mother at age two and was married off at fifteen. When she was unable to have children her husband's family made him divorce her, so she married the cousin of her former husband. He treated her like a slave and her thoughts turned to suicide.

When team members visited Fatima they told her that she was precious to God. She was unable at first to grasp that He could love her, but as it finally sank in she said immediately that she wanted to trust Him. She knelt down and asked

Jesus to come into her life. The team saw her face begin to glow with joy. Without ever before hearing the word 'Saviour' Fatima told them, 'Jesus is my Saviour!'

'When I was fifteen,' she explained, 'I had a dream. I saw a great and beautiful Man with a rod in his hand. He stood in the middle of a circle. A woman invited me to enter the circle but I said I was dirty, and not worthy. So I was taken away and washed. Even my hair grew long and beautiful! I was taken back to the circle again and this wonderful Person took a ring from his finger and gave it to me. When I shared this dream with others I was told that this Man was a prophet. I never forgot the dream. Now I know that He was Jesus, and I have finally entered the circle!'

Life is not easy for Fatima. Her husband is very controlling and she probably won't be able to have a Bible at home. Occasionally she may be able to watch an Arabic Christian broadcast on television, and attend the women's meetings held by the team. But now at last she has a future—and a hope.

—OM France

→ **Fact**: France's Muslim population, about 6.5 million, is the largest of any country in Western Europe. Although thousands of Muslims here have been introduced to Christ, about 150,000 French men and women have converted to Islam.

Bosnia-Herzegovina: Kindling Understanding

The extremely high unemployment rate within Bosnia and Herzegovina leaves many people without the ability to provide for even basic needs. Winters are long and cold. Most depend on wood to heat their houses, so for the last eight years OM has raised money to give firewood to the very poor.

A family in a nearby Muslim village was on the list so the team delivered a good supply of chopped wood as well as food and hygiene items, in the name of the local church. Before going to visit this family they heard that some months previously their youngest child had died in a tragic accident. A gasoline tank had fallen over and ignited; the 3-year-old caught fire and was too seriously burnt to survive.

As they talked with the Muslim father he told them with tear-filled eyes, 'Many of my neighbours and even the spiritual leaders have said nice things to us. But you were the first who have actually helped us!'

Team members are glad to show the love of Christ in practical ways because they know that's what He would do. Sometimes there is no apparent response. But the first entire family to put their faith in the Lord in this part of Bosnia had been introduced to Him, several years before, through the firewood project. Others have also come to faith as the team has blessed the community, and a church has now been born where there was none.

—OM Bosnia

→ **Fact**: Bosnia's two million Muslims are among the least evangelised people in Europe.

Albania: More Than Medicine

The Keneta swamp land is an illegal settlement at the edge of Durres, with areas of severe poverty. The medical clinic there has been running for several years now, shining the light of God's hope into the lives of local people. They know they can go to the clinic and receive a truthful diagnosis of their health concerns at an honest price, as opposed to receiving a dishonest diagnosis that is highly influenced by the amount of money they can give to the pockets of the larger system. This is possibly the first time that many patients are not required to pay corruption fees for the basic right of good health care.

One patient, Albana, told a Christian friend about her experience and she wrote to tell the clinic staff, 'Albana came to the clinic with her daughter-in-law because she was having chest pain and problems breathing. She explained to me later that the doctors actually sat down with her and looked at all the prescriptions and asked her how much and how often she was taking them. They did a thorough examination and asked her many questions. Then they sat down with her and explained that they believed she needed bypass surgery, and clearly showed her how to take her medications.

'Albana looked at me with tears in her eyes and said, "Do you know what they did next? They prayed for me to God."

'With tears streaming down her face, she added, "I've never in my 57 years had a doctor spend so much time with me on a visit. I know I will never be able to afford the surgery, but I do know that when I came home my heart felt so much lighter. I know that prayer had something to do with this."'

Previously, Albana had torn up her daughter-in-law's Bible and burned it in the fire. Now she asks her daughter in-law to read the Bible and pray for her. Albana was given something more than medicine at the clinic. She received real love, and the gift of hope.

Scores of Albanian families with small babies live in poor housing and struggle to buy even basic food. Working with the local doctor, the team visits them with gifts of nappies and baby formula, listening to the new mums and offering health advice.

They also visit families with young children who have disabilities. Such children are shunned in Albania, considered by some to be a disgrace to the family. Since access to equipment like wheelchairs is very limited, disabled people can be trapped inside one room, with only their close families, for most of their lives.

When a few of the team brought a food parcel to one family, the mum cried. She explained that in the morning she had used the last of her flour and had no money to buy more food. This parcel was the answer to her unspoken prayers, the evidence that God loved her and her family.

—OM Albania

→ **Fact**: Albania's 2 million Muslims make up over 62 % of the population, but many do not practice their religion. The country reopened to the gospel when Communism fell in the 1990s; more than 160 of the churches that were started are connected to the Albanian Evangelical Alliance.

UK: The Cost of Commitment

One of our London ministry's team members had many opportunities to share about God's amazing grace with a young lady from the Arab world. Dina is married and has three children. She is also deaf, but that has not stopped her and Carol from forming a friendship, meeting as often as their schedules allow for good coffee and spiritual conversations.

Six months ago, upon learning that Dina had read and reread the Gospel of Luke many times, Carol gave her a devotional New Testament. She regularly reads this; in fact, the Book has become a treasured possession.

One time as she was studying the Testament her husband took notice, and told her to stop reading it. Up until this point he had been aware that she had the Book but had seemed unconcerned. After a long conversation, Dina told her husband that she wanted to become a Christian.—Her husband then divorced her in the Islamic manner by repeating the words, 'I divorce you.'

Such pronouncements are considered legally binding all over the Muslim world. In fact, five sharia (Muslim law) courts as well as at least 85 sharia tribunals are unofficially allowed to operate in England under the 1996 Arbitration Act. Since they began, these tribunals have passed judgments on over 7,000 cases, with 95% of them relating to divorce. Most decisions are highly discriminatory against women, including the ruling that '*no Muslim woman may marry a non-Muslim man unless he converts to Islam and that any children of a woman who does should be taken from her until she marries a Muslim.*'

Dina was forced to flee her family home. Her husband kept the children, and her father threatened her life should she ever return to her homeland. Social Services were contacted and they have helped her find temporary accommodation. They are also looking into the issue of her children's custody.

In spite of all the trauma of what has happened to her, however, Dina has told Carol, 'I want you to take me to church. I want to learn the Bible. I love Jesus! I believe Him. I want to be a Christian.'

New followers of Christ, especially in Dina's circumstances, need a great deal of practical and spiritual support from God's family. Christians also need to ask the Lord to bring reconciliation between estranged husbands and wives. Pray that entire families will be reborn through the One who is the way, the truth and the life.

→ In a May 2010 UK survey commissioned by the Exploring Islam Foundation, half of respondents linked Islam with terrorism; just 13 % thought the religion was based on peace, and only 6 % associated Islam with justice. Some 60 % of respondents admitted they did not know much about the religion, but a third said they would like to know more.

Tea for Two

During the summer, short-term outreach teams often put together children's programmes in London's parks, where people of all nationalities relax. Activities include face painting, balloon animals, parachute games and story times. Families in the park are invited to bring their children to play, and sometimes they join in the fun or sit and watch on the side. This provides a great opportunity for team members to get to know the parents as well as children, and share the love of God with them.

One team member in a recent outreach had the opportunity to speak with a Muslim woman for a long time, over tea. As they learned about each other's lives the conversation led naturally to explaining how Jesus could make a difference. The woman responded positively, saying she would love to come again with her child, and gave her phone number so the team could let her know the next time they would be in the park.

Another woman was also very open to hearing about Jesus and took home a DVD about His life, saying she was looking forward to watching it. She, too, gave her phone number so the team could keep in contact about upcoming events, both in the park and at the local church.

These outreach participants were surprised to learn that sharing their personal faith was the easiest thing in the world when they simply relaxed, and let God's Spirit take over!

OM teams in the UK have been reaching out to Muslim World visitors and some of London's one million Muslims residents for over thirty years. Besides seeing a good number of Muslims embrace faith in Jesus Christ, they have planted two bilingual churches in the London area. Their intensive training programmes have also equipped several thousand men and women to work among Muslim people all over the world. Please ask God to continue to bring fruit through this key enterprise.

→ Befriending Muslims
Alison, who lives in the UK, notes, 'My love for Arab women all started by praying for them. If you see an Arab lady, go over, smile and say "hello". It really is that easy. Ignore the hijab covering; address the woman underneath. Make small talk; the weather is a starting point that we all seem confident with! Compliment her on something.—Don't be disappointed if the conversation is short and insignificant.
'Whether in the queue at a supermarket, on the train or in the school playground waiting to collect children, chat away and see where it leads. God is a master planner and longs to be known. What a joy for us to be a part of it all!'

Tips for Churches Wanting to Reach Muslims[8]

Do:

- *Pray!* Form groups that will pray for Muslims in your locality and throughout the world.
- Highlight obstacles to Muslims finding Christ in your church and *seek training* from those with experience of Muslim ministry.
- Get *books and resources* in your bookstall to inform your church about how to meet and engage with Muslims.
- Consider *identifying some in your fellowship* who would be proactive in helping the church understand how to relate to Muslim seekers.
- Consider *preparing a home group* that is geared to accommodate believers from Muslim backgrounds.

Don't:

- *Become impatient*; it will take time. The gospel challenges several aspects of a Muslim's core belief.
- *Fear!* Don't worry as you watch Islam influencing different parts of your area. Remember that more Muslims are coming to Christ today than in the past fourteen centuries of Islam.
- *Panic!* Love covers a multitude of cultural blunders. A sense of humour will also help to smooth things over.
- *Confuse the ideology* of Islam with all Muslims or assume that all Muslims are the same.
- *Imagine that you are alone.* Seek to partner with other believers in your locality in this ministry.

Islam in Western Europe and the Balkans

Naturally, the impact of Islam on each European country varies according to the density of Muslims in its population. But other significant factors include the nation's history and the differing attitudes of Muslims themselves in each area. Although OM has teams dedicated to reaching Muslims in a number of locations, we have chosen to consider the effects of Islam in one representative country of Western Europe, Austria. We will then look at the Islamic culture in Bosnia and the Balkans as a whole.

Austria: An Uneasy Alliance

Muslims in Austria have increased fifteen-fold since 1971. Turks, Serbs, Bosnians, North Africans and a plethora of other nationalities now make up nearly half a million out of the country's eight million-plus population. The large immigration from the Balkans goes back to the days when Bosnians were citizens of the Austria-Hungarian Empire. Austria developed a legal framework for Islam from the early 1900s and the country is now unique in Western Europe in granting Muslims the status of a recognised religious community. Islam has now become the second largest faith in Austria. Less than half of one percent of the population would claim to be born-again Christians.

For years the government refused to allow foreign workers to learn German in the hope they would not settle permanently. The strategy backfired; most not only remained but sent for their families. Ethnic communities proliferated in every city with shops and services catering to non-German-speaking peoples. In 2006 a government Integration Report quoted the Interior Minister saying that 45% of Muslims in Austria were not integrated, and did not possess any interest in doing so.

A mosque has now been established in army barracks in Vienna (the first in Europe), providing Muslim priests or imams for soldiers. Muslim recruits may also refuse to salute the Austrian flag. Even more alarming was an official survey of Islamic teachers on behalf of the Muslim community published in a leading newspaper, *Die Presse*: 14.7% said they opposed the Austrian constitution. 21.9% opposed democracy because it could not be reconciled with the teachings of Islam; and 28.4% said it was not possible to be a Muslim and a European.

Culture clashes between Austrians and immigrants are becoming more evident as the foreign population swells. For most Austrians, for instance, defacing buildings with graffiti or discarding trash in public areas is taboo, and they are conscientious recyclers. Although only about 10% of foreigners choose to ignore the social norms, their behaviour has fanned resentment towards all foreigners.

In some areas, an estimated 90% of children in local schools have immigrant parents. Even those who are born in Austria often struggle to use good German since at home they speak different languages. Many teens drop out before completing their education, which makes it hard for them to find employment.

Although the government offers vocational training programmes, the financial provision it makes for immigrant families does not motivate people to work.

Muslim girls and women are even less likely to integrate with Austrian society. Whereas males usually blend in with their Western-style clothes, only about half of Muslim females are permitted secular fashions; the rest wear traditional scarves and veils. In Vienna's university area one can find large groups of fully veiled Muslim girls. Wearing a burka (full body covering) is actually outlawed in Turkey, although the law isn't strictly enforced. Many families choose to send their daughters to other countries so they can wear traditional dress! In very conservative areas women keep to their homes except to shop, and men and boys predominate on the streets. Muslim girls may also be expected to marry young, so fewer have the chance of entering university.

Initiatives for integrating the country's foreigners are not common. Even most churches, admits one Christian leader, feel more like exclusive clubs. 'Their friends can join, but they don't go out of their way to invite others. The middle class doesn't like contact with the lower classes. That may be why churches don't grow much.'

In 2007, however, OM Austria found a church in the greater Linz area that was interested in reaching out to foreigners. A former coffee house was opened and named 'i-point,' in a neighbourhood where all but three of the four hundred and sixty people in the immediately surrounding flats are immigrants.—Two are OMers working with the project. The space was donated rent-free and the government provides funding for heat and other expenses.

Community children aged six to twelve are welcomed three afternoons a week for sports, games, crafts and homework help. Turkish women enjoy a weekly gathering, and with the aid of a social worker German language lessons are offered free of charge. Four area churches now send part-time volunteers to work with OMers. When staffing is sufficient the programme will be extended to serve older youth and, eventually, men.

Notes the OMer heading the project, 'Older people in Austria are not so happy with integration, but younger ones know we have to do something. We have a vision for building a network with others interested in working with children and young people.'

OM Austria's field leader is optimistic. 'We shouldn't wait until we have a Muslim-dominated society to share the gospel. We should do it now. I'm excited that we have a growing outreach, but the key is to involve the church so they own the ministry, not OM.'

> Europe finds itself in a contest with Islam for the allegiance of its
> newcomers. For now, Islam is the stronger party in that contest,
> in an obvious demographic way and in less obvious philosophical
> way.—Christopher Caldwell, Reflections on the Revolution in
> Europe: Immigration, Islam and the West

Bosnia: Healing Unhealed Wounds

Visitors driving through the Bosnia-Herzegovina countryside are impressed by stunning mountain vistas, rushing rivers and lush green valleys dotted with neat houses, gardens and haystacks. Strangers are also forcefully made aware of the wounds of war: buildings reduced to ruins or pitted with bullets, the occasional skull-and-crossbone sign warning of unexploded landmines, and the disturbing frequency of cemeteries. Gravestones are instantly identifiable as Muslim, Catholic or Orthodox and to passers-by who stop for a closer look, it becomes obvious that the years 1992 to 1995 signalled a tragedy of staggering proportions.

Much of the world has forgotten the killing fields of Bosnia after it followed Slovenia and Croatia's lead and broke away from Yugoslavia. The explosion of hatred between Orthodox Serbs, Catholic Croats and Muslim-background Slavs left over 100,000 dead, a third of them women and children. But although the grass has grown over those 15-year-old graves, the hearts of survivors remain deeply scarred.

It is said that a house—or country—divided against itself cannot stand. Yet the barriers between ethnic groups in Bosnia and Herzegovina are still very evident. In a land only a third the size of England, Serbs have claimed their own autonomous region. In the remainder of towns and cities, Bosnians and Serbs tend to live on opposite ends. Even the government is divided with not just one elected president but three—Bosniak, Serb and Croat—each one taking four-month terms through the year.

Meanwhile, the country's social and economic situation grows increasingly desperate. Factories that closed during the war have not reopened. A 40% unemployment rate—rising in some places to 70%—means the government gets insufficient tax money to rebuild the infrastructure. Young people see no future for themselves and turn to drink and drugs. Pensioners struggle to survive on a pittance. For many homeowners, wood-burning stoves are the only option for heating during long winter months.

But people are also spiritually impoverished. 'There's a definite sense that "my religion is my nationality,"' explains OM Bosnia team member Trevor, from the UK. 'The words "Serb" and "Orthodox" are used interchangeably, as are "Croat" and "Catholic," and "Bosnian" and "Muslim." Although a person's religion is part of his birthright, only a few are devout followers. However, a growing number are being influenced by Muslim missionaries from outside, and the offer of schools, mosques and other gifts donated by wealthy Muslim countries.'

Only about 25 evangelical fellowships exist in Bosnia. When OM began bringing in humanitarian aid in 1998, church-planting became a priority. The first team lived in a 750-year-old Muslim-dominant town in the northwest corner of the country, which has never had an evangelical church. The first locals to follow Jesus were baptised in a local river in 2001, and although a few more men and women gradually came to faith the situation then seemed to stagnate. The team realised that the act of attending formal services in a church building didn't come naturally to people unfamiliar with Christianity, and decided in 2006 to move from a congregational model to house fellowships. Since then the number of believers has tripled from ten to thirty, and it has been gratifying to see new Christians using their own initiative to reach out to neighbours. One of the several house groups meets for prayer and Bible reading every day.

Muslim-background believer Amir says he first met an American team member when he was a fifteen-year-old student, eager to practice English. 'She prayed ten years for me,' he marvels. 'Then I went to a Christian conference in Sarajevo, and what I heard was like an explosion inside me. I was torn in two.' But today Amir is an enthusiastic follower of Christ, the only one in his family.

'Church-planting is like growing a flower on a rock,' observes another team member from Estonia who has persevered for ten years. 'The only thing that has kept me going is knowing it's God's will. But I agree with what another worker said: "I have only one candle. I'd rather let it shine where there's total darkness than where there's even a little light."'

Most of Bosnia's population are still unreached. Only about a thousand among 4.2 million have discovered a future and hope in Jesus Christ. Few new churches are being planted and most residents, like their government, live passively, unwilling to upset the status quo after surviving the horrors of war. Even believers are slow to see the need for a reconciliation ministry. Although almost all churches in the country cooperated with an OM-instigated 'Pray for Bosnia' focus in 2008, subtle ethnic tensions within congregations still exist. And Baptist and Pentecostal churches won't always work together.

For several years OM's Sarajevo team concentrated on strengthening already-existing small fellowships. Then, in 2006, they felt the Lord leading them to pioneer a new ministry in the unreached suburb of Dobrinja. This Muslim neighbourhood is close to what was known as 'sniper alley' during the war, an area relentlessly pounded by Serbian forces entrenched in the circling mountains. With the blessing of the national church most of the OM team moved to Dobrinja to become part of the community. While no house groups have been established as yet, a twice-monthly Saturday night worship time attracts some interested families.

In 2009 another couple settled in the Muslim section of the old city of Mostar to work directly with the local church in discipleship, coaching and training of local pastors and leaders. Much of their ministry is centred around a purpose-built Bible School in Mostar that serves the whole country.

Many outside observers believe that Bosnia-Herzegovina will not make progress either spiritually or economically without reconciliation between its three main ethnic groups. Humanly speaking, such healing seems impossible. Only the God who knows all hearts can penetrate the barricades of bitterness. And He will only exercise that power in answer to the concerted prayers of His people.

Islam in the Balkans

—We are indebted for the following commentary from Brian Jose,
Executive Director of Radstock Ministries, working in partnership with
OM Albania where he serves as OM's Country Leader.
Brian was captivated by Central and Eastern Europe on his first visit in
1980. His heart has never left. He and his wife, Audrey, live in Durres,
Albania, where, they say, they bask in great weather, great food, great
people and great churches.

Few who are old enough will forget the headlines and images from 1999, when we learned that horrific phrase 'ethnic cleansing'. That was when Slobodan Milosevic attempted, via war and genocide, to extend his power throughout the Balkans in the names of Serbian nationalism and, profanely, the Christian (Orthodox) faith. As the Serbian army occupied and destroyed Kosovo, seeking to expel the majority population, 442,000 mostly-ethnic Albanian refugees fled

Kosovo for Albania.* It has been often said that Albanian evangelicals, less than 1% of the population, cared for about 20% of the refugees. I was there, helping the *Nxenesit Jezusit* (Disciples of Jesus) church in the northern city of Shkoder, and saw it with my own eyes. That church of about twenty people, many of them still teenagers, distributed food, clothing, mattresses and other supplies to hundreds of refugees until they could safely return home.

One evening, at an open-air coffee bar we were operating in the courtyard of the small church premises, a man of about fifty appeared on his own. He didn't want coffee or a game of dominoes. He wanted a Bible. 'I know from history that our people are Christian, not Muslim,' he said. 'I want a Bible to read.' He took one. I never saw him again.

It is important to remember that the Balkans have a mixed religious history, with Islam entering the peninsula with the Turkish occupation in the 14th century. Albania's 3.6 million people are roughly 70% Muslim, 20% Orthodox and 10% Roman Catholic. Montenegro's 667,000 population also divides into two major groups: 74% percent Orthodox and 18% Muslim. Greece's eleven million people are 98% Orthodox, and Kosovo's 1.8 million are the exceptions to typical Balkan diversity. The aftermath of the 1999 war ironically resulted in most of the Orthodox Serbs fleeing Kosovo, leaving the country about 90% ethnic Albanian and Muslim and about 7% Orthodox Serbs, largely clustered in mono-ethnic villages.

Many ask how to reach Muslims in the Balkans, and a few claim to know the answer. There are the usual debates, largely imported from non-Muslim countries, about what vocabulary to use and when enculturation becomes syncretism. Certainly some easily identifiable obstacles exist.

Serbia, often in the news for the wrong reasons over the past fifteen years, is certainly in need of people to bring a message of hope, love and compassion. Not long after American and British bombings during the Milosevic era, a believer stood with me overlooking his family farm on the banks of the Danube River at Novi Sad. He was almost literally 'spitting mad' as he described his anger at watching missiles following the course of the Danube and then diving directly into the bridge, piercing it 'like a nail into a can of Coke'. He despised the West-

---

* Sources: Eurosurveillance, Volume 4, Issue 9, 01 September 1999, 18 Nov. 2010 http://www.eurosurveillance.org/ViewArticle.aspx?ArticleId=79>; remaining statistics from the on-line CIA Factbook <https://www.cia.gov/library/publications/the-world-fact book/index.html>.

ern powers that had destroyed his city. Do we have good news for the people of
Novi Sad? Later that evening over dinner the man's wife told me, as we admired
her baby, 'whenever we look at a newborn baby in Serbia, we think, *"This child
will see war in its lifetime."'* There is widespread need for the Gospel of Peace in
Serbia, particularly in the southern regions. Perhaps Slavic believers from places
like Ukraine and Russia can play a key role here. We need a 'mobilisation operation' for Serbia!

In Macedonia, where some say only five or ten Christians live amongst the
Albanian population, holding on to Islam is seen as part and parcel of preserv-
ing national identity in the face of the majority (and presumed hostile) Orthodox
population. One evening several years ago I shared the *iftar*, the evening meal
celebrated during Ramadan to break the daily fast, with an Albanian man. He
related at length his detailed understanding and admiration of Jesus, the Bible and
the basis of salvation through the cross. He went on to say that on the rare occa-
sions when he admitted his convictions to friends, they would respond, 'Ah, now
you are becoming a Serb (that is, one of those who has tried to wipe our people off
the map)!' For that reason, he could not declare his faith in Jesus.

Family pressures are often enormous. Stories of beatings, burning Bibles,
young people being forbidden to attend any church event and even more serious
threats are easy to come across amongst those from Muslim backgrounds, and
who have chosen to follow Jesus. A church-planter in Kosovo recently shared a
story of how powerful it had been for him to get the youth group from a church in
another city to come and visit his youth club where there was only one, brand-new
believer. 'When they got talking to the young people from the church, the real
questions starting coming. "What did your parents do when you told them you
had become a Christian?" was the first and most important one.'

Probably searching for 'techniques' makes no more sense in the Balkans than
it does in England, where yesterday at my church, three very different people
shared three very different paths to faith before they got baptised. What they had
in common was that Jesus had broken into their lives through other people and
through reading the Bible.—No surprise there.

An Albanian church leader shared with me how his nation had been evangelised in the early days of post-Communism, when there were no churches and
only a handful of Christians. 'We had nothing. We had nothing to lose. We'd
find a car or money for a bus and say to each other, "Let's go to this city or that
city and tell people about Jesus!" We'd go, not knowing where we would sleep,
what we would eat or sometimes even how we would get back home.' In the 1990s

those attitudes took Albania from a place with no churches to approximately two hundred churches, despite (or perhaps because of) a backdrop of poverty, societal corruption and sometimes even violent anarchy in the streets.

In 2000, while walking with a Muslim-background Christian through the war-ravaged streets of Peja in Kosovo, I stopped in front of a row of flattened houses. The whole street, apparently, had been flattened as a Serbian tank had driven down and, one by one, taken point-blank aim at house after house in an Albanian quarter of the city. The particular house we stopped in front of had had a cross crudely spray-painted onto the rubble, to send a message, I was told, that Christianity and not Islam should rule Kosovo.

'Why,' I asked my Muslim-background brother in Christ, 'would you or any Muslim, in the light of this depraved representation of Christianity, decide to follow Jesus?'

'That's easy,' he said. 'When the Serbs started shelling Peja from the hills, we left behind our grandmother, who said she was too weak to travel; and we walked—only at night because it was too dangerous to walk during the day. I remember thinking, "I've seen refugees on TV, and now I am one." We travelled for four days through the mountains. It was cold. We ran out of food and water. We slept in the snow. People were pushing their elderly relatives in wheelbarrows. And when we got to the Albanian border, some were collapsing over the border like some marathon runners do at the end of a race. When I crossed over the first person I saw was an Albanian Christian who handed me a glass of water. That's why I become a Christian.'

So how will the millions of people living in the Balkans be reached for Christ? Probably only as we 'experts' and 'professionals' with our books, techniques, seminars and so-called expertise learn how to partner with national Muslim-background believers, and those who have intrinsic cultural understanding from a lifetime of living alongside Muslim countrymen. There is a place for those from outside the Balkans, for sure. But a Kosovar teenager can best share with another Kosovar what it is like to tell your parents about your new faith in Jesus. An Albanian can best tell one of his ethnic cousins in Macedonia that there is no national betrayal in embracing the Jesus of the Bible for salvation.

But in each case, the costs may be high. One of the handful of believers in Macedonia, the only follower of Christ in his village, was hung by his ankles from a tree by his fellow-villagers because they wanted him to understand that talking about Jesus would not be tolerated. New believers may be partly or completely ostracised from their families. They will need a genuine, functioning family of faith, not just a church service to attend on Sundays. So, the technique, if there is one, is to plant relationships, plant mission and, ultimately, plant churches—all of it in partnership with national churches. That will take humility, submission, patience, creativity and servant hearts.

I'm in. Are you?

Resources

Also see resources listed in the section following 'Caring for the Marginalised: Immigrants/Refugees'

■ Recommended Reading

Adeney, Miriam. *Daughters of Islam; Building Bridges with Muslim Women*. IVP, 2002.

Bell, Steve. *Friendship First: the Manual*. Available from interserve.org.uk

Chapman, Colin. *Cross & Crescent: responding to the Challenge of Islam*. Intervarsity Press, 2003.

Goldsmith, Martin. *Beyond Beards & Burqas; Connecting With Muslims*. Intervarsity Press, 2009.

'Islam in Britain—A Challenge to the Church,' report by the Institute for the Study of Islam and Christianity. [DVD set by Patrick Sookhdeo also available] Isaac Publishing, 2005.

Lowen, Joy. *Woman to Woman: Sharing Jesus with a Muslim Friend*. Chosen Books, 2010.

Maurer, Andreas. *Ask Your Muslim Friend: An Introduction to Islam and a Christian's Guide for Interaction with Muslims*. Gilead, 2008.

Miller, William E. A *Christian's Response to Islam*. P&R Publishing, 1976.

Miller, W. E. *Your Muslim Guest*. (booklet) Fellowship of Faith.

Parshall, Phil and Julie. *Lifting the Veil: The World of Muslim Women*. Authentic, 2003.

Shah, Hannah (pseud). *The Imam's Daughter*. Rider & Co., 2009.

Sookhdeo, Patrick. *A Christian's Pocket Guide to Islam*. Christian Focus, 2006.

Sookhdeo, Patrick. *The Challenge of Islam to the Church and Its Mission*. Isaac Publishing, 2006.

Sookhdeo, Rosemary. *Secrets Behind the Burqa*. Isaac Publishing, 2nd ed., 2004.

Sookhdeo, Rosemary. *Stepping Into the Shadows: Why Women Convert to Islam*. Isaac Publishing, 2nd rev. ed., 2007.

St. Francis Magazine. Free online publication of Arab Vision and Interserve, with helpful articles about Christian witness to Muslims. http://stfrancismagazine.info/ja/

Stacey, Vivienne. *Meeting Muslims*. OMF Literature, 2006.

Steer, Malcolm. *A Christian's Evangelistic Pocket Guide to Islam*. Christian Focus, 2004.

Steer, Malcolm. *A Muslim's Pocket Guide to Christianity*. Christian Focus, 2005.

Swartley, Keith E., editor. *Encountering the World of Islam*. Authentic Media, 2005.

Ulfkotte, Udo. *SOS West: The Creeping Islamization of Europe*. [In German] Kopp Verlag, 2008.

■ Media for Outreach to Muslims

Bibles and Christian Literature

■ Arabic Bible Outreach Ministry   www.arabicbible.com
Online Bible and free materials in Arabic available from other ministries.

■ Arabic Bibles, magazine and other media.

www.vopg.org/library/engl_listsubjects.htm

■ Audioscriptures.org   www.audioscriptures.org
Listen to the New Testament in many languages.

■ Call of Hope   www.call-of-hope.org
Literature, magazine, stories in French, Arabic, Turkish, Bahasa Indonesian and Bahasa Jawa.

▪*Kitab*   www.interserve.org.uk/kitab
Multi-media, multi-language resources, including literature in minority
languages of the Muslim world.

▪Living Word   http://livingwordbc.org/FreeStuff
                                          New.asp
Farsi or Arabic language Bible or Jesus film, available on free-will offering basis.
Farsi New Testament is also downloadable.

▪Farsi Bible, for outreach to Iranians.   www.farsinet.com/injil

▪Persian Bibles, books, tracts, music   www.elam.com

▪Multi-Language Media   www.multilanguage.com/ara/
                                          Default.htm

▪No Frontiers (Multi-Language)   www.nofrontiers.org

▪*Orientdienst*   www.orientdienst.de/english.shtml
German ministry offering Turkish calendars and literature.

▪Pamir Productions   www.sadayezindagi.com
Evangelistic material, books, Scriptures, audio and video for Afghans in Dari,
Pashtu.

▪Persian Literature   www.elam.com

▪Sharif Bible Society   www.sharifbible.com/bible.htm
Free downloadable Arabic Bible.

▪The Truth for Muslims (Misc. Languages)
                                          www.truthforMuslims.com

▪Web Bible (Turkish)   www.wbtc.com

Note: The Bible Society and International Bible Society in many countries and
Amazon also sell Arabic Bibles, New Testaments and audiocassettes

Correspondence or DVD Courses and Bible Studies

For Muslims:

▪Alif course by AWM.   info@alifproject.org.uk
 (Due to be released in 2011.)

▪Free Emmaus Bible College study in English, French, Arabic and Turkish.
www.arabicbible.com/free/free_
course.htm

▪Word of Life (in English)   www.word.org.uk/course

For Christians:

▪Bridges   www.crescentproject.org
6-week DVD-based course by Crescent Projects about Islam and how
Christians can relate to Muslims.

▪Facing the Challenge   www.facingthechallenge.org/
quotes.php
Free online courses include 'What Muslims Believe.'

▪*Orientdienst*   www.orientdienst.de/muslime/
minikurs/minicourse_islam.shtml
Free online mini-course about Islam in German.

▪Perspectives   www.perspectives.org
'Encountering the World of Islam.' Similar in size and weight to a standard
Perspectives course, but focused on understanding and engaging Muslim
peoples. Also 'God's Heart for the Muslims,' an 8-lesson study that uses the
Bible to help participants to reflect on how to share the love of Jesus with
Muslims more effectively.

▪Pioneers   www.encounteringislam.org
'Encountering the World of Islam' book and 12-week course, used worldwide.

▪Seminar on Islam   www.ministeringtomuslims.com/
English%20Pages/seminar.html
Free 3-part online seminar in English or Italian.

▪Sharing Lives   www.sharinglives.eu
Excellent 5-lesson course taught onsite at a church or group's invitation.

▪ DVDs, Videos

▪*A Muslim Journey to Hope* (Arabic)   www.muslimjourneytohope.com

▪Eden Communications (Multi-Language)
www.christiananswers.net/catalog/
translations.html

- Arabic language   www.christianvideos.org/arabicvideo.
  html

- *Dreams and Visions*   http://www.dreamsandvisions.com
  Stories of Muslims coming to Christ, viewable online in Arabic, French or
  English.

- Indigitech   www.indigitech.net
  Multilanguage video, audio, literature resources.

- *'More Than Dreams'*
  www.visionvideo.com/detail.taf?_function=detail&a_product_id=33171
  DVD with dramatic stories of Muslims meeting Christ in 5 countries; several
  languages.

- *'The Life of Jesus'*   www.jesusfilmstore.com/JESUS-film/
                                           products/17/
  Special DVD editions of *Jesus'* film in Middle Eastern or Horn of Africa
  languages, or watch the film online: http://www.jesusfilm.org/film-and-media/
  watch-the-film

- World Christian Video Directory   http://christianvideos.org/arabic
                                           video.html

▉ Radio

- Call of Hope   http://call-of-hope.org
  Downloadable radio programmes in Arabic, music and books.

- *Orientdienst*   www.orientdienst.de/english.shtml
  Programmes in Turkish and Kurdish.

▉ Television

- ABN (Aramaic Broadcasting Network) www.abn-international.com/abnnew

- Al Hayat (Life) TV   www.lifetv.tv

- Arab Vision   www.arabvision.org

- Sat7   www.sat7.org

- TBN (Trinity Broadcasting Network) www.tbn.org/watch-us/broadcasts-on-
                                           worldwide-satellite

■ Other Useful Websites

■Arab World Ministries   www.awm.org
AWM's vision is 'to see mature, multiplying churches among all Muslim
peoples of the Arab world.' Websites in English, French and Dutch.

■*Asdika* (Friends)   www.toxethtab.org.uk/
'Ordinary Christians sharing Good News with ordinary Muslims.'

■Barnabas Fund   https://barnabasfund.org
Many good resources.

■Directory of Arabic Christian Churches, seminaries and other organisations in
a number of countries: www.arabicbible.com/directories/
                                           org.htm

■FaithFreedom.org   www.faithfreedom.org
A grassroots movement of ex-Muslims who want to promote secularisation and
human rights in Islamic countries.

■Fellowship of Faith for the Muslims   www.ffmna.org
To understand, pray for and relate to Muslims.

■Ministering to Muslims   www.ministeringtomuslims.com
Resources for those who want to understand Islam and share their faith with
Muslims.

■Operation Nehemiah   http://barnabasfund.org/US/Action/
                                           Campaigns/Operation-Nehemiah
UK initiative by Barnabas Fund.

■The 30-days Prayer Network   www.30-days.net
Christian guide to praying for Muslims that coincides with Ramadan each year.

■ More about Islam, for Christians

■Answering Islam   www.answering-islam.org
■Christian Answers   www.christiananswers.net/islam.html
■Reach Across   http://uk.reachacross.net

■   Apologetics, for Muslims (in English, Arabic or other languages):

www.acts17.net
www.alnour.com/
www.answering-islam.org
www.arabicbible.com
www.christiananswers.net/catalog/idx-islam.html
www.debate.org.uk
http://isaalmasih.net/
www.itl.org.uk/sitemap.htm
www.maarifa.org
www.the-good-way.com

■   Christian Websites for Turkish Friends:

http://incil.com
http://incilturk.com
www.islamacevap.net
http://isamesih.com
www.kampusweb.com
www.kutsalkitap.org
http://mujde.org
http://yeniyasam.com

Section 3

Empowering Kids and Youth

Introduction

The Rising Tide

If I were to describe the spiritual situation of the over one hundred million children and youth living in Europe today, two opposite words spring to mind: 'hope' and 'despair.'

The fact that Christianity is declining in Europe and Christians are becoming a minority has had a profound affect upon young people. Large numbers of Europeans no longer know what Christianity is really about; in some areas they would rather discuss the merits of cheese than Jesus, the Son of God. The 21st century is not only called Europe's post-Christian era but the anti-Christian era. At the same time there is a definite rise in spiritual hunger, and people of all ages are looking everywhere to satisfy an urgent, inner restlessness.

The breakdown of Christian morals and values has had massive consequences for our society, leading to various degrees of corruption, exploitation, abuse, abortions and human trafficking, to mention just a few of the problems. Without the acceptance of common values, families—the foundation of society—break apart, and children are often brought up in alternative homes or by single fathers and mothers. Some accept this is an everyday reality, for others the brokenness is internalised, causing permanent emotional damage.

'Home' is for too many of today's kids and youth simply a place to stay overnight. Friends are much more of a family to them than people they're related to. Depending on their parents' educational background and their own upbringing, each one expresses their yearning for satisfaction and fulfillment in a different way.

Youth in general have become strongly individualistic. Often they do not think of the consequences their behavior will have on other people and, in the long run, on all of European society. As the gap between rich and poor widens, we also see increasing divisions between the less educated, underprivileged youth and those who are better off. The underprivileged are often very consumption-oriented. They seem to have little personal ambition or social concern and are more focused on survival. Their main consideration is how much they can consume with the least effort and investment. Entertainment, drugs and sex dominate their lives. Sadly, this tendency often starts in childhood and leads to a future of criminality and abuse.

More advantaged young people, on the other hand, tend to be influenced by modern communications and the media. iPods, mobile phones and PCs rule their lives. They are more likely to pursue academic and social achievement and, as they become older, become involved in environmental and political action. Provided with a cause to live for these youth can be committed and radical; but they may not remain enthusiastic for very long.

This latter group in our society is very much shaped by post-modern thinking that construes everything, including faith, as relative. Secularisation and falsely-constructed notions about Christianity have made a huge impact. They disengage from anything that poses as an authoritative truth. Truth is no longer to be discovered but created. Everyone has his or her own belief. This crisis of truth leads to a climate of tolerance, where all values, beliefs and claims to truth are equal.

In their quest for satisfaction and fulfillment, what can Christianity offer to these two very different groups of young people? How can we empower them?

- Each young person has a longing to be *part of a family*, to belong to a community. Involving this generation in a church or fellowship where they can find their place and are accepted and loved unconditionally will bring healing to their souls. Where there are spiritual fathers and mothers, role models who coach them through the early stages of adulthood, a new generation of good leaders will develop.

- Each of them wants to be *part of something important*. Wherever churches offer not only a place to go but a place for action, making them part of a reformation process, these young people will be highly dedicated. We need to offer social transformational projects where they can be involved and help bring about change.

- Each of them has a longing to know the *meaning of their life*; their calling. When the church offers the answers to these big questions of life—where do I come from, why am I here on this earth, where do I go after life?—they find satisfaction and true fulfillment, and they will be freed from dependencies.

- We can help them develop *a missional lifestyle*. Once youth have become Christians their churches should not just absorb them into their communities, but pave the way for them to be witnesses in their schools, universities and workplaces. Above this, they should be encouraged to engage in social, political and environmental causes as well as world missions. At the same time we can invest in teaching and guiding them to develop their own personalities, based on Biblical truth.

- We can inspire, mentor and train Christian *youth leaders* who will be positive examples to their peers.

Before we can hope to win this generation for Christ, our challenge as Christians is to understand what drives them. Once we do that we can help the youth around us identify their own deepest needs, and lead them to the forgiveness, repentance and salvation found only in Christ.

Without encountering their real and living Creator, they will not grasp who God truly is—and who they are meant to be. So, what venues can we provide where children and older youth can meet God in a language and culture they understand? Where can they experiment and discover new ways to live out faith in their generation? How can we use today's technology and media to share the Good News?

Far more than ever before, it is essential that we as Christians pull together. Reaching the next generation cannot any longer be about your denomination or mine, or about our different opinions on various issues. In all our diversity we need to portray unity in faith and live it authentically before our youth. They care far less about our denomination than how real we are in our lifestyle. What changes has Jesus made in us? Do our whole lives reflect what He did for us?

We are also challenged to mobilise fellow-believers and help them understand that young people without Christ are lost. Though some like to debate the 'spiritual state of lostness' these days, let's have the courage to be less post-modern on this issue. The consequence will be finding appropriate ways to reach youth.

As Christians we need to boldly cross barriers into local social institutions, government youth departments and secular kids and teen networks, working alongside these agencies wherever possible in order to bring Christ into the equation. This is what a missional lifestyle is all about, living out our lives with Jesus wherever God places us. Too long we have kept to ourselves and tried to build our own separate Christian culture with our Christian kindergartens, schools, and so forth. These things are still valid in some areas, but more than ever we as Christians are challenged to go where young people are and live our values in the midst of this world. As European Christians now in the minority, we need to encourage each other to be Christ-followers with confidence—in word and deed.

The question that continues to haunt me is, how does God look upon the people he has created and loves? Although his heart may often despair when looking at the misery of man, he also has hope for this generation. Europe has thousands of young men and women who seek the Father's heart and want to become radical Jesus-lovers and history-makers. These young people care about the spiritual status of their families, neighbourhoods, countries and the rest of the world. Where youth fall in love with Jesus and his body, the Church, there is an explosion of new initiatives, new methods and new churches—and they will excel, with the blessing from the older generation!

One of the new, very exciting initiatives that I'm involved in is Mission-Net. Mission-Net is commissioned by the European Evangelical Missionary Association and European Evangelical Alliance, and has at its heart a two-fold agenda: a biannual, pan-European training and mobilisation congress; and kindling a movement among young European Christians.

Mission-Net is primarily aimed at those aged between 16 to 30 who are willing to consider a Christian missional lifestyle, allying spiritual expressions of their faith with practical contributions to the society's common good. We encourage young people to once again become transformers of society; therefore our slogan has become 'Transforming our world'.

The first Mission-Net Congress held in 2009 in Oldenburg, Germany, attracted about 3,000 young people from 47 different European nations. Encouraged to make their lives count for God, participants wrote letters to the EU, collected clothing for Latvia and donated money to Ugandan and Latin American youth projects. They also visited elderly people's homes in the city and played soccer with kids on the street. Following the congress a number joined short term service trips in various European nations, putting into practice the evangelism skills they had learned.

More Mission-Net Congresses are expected to be held on a regular basis. Meanwhile, young people are urged to get involved in promoting new 'Mission-Net movements' on a national and regional level across Europe.

The question we need to ask and answer while reading through the next pages is: how much will we allow God to speak to us and break our hearts anew, as his own heart is broken by this young generation? Europe's future holds enormous potential, but only if we choose to give the rising tide of youth our love, passion, prayers and lasting commitment.

—Evi Rodemann
Director, Mission-Net

Hard Facts

Suicide

- Among the 15–34 age group, suicide is today one of three leading causes of death in all countries. The latest available data for 15–24 year-olds in Europe, collected from 33 countries, shows that the Russian Federation is at the top of the suicide list with 32 per 100,000 young people, followed by Lithuania, Finland, Latvia and Slovenia.[9]

Self Harm

- The UK has one of the highest rates of self-harm in Europe.[10] Over 2,700 young people under 25 were admitted to hospitals for self-harm with a sharp object/cutting in 2008/9; a 50% increase over the last 5 years. A 2008 survey for a mental healthcare provider suggested that a third of UK girls aged 11 to 19 have tried to harm themselves because of depression. 73% of young people who self-harmed admitted to cutting, 48% to punching themselves, 14% to burning and 10% to self-poisoning.[11]

Binge Drinking

- The EU is the heaviest drinking region in the world. Nearly a quarter (24%) of European young people aged 15–24 reported binge drinking at least once a week in 2006. The highest levels of both binge drinking and drunkenness were found in the Nordic countries, UK, Ireland, Slovenia and Latvia. Across the whole EU, more than 1 in 8 of 15 to 16-year-olds have been drunk 20 times, and 1 in 6 have binged 3 or more times in the last month.[12]
- The UK is the binge drinking capital of Europe, with 12% of the population admitting to having up to 10 drinks in a single night out.[13] Over 50% of British 15 to 16 year-olds have participated in binge drinking. 44% of 18 to 24-year-olds are regular binge drinkers. Joseph Rowntree Foundation International health surveys show the UK has unusually

high levels of 'risk' behaviour in teenagers, particularly in relation to alcohol, illegal drugs and sexual activity.[14]

Drugs

- The most recent survey of 15 to 16-year-old school students (2007) showed the highest use of cocaine in Spain, France and the United Kingdom, with 5% using 40 or more times.[15] The UK has been labelled the cocaine, ecstasy and amphetamine capital of Europe [European Monitoring Centre for Drugs and Drug Addiction, 2008].

Street Kids

- Over 300,000 orphans roam the streets of Romania[16] A few thousand live in pipes under Bucharest's streets. The majority of street children in Bucharest are raped on their first night.[17] Most are addicted to inhaling toxic glue that can permanently damage the brain.
- About 130,000 children in Ukraine live on the streets according to state estimates, but numbers are extremely hard to track and may be much higher. 300,000 children are outside the school system in Ukraine and are not accounted for.[18] 1 out of 100 children is brought up in a broken family.
- Estimates in 2006 gave a figure of 1,500 street children in Prague, Czech Republic. The majority of these children come from children's homes (70%), the remaining part from broken families.[19]
- Russia has at least 1 million street children, although the government's official number of children without supervision is 700,000. Kids usually find a home in underground pipe and cable collectors during the harsh winter.[20]

Runaways

- 100,000 children under the age of sixteen run away from home or care every year in the UK.—That's 1 every 5 minutes. 1 in 12 young runaways are hurt or harmed while they are away. 1 in 6 young runaways sleep rough. There are only 11 safe refuge beds for runaway children in the whole of the UK.[21]

- Ireland has 500 to 1,000 street children [Council of Europe]. In the past 5 years, up to 300 children go missing from state care in Ireland and an unknown number of these are feared to have been sex trafficked.[22]
- Every year in Germany an estimated 9,000 young people run away from home: 70% are boys, 30% girls.[23] Up to 20,000 runaway children, teenagers and young adults live on the street at some time.
- Each year in the Russian Federation more than 120,000 children run away from home, become vagrants, take up alcohol and drugs, or become participants or victims of crime. 1 in 4 crimes involves underage youths.[24]

Poor Health

- An estimated 13,000-plus deaths of children 0–14 years of age in the European Region are attributable to diarrhoeal disease due to water, sanitation and hygiene. Most deaths occur in the countries of Eastern and South Eastern Europe and Central Asia.[25]
- 1 in 100 children in Ukraine is an invalid. Residual radiation contamination of soil and water from the 1986 Chernobyl nuclear disaster is still breeding illness in Belarus, Russia and Ukraine. It is expected that the increased incidence of thyroid cancer will continue for many years.[26]

Disabled

- Many parents in Eastern Europe are forced by the State to hand over their children at the moment of birth, if a disability is diagnosed. Russia and Bulgaria have the highest rates of placement of children in institutions in Europe.[27]
- In several countries, severely mentally and physically disabled children are still kept locked up for years in 'cage beds,' bars five feet high built around their bed.[28]

Forced Labour

- About 900,000 of Romania's children are exploited and forced to do manual labour to support their poverty-stricken families, according to a UNICEF study in 2004. A third of these children do extremely hard work; most are illiterate as they were withdrawn from school.
- The government of the Russian federation estimates that up to 1 million children (aged 5 to 17) may be working in that country.

Trafficked Children

- The trafficking of Albanian and Bulgarian children as young as 6 years old to Western Europe for prostitution and other forms of exploitive labour, such as begging and domestic work, remains a problem. Some cases of illegal traffic in child organs are also suspected. Roma (gypsy) children are particularly vulnerable.
- UNICEF[29] estimates that 1,000 to 1,500 Guatemalan babies and children are trafficked each year for adoption by couples in North America and Europe.

Child Marriages

- Girls in Roma (gypsy) communities, especially in Eastern Europe, are often married off before they reach their teens.—Some are as young as eight. In 2010 a 10-year-old Romanian girl made news when she gave birth in Spain, after being married to a 13-year-old.
- Under Islam, girls can be and are forced into married as young as nine, even in EU countries where underage marriages are illegal. Several thousand very young Muslim girls in immigrant families are also secretly made to undergo genital mutilation in the belief that it ensures respect for the girls.
- Many girls from Eastern Europe as young as 13 are trafficked as 'mail-order brides.' In most cases these girls and women are powerless and isolated and at great risk of violence.[30] Services that specialise in selling European child brides to clients are readily available on the internet.

Unborn Children

- 1.2 million abortions take place each year in Russia alone.
- 75% of pregnancies in Romania (3 out of 4 babies) are terminated by abortion.
- 570 babies each day are deliberately prevented from birth in Britain, at all stages of pregnancy.
- In Eastern Europe there were more abortions than births in 2003: 105 abortions for every 100 births. This has now dropped to about 44 abortions for every 100 births. In addition, one quarter of reported maternal deaths occurred as a consequence of abortion.

Child Abuse

- Studies show that an estimated 10% to 20% of European children will be sexually assaulted during their childhood.[31] Some kinds of abuse are on the rise, including websites devoted to child pornography.

'Invisible' Children

- Thousands of boys and girls, many born in developing countries, are sent to live with relatives who have emigrated to Europe. These privately-fostered children—at least 10,000 in Britain alone—are unregistered and 'lost in the system,' invisible to local authorities. Welfare groups are finding more and more cases of such vulnerable children suffering neglect or abuse.[32]

Poverty

- Child poverty in Europe has increased over the last 20 years. Around 1 in 10 children live in a jobless household.[33]
- The economic crunch has led to the highest-ever youth unemployment numbers all over Europe. Some 5 million under-25s are unable to find work, contributing to the poverty of families, social exclusion. discouragement and decreased career prospects. Young women are the hardest hit.

- Nearly one-fourth of the population of South-Eastern Europe (Albania, Bosnia-Herzegovina, Montenegro, Serbia and Kosovo) are children. About 855,000 of these boys and girls live in poverty, not getting enough to eat, not going to school and not receiving medical aid when needed. Some 13,500 are not looked after by their parents.[34]

> O Lord, you took up my case; you redeemed my life. You have
> seen, O Lord, the wrong done to me. Uphold my cause!
> —Lamentations 3:58–59, NIV

Children's Ministries

Research shows that the vast majority of European school children are un-educated about even the basics of Christianity. In this section we look at a variety of effective ways that they can be introduced to the good news of Christ, at an age when they are most open to receiving it.

UK: Empowering Children in Schools and Through Holiday Clubs

How many children in the United Kingdom, at a guess, regularly go to church? Probably between 5% to 8%. How many attend school? Close to 100%! It doesn't take rocket science to reach the conclusion that if we want children to hear the good news of Jesus, we need to take it to the schools. In Britain, unlike many countries in Europe, religious education is a compulsory subject that all state-supported schools must teach.—And the main content of primary school assemblies must be Christian!

OM Lifehope's 'Kids 'n' Things' programme began back in the '90s when OMer Joe Ridgely asked himself, 'Why should we wait until our children have become hardened to the things of God? Children are very open and willing to listen and to accept spiritual things with a child-like faith. Many key leaders today became Christians as children.'

For over fifteen years now, the 'Kids 'n' Things' team has been making use of the great open door of reaching tens of thousands of children in primary schools. These volunteers recognise that it's not enough that children hear the message.— The message needs to be presented in a way that holds their attention, explained in ways they can understand and remember. Kids 'n' Things does this through thirty-minute theatre performances linked with the year's main Christian festivals—Christmas, Easter and Harvest—which students are required to learn about anyway. Each professional-quality show is packed with puppet songs, stories, mime, drama, conjuring and a clear Christian message.

Explains Julian Wolton, the current leader of Kids 'n' Things: 'Most school children are ignorant of the meaning of the main Christian festivals. This gives us a tremendous opportunity to be invited into schools and to present Christian truths in a clear and entertaining way.'

The vast majority of people who respond to the gospel do so before the age of twelve. Since childhood is such a key time it's essential to take the message to children where they are, in child-friendly ways. Kids 'n' Things strongly believe that if children hear and understand the truth about Jesus, many of them will choose to follow Him for the rest of their lives.

School holidays also provide valuable times for reaching children and their parents. Many parents are desperate to find interesting activities to keep their children happy and safe. Over the years, Kids 'n' Things has developed one-week holiday clubs which are run in partnership with churches across the UK. A typical club may be attended by 30 to130 children, usually 80 % of which have no regular church contact. Through stories, puppets, conjuring, music, drama, crafts and games these young people learn important truths about God. Daily themes cover issues like 'fear,' 'image,' 'making choices' and 'saying sorry.' The aim is to show the children that God is real and relevant, and that He wants to get involved in their everyday lives. Each club ends with an opportunity for children to respond. Often they write letters to God as their way of acting on the lessons they have learned. The team has been deeply touched by the honesty and simple faith expressed by the children in these letters.

Holiday clubs also act as a bridge for introducing entire families to the life of the church. Although fewer and fewer people in today's society are attracted to meetings in a church building, says Julian Wolton, children continue to be the great exception. One church member who wrote to the team after a holiday club reported, 'Several children came to church with their families because of the club. There are probably lots of children at home too, still remembering your messages. My own son told me he wouldn't mind having the holiday club every day!'

Another church's children's worker commented, 'After last year's Lionheart Club, sixteen new children started attending our weekly kids' club. Fourteen of them have now made decisions to follow Jesus.'

Julian recalls a story dating back several years to when he was running a week-long Lionheart holiday club. 'A teenage girl called Rachel, one of the group helpers, told me the first time she really heard about God and Jesus in a way that she could understand was at a Lionheart club, when she was younger. Her faith had continued to grow since that point and she had recently been baptised.

'Two years later we ran another club at the same church. This time Rachel was leading a youth programme for other teenagers who used to attend Lionheart clubs when they were younger. She met with our team every morning and asked us to pray that God's Word would come to life for them.

'I like this story because it demonstrates how someone's life was changed to the extent that they are now impacting the next generation.'

Kids 'n' Things is committed to encouraging church members who are responsible for children's work. The team runs regular training courses, both in churches and at the mission's Halesowen centre. They hope that believers will be inspired to continue their vital task of caring for youth within the church. As Julian notes, 'Many people who work with children week by week have great commitment but little or no training. By training these men and women to be more effective, our ministry can have an effect way beyond what we can do just by ourselves. Our training includes traditional methods of reaching children such as storytelling, along with newer ideas like puppets and gospel conjuring.'

Kids 'n' Things team members join OM from all over the world. As they lead creative programmes before an average of ten thousand children per year in UK schools and churches, they gain understanding, experience and skills that they can take home or apply elsewhere. Former team members have now gone on to establish and develop successful children's ministries in a number of countries, spreading the impact far beyond the shores of Britain.

Ukraine: Empowering Children Through Summer Camps

Week-long summer day camps for 600 to 800 children in rural villages each year are part of OM's strategy for reaching Ukraine's next generation. The camps are intended to be the first step in getting young people linked with local churches.

Explained team leader Tanya Morgunova, 'Most village churches don't have Sunday Schools because pastors may not see the need or do not know how to start one. Few children attend, mostly it's just a few grannies. Many of our OM team members received their children's ministry training from a Christian centre in Kiev. After qualifying they were given permission to train potential Sunday School teachers in our area of Ukraine. So we hold our camps where these teachers live. Two months after OM has a camp we re-visit the village to support the teacher. The next year they may hold their own camp. If they're not yet ready for that, we hold another one.'

Teams occasionally encounter stiff opposition from religious leaders in the villages. 'We use the Wordless Book flag that has a cross in the centre at our children's camps. One man told everyone it was an American flag! Another claimed that when we had children put their hands together in prayer they were being hypnotised. Team members have even had death threats. But sometimes it's the parents who come to their defence, asking the opposition why they don't do something for the kids!'

Ukrainian volunteer Ira recalls one particular camp where none of the children who attended were Christians. 'Little Natasha was a complex little girl who didn't seem to care what people wanted to say to her, at least at the beginning. But by the end of the camp I noticed that she was being attentive during the Bible lessons, and speaking openly in the small group discussion times. I didn't know it, but Natasha was going home every day and telling her mother, Luba, what she was learning about Jesus.

'On the last day of camp, Luba came to the closing ceremony. She approached me and shared how tired she was of her life of cigarettes, alcohol and scandals. Then she told me some of the things she had heard about Christ from Natasha. Luba knew she wanted to accept Him. After we talked for a little while I prayed the prayer of repentance, and Luba repeated it after me. "I felt a huge, heavy burden fall off of my shoulders," she told me afterwards. "Now I'm free, and I want to live with God!"'

Adds Ira, 'That turned out to be one of the most wonderful days of the whole summer for me.'

Ukraine: Empowering Children in Orphanages

Ukraine has over 130,000 orphans living in 450 orphanages or homes. The vast majority of these children—around 90%—are actually social orphans. They may have living parents but they have either been abandoned or removed from their parents' custody because of alcoholism, prison sentences or other circumstances. Many hundreds of new mothers simply leave their babies behind in maternity hospitals.

The Vinnitsa area, where an OM team has been based for a number of years, has about 30 orphanages including shelters for mentally or physically disabled children. The team distributes practical aid such as shoes and clothing, plus sports equipment and Samaritan's Purse Christmas shoeboxes. The children are also delighted by the special programmes they offer. Because of the overseas gift of a professional puppet theatre stage with props and 48 puppets, OM's professional quality shows-with-a-message are welcomed even in state-run institutions. Team members write and record their own scripts, and local church youth are happy to volunteer their help as puppeteers.

The medium of puppetry has proven to have a remarkable impact even on those who are using them. Admitted Olya, 'I never thought that something that was designed simply for fun could so powerfully influence my life. When I put the puppet on my hand for the first time, I was able to bring it to life—to move, to talk, to show emotions!'

Since Vinnitsa orphanages house nearly 3,000 kids the team cannot work with them all one-to-one. In spite of this they say they have seen some very positive results. 'The orphans are so much more open than kids in regular schools and enjoy the programmes very much. They learn to pray—learn to forgive. God has changed both kids and staff. This was recently confirmed when we met a young man who had once been in an orphanage school. He told us that it was the programmes and Bible lessons that had moved him to become a Christian many years ago.'

The CoMission for Children at Risk found that each year about 15,000 children who reach the ages of sixteen to eighteen are turned out of their institutions, most of them totally unequipped to meet the real world and nowhere to turn for help. Approximately 6,000 become homeless, 3,000 resort to crime, and roughly half the girls are forced into prostitution. Approximately 1,500 teenagers commit suicide.

State agencies are now doing more to make further vocational training available, and some Christian organisations are involved in assisting young people with post-orphanage transition and training. However, more halfway houses are critically needed.

Moldova: Empowering Children Through Day Centres

Vlad's Dad is in a Moscow prison; his mother is working abroad. The boy himself has lived some time with his grandparents, but this week his mom is home for a visit. Vlad's eyes shine as he talks of her and the surprise she promised him. But then his face clouds over. *'I would rather have her come home without money, but stay and live with us. At night I dream of her leaving again, and then I cry.'*

About 25% of this very poor country's 4.3 million population—almost a million men and women—seek employment outside Moldova. Parents commonly leave their children behind with grandparents and sometimes end up with new partners. The number of broken families has reached epidemic proportions.

A few years ago OM decided to work with churches to provide day centres for some of the thousands of children who have never experienced a normal family life. The centres start when local schools finish each day and offer a healthy lunch, homework help, Bible stories, games and crafts in a safe and happy environment. OM's international teams have also built outdoor playground equipment for some of the centres.

'Any child aged 7 to 12 who needs help is welcome,' states Agnesa, who leads a centre in the north of the country, 'They don't have to be from a Christian family.'

Often the centre attracts kids who are abused by alcoholic adults or live in overcrowded rooms, sleeping in their clothes and eating whatever scraps they can find or steal. Although they can attend public schools, they are required to bring their own notebooks and other supplies, even toilet paper. Those who are too poor to afford such things are made to sit in the back row of class, totally ignored by the teacher. As a result many children fall behind or give up trying to learn.

So far, ten day centre projects are currently bringing hope to 171 children. In Rezina the centre uses the church premises and opens every weekday from 1 to 5 pm. 'But the kids don't want to go home,' Agnesa smiles. 'They are always hanging around the church, hoping someone will come. One holiday we wondered if we should close, but when we arrived the kids were already standing outside, waiting for us.'

She adds: 'Eighteen months ago I wasn't convinced there was a need in our city. Now I'm very glad we started this work. It isn't easy.—These kids are always seeking attention, trying to find out how much we love them. But we need to keep this work going!'

Empowering Kids and Youth Through Sports

Since 2000, the global sports initiative KidsGames has introduced over three million children in 150 countries to the possibility of new life in Christ. Using sports, games and Bible stories, the event encourages churches, schools and other local groups to work together for the benefit of 6 to14-year-olds and whole communities.

OM Ukraine hosted the first-ever KidsGames to be held anywhere in the former Soviet Union in September 2002. Over 3,000 children spent five weekends in Rivne competing in soccer, basketball, track and field, table tennis and even chess.

Although the idea was initiated by OM's Dirk Human, the games were organised and supported by eighteen local schools and sixteen churches. It was the first event where Rivne churches, schools and government worked together, all for the sake of the children.

The first KidsGames carried an Olympic-type theme and also stressed a 'Healthy Way of Living,' through the teaching of Bible-based lessons on the life of Joseph. All children who successfully completed the programme received certificates, a Ukrainian New Testament and a book about a Christian sports figure. Medals for top competitors in each category were designed with blue and gold ribbons representing Ukraine's national colours and a gold medallion with 'Kid'sGames' inscribed in Ukrainian.

Before the programme was even halfway through, however, it was clear the event was making a positive impact on the entire community. City officials asked if KidsGames could be regularly scheduled in Rivne, and churches witnessed a two to three-fold increase in their children's clubs and Sunday Schools.

Observed OM's National Director, Oleg Abaturov, 'After KidsGames a hundred new people came to my church. We started a new church for youth. Parents came to church, too, to find out what was happening to their kids!'

Pasha Rozhkov was just one of those children. His teachers knew him to be a trouble-maker.—Cigarettes, alcohol and glue-sniffing were this boy's preferred ways of escape, and he had no interest in changing his ways. But Pasha signed up for KidsGames, competed with other children and participated in small group discussions that followed the Bible lessons. The leader's thought-provoking questions challenged his rebellious heart.

Hungry to know more, the boy began attending a church youth group. For months, a battle ensued between the quick highs of his old life and the promises of something greater through Christ. Then one night his youth group leader illustrated the hope of the gospel by nailing individual 'sins' to a wooden cross. In the back of the room the boy who used to make his teachers weep was himself in tears. With a heartfelt prayer of repentance, Pasha accepted Christ as his Saviour and Lord.

This wasn't just a temporary fix. Pasha remained actively involved in his youth group and in the ministry that first brought him to Christ: sports. He has since served as a trainer in OM's summer camps and when KidsGames returned to Rivne, Pasha's smiling face could be seen at every event. This time he was a coach, cheering for his team and sharing hugs and high fives at the end of each game.

But KidsGames and the teen version, TeenGames, are only two of the many ways sports ministries are connecting with young people across Europe. OM SportsLink is partnering with the Fellowship of Christian Athletes (FCA) and Ambassadors in Sport to facilitate an exciting variety of sports camps and clinics.

A golf outreach to youth in Athlone, Ireland, for instance, has been enhanced by the FCA Golf Team sending professional golf instructors and PGA Tour professionals like Anders Forsbrand. The pros deliver invaluable golf tips as well as powerful testimonies of their faith in Jesus Christ. Both participants and their families are impacted. The golf outreach has now become an annual event, and sports ministries in Ireland have mushroomed to include European Triathlon Championships and summer baseball and soccer clinics.

The Baseball Phenomenon

Baseball may not be the best-known sport in Hungary, but American OMer Terry Lingenhoel decided that neighbourhood baseball games might be just the ticket for involving his children in ministry. As time went on the games surprised everyone by becoming a successful model for evangelism and tool for discipling new believers. The sports pastor and a team of enthusiastic volunteers from the Lingenhoels' church in Ohio supported the venture, crossing the Atlantic with equipment and offering training. After this first 'Spring Training,' informal practices in the Budapest suburb of Erd immediately caught on. The next year's camp in 2003 attracted seventy-four children, twenty adults, and even a local TV station, resulting in the formation of three teams that joined the Hungarian Baseball leagues.

OM's baseball ministry went nationwide with four days of Winter Baseball Training in 2007 assisted by Unlimited Potential International, drawing no less than twenty-seven Hungarian coaches plus seventy teenagers, thirty children and fifty adults! Besides receiving top quality instruction, participants heard the gospel message presented by professional baseball players. Later, a 'Sports Envisioning Day' attracted about sixty Christians, most of them church leaders, wanting to learn how to use sports as a springboard to mission. After five years of seeking permission, the local government in Erd gave Terry and his team land to build their own baseball field.

Thanks to these pioneering initiatives there are already eleven 'mission' teams officially registered with the Hungarian Baseball Association (HBA) among the adult men's baseball, women's softball and youth baseball teams. Terry has been elected to the board of the Association to head up the youth development. He also helps to coach the HBA's national teams. The government is excited that he is willing to give baseball instruction in schools.

'With most of those playing baseball being pre-Christians, the opportunity to share our faith through relationships has been great and very natural,' observes Terry. 'The unexpected bonus has been the opportunities to share our lives and testimonies with the teams we play against. Our vision is to place a missionary player/coach with each club in the Federation!'

Perhaps most encouragingly, a Sports Ministry Network has become part of the Hungarian Evangelical Alliance. The network's role is to promote, train and help facilitate sports ministry in churches and camps throughout Hungary. An increasing number of churches across Europe are waking up to the exciting potential of sports, and the European Christian Sports Union, along with a host of sports missions from around the world, is supplying valuable backup.

Empowering Youth Through Clubs and Drop-in Centres

Netherlands: Unconditional Love

> —Ewout van Oosten shares three stories that explain how OM Netherland's youth workers are learning to be God's vessels, alongside the Church.

In our Delft youth centre, called The Mall, our aim is that every young person will be seen, heard and touched. We welcome them as they come, give them our hands, look in their eyes and call them by name. We also try to say goodbye as they leave and offer our hand or touch their arm or shoulder. We've noticed how important this is. Some guys even like to be hugged.

Last Friday I put a friendly arm around a young one and made a joke. The boy, let's him call Sjors, also put an arm around me and then gave me a hug—and then another. Then he said, 'You feel like my father.'

I chuckled and walked away but Sjors walked along with me. He told me quietly, 'My father is dead.'

I learned that Sjors's father had died three years before after a baseball struck his skull, causing damage that went undiscovered until too late. My hug had reminded 13-year-old Sjors of his father, who was no longer there for him. This incident affected me enormously. Seeing, hearing, touching—they're basic needs for all of us. A hug from your father tells you he loves you, that he is there for you, that you're his guy or girl.

■■■■■■

Fritz stands opposite ten other Antillean youngsters on the football field: big, strong, angry and frustrated. Sometimes his father doesn't talk to him for days. The teenager feels ignored. He was not invited to the football game.—Ignored again. So he shows up to let everyone know that he cannot be treated this way. It's him against the rest of the group and he plays hard, taunting and kicking. Better to be hated than ignored!

For some of our young people this defensive behaviour is all they know. They cannot believe that things in life can go well, that dreams can come true. Nor can they believe that unconditional love exists.

We hope they see Jesus' love in us. Fritz has run away from us, angry. We pray for him and hope that the sanctions and limits that we set show him Jesus. Show that unconditional love exists. *God, help Fritz, and help us.*

■■■■■■

Rogy is about to leave the centre after a one-on-one conversation with one of our workers, Gerard. Before he leaves, Gerard gets a long hug from Rogy that lasts twenty seconds and speaks to us more than a thousand words. The teenager has just come to the centre because the police are after him. He's not quite sure what to do, but above all he needs someone to talk to who will really listen without immediately judging him. Eventually he concludes himself that it is best to show himself to the police.

Rogy got twenty days in detention. He is not a sweet boy, but if we do not love him, who will? That twenty-second hug showed that he knew he was not alone, that our attention and help made a difference in his life. The centre is a place where Rogy dares to be vulnerable, speaking to us face to face. It's a place where we can slowly help him—and others like him—make better choices for the future.

We ask another youth how much he wants to know God. He answers, 'On a scale of 1 to 10, I give a 9.' We hear yet another teen honestly pray these words in their first prayer: 'You know that I am interested in faith, God, but would you still please have a little patience with me?'

Patience. Love. God is working in us, too, and we are giving more and more time to the individual trajectories of young people, besides organising the usual 'open house' for them. This is what is making a difference in the lives of youth outside the church.

God's love for us and for our neighbours has inspired us to pioneer youth work in co-operation with local churches and partner organisations, and to mobilise fellow Christians by sharing our knowledge and experience. We commit ourselves to do nothing unless we can partner with a local church. There are enough churches in the Netherlands!—We don't want to steal their responsibility, but empower and inspire them to be missionary churches, willingly and ably reaching out to neighbours. If we do our job properly, the result should be that we in OM 'work ourselves out of the job' after a couple of years.

At the moment we're working in six cities in the Netherlands. The youth ministry consists of drop-in centres through which we are in touch each week with about 200–250 teens, both Dutch and immigrant—many of them Muslim. Sports and computer games are just two of the ways we use to attract them. In one place where the work only started two years ago teens have already become interested in Jesus, and are joining the youth ministry of the church we've partnered with. We want to stress that youth centres are only a vehicle—not the goal. We are building relationships so that we can share Christ.

We are learning more about how to evangelise here in the West. We have developed some blind spots as Dutch among the Dutch. The fact that we've now got non-Dutch people working with us has really opened our eyes as to how secular we've become. It's especially refreshing to have people who formerly worked in a country where being a practicing Christian is the exception rather than the rule, and where Christians really have to pay a price. That is something we want to learn again. I really believe that we can help the Church to be relevant once more. OM's pioneering spirit and cross-cultural experience is key to Western countries like ours, that are more and more a melting pot of all the cultures of the earth.

Finland: Mixing it Up

In 2009 OM looked at the challenge of reaching un-churched children and teens in Finland. Although the national Lutheran Church has been a strong influence and almost 90% of teens attend confirmation camps, nominalism is rife and traditional services no longer attract young people in the grip of a secular, postmodern worldview. OM came up with a youth initiative in Tampere called MIX ministries. MIX clubs in schools and youth centres have been well received, not only by local churches and authorities, but more importantly by the kids themselves.

Clubs are run in partnership with local churches. Primary schools are used in the afternoons and teens are welcomed to evenings at a city-run youth centre. Since Finnish schools are open to morning assemblies at Easter and Christmas, the MIX team enjoys presenting the gospel message with the help of puppets. Clubs mix fun activities with strong, Bible-based input designed for youth who have no other Christian connection. Recently, a pilot project was added to incorporate disabled children.

After the first few weeks of running the programme in six different parts of the city, workers were amazed to see up to 150 kids and teens flocking to the centre each week. At Easter they showed the 'Jesus' film. Initially only a few teenagers were interested in watching, but soon everyone in the centre sat glued to the screen—a couple of Muslim boys among them.

'That film drew teens like a magnet,' marvelled leaders Miika and Riitta Parkkinen. 'The Holy Spirit was present.'

After the movie the team discussed the true meaning of Easter with the audience. A boy from Central Asia admitted that he'd like to read the Bible, but he was afraid of his dad's reaction if he found out.

The youth centre has a karaoke machine, so Miika and Riitta bought a set of hymns for the kids to sing. A boy dressed in goth black and listening to heavy metal music wanted to sing a hymn with Miika! The song he requested is commonly sung at the end of Finland's school year, before the summer holidays start, and reflects on how God has created the beauty of summer. It also speaks of how people have life and joy in Jesus Christ.

Observed Miika, 'This boy was very withdrawn and suspicious to start with when he came to the club, but now he is actively involved in the Bible and prayer sessions.'

The team has learned that connecting with a child or teen even once a week for an hour or two makes a difference. Each time the club meets the kids learn a lesson from the Bible and pray together. They have every confidence in God's healing power and ask for prayer for sick friends and family members.

'The Mix Club is my son's favourite hobby!' the mother of an 8-year-old called to tell the staff. 'He memorises each week's Scripture verse and we talk about it at home.'

One evening the team were clearing up after the chaos of an activity session, while thirty teenagers waited in adjacent room for the spiritual side of things to begin. 'Hey, when will the Jesus thing start?' they yelled impatiently.

'These teens are not easy to handle, but beneath their restlessness is a hunger for truth and love,' Miika said. 'After one of the meetings the teens hung around outside the building, talking with some of the volunteers. That evening, five of them prayed to ask Jesus into their lives.' Some continue to attend church youth groups. It's a beginning.

—Heidi Alajoki, OM Finland

Germany: The Xenos Team

The programme starts at 4:30 pm, but when we arrive at 4 the mothers are already sitting at tables and the children are jumping around. As the ladies drink their tea we make last minute preparations.

This weekly meeting began when we saw our Xenos Café—where foreigners can meet Germans and Muslims can meet Christians—gradually flooded with children. These were not only the boys and girls of German church members but also from neighbourhood families: Kurdish, Turkish, Albanian and Italian. Sometimes there were more kids than grownups, so we decided it was time to start something just for them.

Most of the Muslim women accompany their children to the Tuesday afternoon meetings. If they can't their children don't come at all and we don't want to put up barriers. We welcome tiny tots to primary school age: some who can read and others who can't; some who talk, others who don't. Some kids can't even understand German.

When the crowd quietens down a bit we sing some songs. Even the mothers sing along with great enthusiasm, copying the actions! Then comes a Bible story. While the tiny tots cry and the 4-year-olds knock chairs over we hope that the older ones are getting something from the story of Abraham.

After five or so minutes of storytime we move on. The oldest children play UNO while the youngest crawl around on the floor with cars and blocks. After a while we all go outside and play in the yard.

The mothers then serve the cooked noodles or Turkish-style pizza they've prepared for a snack. All are hungry and eat their full—after we have given thanks to God!

Up to eighteen teenagers aged 12 to 16 storm our 'bistro' on Monday evenings. This is an urban youth centre, and in the immediate vicinity are two Turkish mosques and a Kurdish cultural centre. The surrounding area is peopled almost exclusively by foreigners. A number of teenagers who join us are Russian Germans but the majority have a Turkish background. During the first hour we play group games that begin and end in chaos, but everyone has fun.

The second hour has no formal structure. As music plays we engage the teens in games or table football. They buy cans of Coke and when we have opportunities, we talk to them about life and faith issues. Because this is a state-run centre we can't have a Christian programme, but it is a good place to make contact.

Some volunteers find the ground too hard. One person emailed the team saying that he was shocked at the kids' language, loudness and behaviour. But Christians from various communities continue to help out.

In addition to the Bistro Mondays we offer other days for activities like crafts, dancing and frisbee. OM's Xenos team takes its name from the Greek word for 'stranger' and is one of three outreach teams in Germany, working with immigrants and asylum seekers in the hope of introducing them to Jesus. Xenos workers also offer workshops to churches and those interested in showing the love of Jesus to minority groups. Pray that more Christians in this country will catch the vision for reaching out to youth who are caught between two cultures.'

—Alexander and Sarah Pfisterer, OM Germany

Sweden: Going Underground

'I was already about ten minutes late,' related Korean-American OMer Ja-Kyung Moon. 'As I ran to the centre I made good use of the time praying that God would somehow use me to build His Kingdom.

'At first I couldn't even find the right entrance. I asked for directions from some of the youth who usually came to Underground, but the doors were locked. So I had to take the stairs behind the building. Three girls were hanging out there, smoking, and they asked if I wanted to smoke some weed, too. Actually they had only cigarettes and maybe they didn't realise that I was one of the leaders, because they started making racy suggestions about what they could do with me. One girl pointed to her older friend and announced she was a stripper, which I figured was a lie.

'A boy showed up and joined our conversation for a little while, but soon went inside to the centre. Somehow I felt led to stay outside and continue my conversation with the girls. At first I just talked about what smoking could do to us. I knew that most of what I was saying to them was just going in one ear and out the other.

'Later I found out that the two younger girls were Syrians and nominal Christians. The older one, 19, was half Syrian and half Swedish. She told me that she wanted to go to Stockholm to study rehabilitation for criminals and addicts. During the conversation I also found out that this girl was actually a cousin of one of the youth at the church. Somehow her heart opened then and she shared her story with me. I learned that her mother was in jail for selling drugs, her father was in a gang and had also been in and out of prison for pushing drugs. So she had been living with her uncle for the last sixteen years.

'Soon I was sharing my testimony. When I was about to tell her what kinds of changes God brought to my heart and my life after meeting Jesus, however, she sprang up and started to run away.

'"I can't take this any more!" she screamed.

'Her two friends physically grabbed her and brought her back. "You're not going anywhere," they told her. "You gotta listen to this."

'So, I got to finish my testimony. At one point I felt like sitting down on the steps, but they were so filthy with spit, garbage, cigarette stubs and melted snow I couldn't. So I just stood there. I could not believe there was a place like this in beautiful Sweden.

'When I told the girl that I would pray for her, she shook her head. "I don't want your prayers," she said defiantly. Then she added, "When I needed it, no one came to help!"

'As she fumbled for another cigarette she claimed that she loved the devil. I sensed the deep hurt, disappointment and anger in this girl's heart. All I could think of to say at that moment was that I wished the best for her, that I cared about her sufferings. I wished her success in Sweden and hoped she would accomplish her goal of studying so that she could help others.

'In the middle of our discussion the girls asked me why I had come to Sweden, and a city like Råslätt. Eventually I could explain that I came because I cared for the youth here, and I wanted them to know how much God loves them. I wanted them to have the same hope I did, to experience transformed lives. The two younger girls said that Sweden needed more people like me, that Jesus was shining through me.

'This is just one of the stories of what many of the immigrant youth face in this community where I am serving. When I see their lives—directionless and without proper adult care and love—it breaks my heart. I believe that it breaks God's heart, too. Many families here are broken. Nor do the problems just belong to immigrants. The Swedish youth, even in some of the churches, are just as much a mission field. They are so much in need of healing, unity and the fresh infilling and empowerment of the Holy Spirit!'

OM's Peter Magnusson calls Sweden and Denmark two of the most secularised societies in the world.

'Christian organisations here are often looked upon with suspicion,' he observes. 'The fact that OM Sweden has worked twenty-four years with the local church in Råslätt, Jönköping has, however, created a lot of trust. When the city-owned housing company got a new CEO in 1995 he called me and a local pastor to his office and stated: "You represent two organisations that have made the community a better place to live. So what can I do for you?" This led to starting a secondhand shop to create job opportunities and provide a place to buy less expensive household goods and clothing. The rent we pay is only a fraction of the normal cost and we also get help from the company. Even our OM office and other property got a significant rent reduction.

'Then about two years ago we were asked by the city to run the local youth centre on Saturday nights. They kept it going the rest of the week but could no longer afford Saturdays. So OM started running the centre every other week, at first, and eventually every Saturday, with the help of church members. The city-owned facility gives us access to a lot of resources, including two sport halls.

'This particular area is the poorest in this region of Sweden, with many large families living in small flats. Over 95% of the local school students are foreign, from about sixty countries. Several of the fifty-plus regular teens that attend the centre have serious social problems. Some also have issues with the police. At the beginning we had to focus a lot on boundaries, since these kids had never learned what was acceptable behaviour. We had almost only boys to begin with since girls were either not allowed to go, or they didn't want to because the boys mistreated them. But after we were very clear about what we would allow the atmosphere improved.

'Now we hardly ever have to deal with boundaries, as the kids tell each other to behave! The trust in the community and good atmosphere has also made it possible for girls to come. Fifty percent of the group is now girls, which is quite unusual in such a Middle Eastern/Asian context. The kids evaluate what we do, and comparing Saturdays with weekdays when the centre is run by the city they say they like the weekend environment a lot better. Recently I overheard one of our boys, who has a lot of problems and robbed a shop last year, earnestly telling others they should behave at the centre and be careful with the equipment!

'The local manager from the city who is responsible for youth work is himself a Muslim. He admitted recently that he had been a bit doubtful when his boss first suggested co-operating with the church and OM. He said the main reason was that he knew most adults couldn't handle these kids, and in his opinion having more adults in their lives that couldn't command their respect was worse than no adults at all.

'But very soon kids from all backgrounds were telling him how well it worked on Saturday nights and how good the atmosphere was. So now he is our biggest supporter, always telling us how much our work means to the community. He relates what we do in all kinds of official meetings, adding his opinion that these Christian are doing a great job! This man is committed to raising all ministry funds for us and makes sure we have all the support we need. Last week we got a thank-you gift from him—cinema tickets and other items for each person who has been involved with us as staff.

'So we are very encouraged. We truly believe that the holistic approach to youthwork—focusing on emotional, social and spiritual growth and change—is a model that could work very well in many of our countries. If we do not have hidden agendas and make a real impact in society we believe that money never will be a problem, and as Christians we can make a huge difference. We are not only appreciated in immigrant communities but among personnel working in schools and social services, some of whom are at the highest official levels and may be from a very secular if not atheistic background.'

Peter admits that as yet no teens have accepted Christ. However, they know they have built many firm relationships with young people in need, and believe a spiritual commitment is the next step for some.

'We have also built a lot of trust in the community,' he notes. 'Often we get the chance to talk about our values and what motivates us. Last weekend some boys asked me if I make a lot of money as I travel for my other responsibilities, and I had the chance to tell them that I do that work for free as well, and that I believe it's more important to make a positive difference than make a lot of money.

'Besides the youth centre ministry I have been giving free private driving lessons. This creates great personal relationships, keeps kids from driving illegally and makes a huge difference to those who are from poor backgrounds and can't pay for a driving school. We hope to develop this idea and recruit more people.

'We are also looking into how to help teenagers with schoolwork, find them part time work, and meet some of their other needs. We are developing a special working relationship with the Department of Social Services which supports immigrant young people and their families. Our hope is that they will employ some of our people on a contract basis for a few support hours per week, in order to meet with individual teens in need. My wife and I are already doing this for a number of kids from Middle Eastern backgrounds.'

OM Sweden is slated to start a training programme for potential youth workers in the near future. The vision is to combine course and practical work for youth
from about sixty different nationalities. Europeans who don't need work permits
and want to stay a second year to work with needy youth may be offered small
salaries through social services, as mentioned. Since many immigrant teens speak
good English, trainees will be able to manage in that language or their own. They
will learn a lot about youth culture, foreign cultures, child protection and many
other issues.

But the focus, stresses Peter, will be on how to build relationships rather than
programmes; how to generate lasting impact instead of excitement, and how to
empower instead of entertain. They would welcome your prayers for this initiative!

Empowering Through Training and Exposure

Youth conferences, training camps, adventure teams and short-term mission
opportunities have proliferated in recent decades as churches and missions have
come to recognise their long-term benefits in promoting spiritual, social and educational growth. An exposure trip, whether lasting a day or several months, can
leave a big impression. Thousands of organisations that have invested in teens and
young adults are seeing graduate short-termers go on to lifetime service all over the
world. OM is one of them.

Below, OM Germany's Corinna Scharrenberg describes how an initiative to
reach Europe's teens has become a prototype for use in other continents.

A Walk on TeenStreet

It all started in a Dutch pizza parlor back in 1992. Dan and Suzie Potter were
challenged by senior OM leaders Stuart McAllister and Dennis Wright to start a
conference for teenagers that could run parallel to OM International's Love Europe congress. The creative couple from America had developed an empathy with
youth, as they both grew up in families where youth ministry was part of everyday
life. Suzie's evangelist parents had started a church in their home, and she was the
third generation to work with young people. Dan's parents had also come from

a line of youth workers; they began to help teenagers full time when he was four years old. Small wonder that the couple were ready to accepted this new venture.

With the help of co-workers in OM Germany who agreed to provide practical support, the first teen congress took place in 1993 in Offenburg, Germany. TeenStreet was born.

'We gave it the name "TeenStreet" for two reasons,' explain the Potters. 'The whole purpose of the event was to give teens a street to travel upon … a way to live. Also, the words 'Teen' and 'Street' were international enough that they could be used anywhere in Europe without translation.'

Only 56 participants came to that first congress. Ali was 15 years old at the time and recalls, 'TeenStreet was an unknown camp for Christian teens from around Europe. Everything was in one big building: main meetings, accommodation, dining room, sports and so on. It was all done in a creative way and so much fun! I was touched to hear stories from people not much older than myself, see how God was using them and learn how He could use me, too. I really feel like it was a turning point in my relationship with God and my decision to live more fully for Him.'

Now an adult, Ali works among teenagers in the Netherlands and is part of the TeenStreet leadership team.

During the following years the number of participants grew rapidly. In 1997 over 1,000 signed up and from 2003 on, between 3,300 and 3,900 teenagers have gathered annually from all over Europe. Even the small, far-flung Faroe Islands sent 318 teens and adults from different denominations in 2010. Soon new congresses were being launched in Uruguay, Brazil, India, the Czech Republic, Malaysia, South Africa and Australia. More are in the works for other countries around the world.

But TeenStreet is not about numbers or places, it is a vision to see teenagers transformed. TeenStreet exists to work with the church to motivate and equip Christian teens to have a real friendship with Jesus—and to reflect Him daily in their world.

The mother of a German teenager girl who had attended the congress confided, 'My daughter filled in a piece of paper, writing down what she wanted God to do with her life. Her wish was that her classmates would come to faith and that she could be a witness for the Lord. Now she rejoices because a girl from her class came to know Jesus, and a boy wants to join the royal rangers [Christian scouts]!'

A number of countries hold mini-TeenStreet events and reunions through the year. Swedish co-ordinator Anette tells of a reunion in Jöngköping, Sweden, with everyone singing the song '*Hosanna (I see a generation)*' by Hillsong. 'As I looked around, I felt convinced that those teenagers *were* going to change the world. But I was more excited when I saw how God was creating a lasting change in their lives. A girl came up to me and said, "For the first time I understand what Jesus did for me at the cross." To sit next to her and see tears running down her face made all the work worthwhile!'

Dan and Suzie led the TeenStreet Germany programme until 2006 and call it the best and hardest times of their lives. 'God trusted us, and OM, with something much bigger than any of us. He could have given His dream to anyone, but He chose us and we pray that we are always faithful to his call.'

The couple particularly recall an evening during TeenStreet 2002.

'We challenged the young people in the audience that night to commit themselves to making a difference in their world. We now meet hundreds of men and women who stood up in that particular meeting, who lived that choice; and today they are serving all over the world. We would have to point to that evening as the moment we realised our small part in God's great call of young people.'

In 2007, Irish-American couple Josh and Debs Walker took over responsibility for the programme at TeenStreet Germany. The two of them had been attending since the second congress, helping the sports team and doing on-stage interviews. Later they worked together with the Potters to plan the main meetings. They say their heartbeat for TeenStreet is 'to see teenagers reaching others, taking over responsibility. Teens who know and live their gifts and become the people God wants them to be.'

TeenStreet has always been built upon small groups: six to seven young people of the same age, gender and home country. Together with their group leader they spend mornings discussing the Bible and engaging in the 'Big Adventure,' a personal study time in which they go deeper into what they have heard in the main meetings. Through these Big Adventure experiences, teens learn to spend time alone with God, to read His word and listen to Him.

After several years the congresses added half an hour of total quietness to this programme; thirty minutes during the morning in which teenagers and adults are challenged to listen to God in silence, and experience His presence. Many adults express amazement that two thousand or more teenagers can actually be quiet for that length of time! The rest of a typical TeenStreet day is filled with creative activities including sports, workshops and seminars; an art-zone, where teenagers are encouraged to use their artistic skills; and of course a lot of time for communication, getting to know each other and relaxing.

The evening's highlight is the 'Throne Room' worship event. For many years the Dutch 'World News Band' led teenagers into praise and worship. Again and again, spontaneous shouts proclaiming the name of Jesus fill the huge meeting centre.

The strategy of using small groups with a group leader makes TeenStreet very attractive for church youth groups. Youth pastor Marc from a church in southern Germany shared, 'Since 2002 we've gone as a church to TeenStreet. The first year we had three group leaders and five participants. The following year we had nine group leaders and 35 teens! The word must have spread that TeenStreet is cool.

'Since then, the event has become part of our annual plan and for many it is the highlight of the year. TeenStreet fits perfectly into our church concept. We have arranged our youth into small groups and those small groups go together with their leaders to the congress.

'Of course, we also have other teenagers joining our small groups at Teen-Street. But this is good because we get to know other teens and churches. The programme and atmosphere at TeenStreet is special and we all are excited about it.'

He added, 'Throughout the year we have our own youth service at our church, where nearly everything is "just like TeenStreet": food, worship, fun and message. You can learn a lot from that event concerning method, content and programme. And if you ask about an encounter with Jesus, nearly all of our young people can share a story from TeenStreet of how Jesus became important to them.'

Jarle Skullerud, Director of Youth Ministry of the Evangelical Lutheran Free Church in Norway until 2011, has brought groups to TeenStreet for several years. He commented, 'Although there are many youth conferences in Scandinavia, none are able to offer Christian teenagers what TeenStreet does. TeenStreet has a unique way of combining Biblical truth with secular issues.'

The week-long programmes focus on three core values: impact, relationship and empowerment. TeenStreet seeks to have a lasting impact on teenagers' lives, to empower them to make their own decisions and to fulfill their potential. The small groups focus on relationships: a real relationship with God and healthy interaction with each other.

Teens in Mission (TiM) is an offshoot of TeenStreet that started in 1998, when a group of 20 teens took what they'd learned at the congress to the streets of Poland. The next year TiM training took place at TeenStreet before 130 participants spread out to Poland, Czech Republic and Italy, where OM had organised practical outreach projects. During the following years TiM offered more options to the growing numbers joining teams in Switzerland, Czech Republic, Belgium, Ireland, Italy, Sweden, Hungary, Ukraine and the UK.

TiM has now moved beyond the TeenStreet setting, taking place at different times of the year and in other countries in the world. In addition, tailor-made TiM experiences have been launched so that whole youth groups can go together to serve in other countries.

It is the desire of both TeenStreet and TiM organisers to see a new generation rise up, a tidal wave of young people fully trusting that God can use them now and not sometime in the future, equipped to reach this fallen world.

The idea birthed in a Dutch pizzeria so many years ago has grown into an international movement that is building the kingdom of God. Countless lives of teenagers as well as group leaders and adults have been transformed over the last seventeen years.

In the summer of 2010 TeenStreet turned eighteen and came of age. Please join us in expecting great things for the future! With God's help, history is being written for eternity.

Empowering Students

Ministries like UCCF (Universities and Colleges Christian Fellowship) and IFES (International Fellowship of Evangelical Students) have long served as lifelines for young men and women at a pivotal time in their lives. But too many churches miss out on the blessings of reaching out to nearby student populations. One UK-based organisation called 'Fusion' has made it their business to serve the church by developing student workers and linking students to local churches. Fusion Student Missions Developer James Hewitt explains below how we can help to generate a 21st Century student movement that will see many thousands of students respond to Christ.

A Manifesto for Church-Based Student Mission

At the end of his time on earth, in his final meeting with his followers, Jesus gathers his disciples on a mountain. Here, against this dramatic and rugged backdrop, Jesus invites his disciples to meet him and receive their commission. Then he speaks. *'All authority in heaven and on earth has been given to me. Therefore go and make disciples of all nations, baptising them in the name of the Father and of the Son and of the Holy Spirit, and teaching them to obey everything I have commanded you.'* (Matthew 28:18–20, NIV) Incredibly, Jesus chose his followers—including us, the church—to fulfil the ultimate renovation project.

Today, in local churches across Europe, followers of Jesus continue to take responsibility for this great commission. Matthew used the Greek words *'pas ethnos'* to describe the call to 'all nations,' which could just as easily be translated as 'every tribe, nation or people group.' In Europe today is a unique and growing people group representing almost 2.5 million people in the UK and many millions more across the continent. They can be found in every major city and many smaller towns. Members of this group consistently go on to have a significant impact on society, often taking positions of great responsibility in business and politics. This community is often stereotyped, sometimes marginalised; currently less than 2% of them know Jesus, making them one of the largest unreached people groups. Hundreds of local churches find many of them living, working and socialising on their doorstep. Many fellowships are trying to engage with this particular culture in spite off its quirks and unique patterns of sleeping, eating and working. What is this people group? Students, of course.

> If I hadn't met Jane giving out bottles of water to students after their night out, and if she hadn't taken the time to invite me and welcome me into her life ... then I'm not sure that I would now be involved with a church, and engrossed in the learning and love of Jesus that I now feel.—Student who was introduced to Christ at university

Local churches are uniquely placed to be able to reach the student population. Whilst the average student may only be at university for three or four years, the local church has the opportunity to build year on year, making a long-term investment in the student community. Every local church within a five mile radius of a university has a part to play. Students represent a diverse mix of personalities and consequently will be attracted to a range of different church cultures, styles and denominations. If a church has even a single student as a member, it has a missionary on campus with access to their hall of residence, their course mates, lecture theatres, student unions and friends. However, as universities have expanded, the emphasis is now no longer just on the campus. The church needs to look for ways to engage with the spectrum of student life: student housing in the town, clubs, societies, shops, cafés and bars.

→   See loveyouruni.org for more ideas about how local churches
     can engage with student life.

The church was God's idea, and it is still the most effective missional tool. In local churches, students can grow in leadership and responsibility, taking charge of initiatives to reach their fellow students. They can also serve the church and be positively influenced by its more mature members, developing values which they will carry into whatever spheres of influence they enter in the future.

Where some reports continue to suggest that universities are becoming increasingly secular and closed to churches, there are many stories illustrating how, when relationships are cultivated, universities are often open to the work of churches and their students. Fifteen years ago a congregation in Britain's East Midlands was inspired to see God transform the local university culture and draw thousands of students to himself. They began with a commitment to pray, often rising early to walk around the campus and intercede with God on behalf of the students and staff. Over the years, the church has seen hundreds of students become disciples. They now hold a weekly Sunday gathering in the student union building as well as enjoy a fantastic relationship with the student union executive. The church also began an initiative called Club Mission which has inspired a number of similar projects in other churches around the country.

'The vision of Club Mission is to help students on nights out in the student union in any way they can, embodying Jesus' love,' says Paul, who headed up the Club Mission team whilst he was a student. 'It's now become an official part of the student union, working alongside the security staff. We've also been given a room to chat to people and another one to pray in, as well as having a mobile prayer team walking around the venue.' The initiative went on to be voted 'Loughborough University team of the Year' by the student union staff.

> Last night I found a guy weeping outside the student union. He
> had just found out that his dad had been involved in a serious
> car accident, and was in a coma. We managed to help him back
> to hall … and had an amazing opportunity to pray with him, and
> tell him how much God loved him and his family. We then let him
> get to bed, and encouraged him to pray, which he did.—Students
> involved in Club Mission initiative

Student life presents many challenges. Loneliness, stress, broken relationships and struggles with emotional and spiritual health are commonplace. A million young people come from other countries to study in Europe every year; often they feel isolated and homesick, and many have never encountered Christianity. Christian students and the local churches they attend can play an important part in walking with people through these difficult times, helping them grow in wholeness and introducing them to Jesus for the first time.

Whilst the ultimate goal is clearly for people to start a new life with Jesus, 'declaring the Word and the name of Christ, the call to repentance, and faith and obedience'[3], Scripture records a variety of ways that people initially encountered Jesus. Nicodemus, laden with theological questions, began by seeking understanding in a secret night time meeting with Jesus. For many their first encounter was being miraculously healed; for a woman caught in adultery, it was an act of forgiveness and new freedom; Zacchaeus found his Saviour inviting himself to his house for a meal!

> I'm really interested in encouraging friendships cross-culturally.
> I heard about a church that hosts meals every fortnight with
> storytelling sessions. They've had about 20–30 students coming
> along, including Muslims and Hindus. The team have been
> trained in storytelling (see www.cafecredo.org.uk) and use a mix
> of Bible and other stories to encourage discussion and slowly
> explain who Jesus is.—UK Student

Similarly, students will encounter Jesus in different ways. Where one student might feel the need to engage with philosophical and theoretical questions with regard to faith, another may be impacted by a simple act of kindness. Students and their churches can invest time in creating a myriad of possibilities for students to encounter Jesus. From informal chats with housemates at 2 o'clock in the morning to running a mini Student Alpha[4] course with friends in a hall of residence, from leading apologetic events to offering free water outside student nightclubs, we need many approaches. We also need to get everyone involved, committing to share the Good News of Jesus with the millions of students who are yet to encounter or even hear about Him.

Every local church, every Christian student, has a part to play. We have a mountain to climb but we move onward and upward, empowered by Jesus' great promise in Matthew: *And surely I am with you always, to the very end of the age.*

Russia: Empowering Through Discipleship

Colin and Bron Cleaver are leaders of OM Russia and the founders of OM's Discipleship Centre in Novosibirsk, Siberia, which operates in partnership with the Russian Baptist Union.

'The idea is to provide a place where young Christians can spend an intensive six months studying and grounding themselves in the Bible,' explain the Cleavers. 'They also learn how to develop their gifts through a mixture of classroom teaching and practical ministry experience, using their training to reach out and disciple others.'

Of the 32 young people who have studied at the Centre during its first five years, 11 were formerly drug addicts, 2 formerly alcoholics, and 4 were orphans. These same young people are now planting and running churches, children's camps and clubs, serving in rehabilitation centres, and preaching and teaching.

Many churches in Russia are working together to run a number of well-organised drug and alcohol rehabilitation schemes. These programmes, combined with a growing evangelistic work amongst students, are ensuring a steady trickle of young converts into the churches.

'God is at work choosing and saving the "foolish, weak, lowly and despised,"' affirm Colin and Bron. "He is transforming them to become mighty warriors in his army, fighting against the very same kingdom of darkness that once held them in captivity!'

Here they share the true story of just one of those young people.

Losers No Longer*

'So, what do you think Satan has for us today?' Andrey Barkov smirked at Georgi, his best friend and partner in crime.

'Let's find out,' he shrugged. The pair took off in search of money, drugs and oblivion.

Andrey had hit an all-time low. Over the last year he had been through three Christian drug rehabilitation centres. Each time, once he was away from his old

* Andrey's story is included in a booklet written by Colin and Bron Cleaver called 'The Siberian Six,' which can be ordered from the website, www.ru.om.org

friends, he was able to stop taking drugs and even experienced God's forgiveness and peace in his heart. However, every time he went home his friends would drive up in their car and invite Andrey to join them on a drugs run. Andrey was powerless to refuse. It was the same story for Georgi, who had also been through a Christian rehab centre. He, too, had prayed a prayer of repentance and experienced the joy and freedom that only God can give. But then he had capitulated for the sake of a high which would last only a few hours. Now they had given up trying. Both had abandoned themselves to whatever fate Satan had in store for two drug users who had turned their backs on God.

A car drove up and Andrey hopped in eagerly, anticipating the high he would experience once he got his hands on what he needed. He had already stolen his father's phone and work tools so that he would have enough money to really go for it this time. He and his friends got hold of the drugs—never difficult to find—and Andrey started to enjoy his purchase as they drove back. With the music booming in the back of the car no-one noticed when his head was slumped between his knees, his breathing rasping and irregular. One of the others complained of a headache and insisted that the music be turned down. Only then did they hear the sound of death approaching as Andrey, already unconscious from an overdose, started to make a strange noise deep in his throat. They stopped the car and threw him into the snow, rubbing it in his face and on his chest, trying to get him to come around.

Growing up, Andrey had been one of life's losers. Seeking the respect of the older boys at school, he soon got mixed up with a gang who went around bullying and beating up other boys, stealing cigarettes, smoking soft drugs and taking tablets. For a real kick in the holidays they experimented with intravenous drugs. Upon leaving school he got a place in a local college, but could never see the point of studying. For instance, on the day of his final exams, instead of trying to pass them he shrugged his shoulders, turned his back on the college and went fishing. He just didn't care. There were surely many easier ways of making money than getting an education and working for a living!

Gradually, however, Andrey felt that he was on a conveyor belt that was running backwards. He saw friends around him growing up, getting jobs, getting married, starting families, moving on in life. Try as he might to get the same things his conveyor was steadily rolling backwards, taking him with it. If he found a girl he liked and started going out with her, it was never long before she realised that he was a drug addict and would have nothing more to do with him. His former classmates started turning their backs on him. Who wanted a friend who was a drug addict? Then Andrey's conveyor belt began to accelerate backwards. As the realisation slowly dawned on him that he wasn't wanted by anyone, he felt the cold grip of despair. The only way he knew to free himself from his depression was by taking more drugs, which in turn drove him further away from what he wanted: a steady job, a soul mate and a place in society.

Sometimes he would try to outrun the conveyor belt, giving up drugs for a time and earning some honest money. But even when he could make up some ground, sooner or later he would look at the wage packet in his hand and imagine the temporal ecstasy he could convert it into. Then he'd stop running and allow himself to be carried even further backwards into his old life.

There was one day, however, when a tiny spark of hope came alive in Andrey. He was lying in a dark room in his parent's house, disappointed and despondent, when his fellow drug-addict friend, Georgi, came around. Yet, this wasn't quite the Georgi that Andrey knew. When Georgi had been invited to a Christian reha-bilitation centre a while back Andrey had laughed. 'He'll have all of those church people taking drugs before you know it, and then he'll steal all their church bells and icons!'

Now his old friend had returned and was insisting that the whole family gather together in the sitting room. When everyone had assembled and they sat looking at him with puzzled expressions, Georgi pulled out a large black Bible and started reading to them. Looking back now, Andrey realises that Georgi was bluffing his first-ever sermon. He didn't really know what he was talking about, only trying to repeat bits and pieces he'd somehow picked up. Yet even though his words didn't really make any sense, everyone in the room was struck by the change they saw in this former addict. His eyes were shining, and there really was something different about him.

Georgi told Andrey eagerly, 'You really need to come to the Baptist church, to the rehab centre!'

'Will they make me like you? Can they change me, too?' asked Andrey.

'Of course. Let's go!' his friend replied, and off they went.

Russians can be extremely suspicious of anything to do with a Protestant church, especially a Baptist one, since they had been programmed to believe many lies about believers. Andrey was no exception. Although he had walked past the church building many times because it was located in the area of town where drugs were on sale, he had no idea what it was about. He thought that Baptist Christians were English people living according to 200-year-old traditions. Surely nothing could be more irrelevant?

When he finally crossed the threshold of the church building and sat down, his worst fears were confirmed. The first man who spoke didn't have any teeth at all, and the next one to speak had a ridiculous haircut. He shifted anxiously on his seat and at one point seriously expected poisoned gas to be released through the ventilation system. After the service, however, people started to approach Andrey in a way he wasn't used to, as if they truly cared about him. It was as though this was one big family and they were extending their love to him. They even showed their love practically, offering to buy him a train ticket to an outlying drug rehabilitation centre where he could get help.

Andrey agreed to go, and with his parents' agreement, started on the 36 hour train journey to the small town of Yelisyesk, in the North of Siberia. As the train drew nearer to his destination he panicked. He had never been far from his hometown before. How would he ever find this rehab centre? He knew nothing about it and didn't know anyone there. When he had expressed his doubts before, Georgi had suggested that he pray.

'But what is prayer?' demanded a frantic Andrey.

'Prayer is when you tell God what you want and then, when you've finished, you have to say "In the name of God the Father, the Son and the Holy Spirit. Amen,"' his friend had advised.

Equipped with this useful information, Andrey prayed continually over the next hours and eventually made it safely to the centre.

Once there he quickly made new friends and realised two things. One, it wasn't only old grandmothers who were Christians; and two, he was sinner who needed to ask the forgiveness of God. Andrey did repent and felt something change in his life, but before his rehabilitation course was over he became very ill with what later turned out to be hepatitis, and had to return home. When he got there he found out he wasn't the only one now going to church. While he had been away his parents had started to go along on Sundays and take part in church life!

However, for Andrey this wasn't enough. When the crunch came, he still couldn't say 'no' to the promise of a drug induced euphoria, and neither could Georgi. Their downward spiral became ever steeper. They had encountered truth, light and love but turned their backs on it. And eventually it led to Andrey lying near death on the roadside, with his friends desperately rubbing snow on his body in an attempt to revive him.

Fortunately, they managed to bring him back to consciousness. As Andrey emerged two thoughts came into his head. The first was, if he had died, where would he have ended up? But the second thought quickly shoved the first out of the way: *I know that there are still more drugs in the car, but now I've overdosed I won't be able to take any more. The others will get to enjoy them and I'll miss out!*

As he caught himself thinking like this he came to his senses, in just the same way as the prodigal son suddenly came to his, while pushing the pigs aside to get at their food. What was he thinking? A crowd had gathered to see what was happening. Was this young druggie alive or not? Ignoring the people around him Andrey got on his knees in the snow, and began to ask God not only to save him, but to become Lord of his life.

Something definitely changed inside him that moment. He went back to church and started to get more and more involved in church life. The young people there were invited to a youth conference in a neighbouring town and Andrey went with them. He had a packet of cigarettes with him, but couldn't get away from all the other Christians to have a quiet smoke. When he returned home he finally took out his packet of cigarettes, held it in his hand, and realised that for the first time in his life he didn't want to smoke. He threw the cigarettes away and bought an ice-cream instead.

Soon afterwards, as he was walking to a church prayer meeting, his old friends pulled up alongside in a car and nodded for him to get in. They were on a drug run. It was the moment of truth, the point he had always fallen down in the past. Would he be able to fight against the temptation? But then he did a double take and realised that there was actually nothing to fight against! He simply didn't want to go with the gang anymore. It was as easy as that. God really had changed him from the inside out.

His friends tried to persuade him, but Andrey only smiled. There was no way they could persuade him to do something he simply had no desire to do. Eventually they drove off without him and he finished walking to the church meeting, full of joy. For the first time in Andrey's life, he understood the meaning of victory.

Now that he was finally free of the addiction which had controlled so much of his life, he started to grow spiritually. Andrey was asked to become the leader of a nearby drug rehabilitation centre which had lost its former manager. Although he had just started a new job with his father's construction firm and didn't want to let him down, he realised that there were people in need in this centre who could literally die if he didn't help. So off he went.

While working in the centre, Andrey met an older Christian in a nearby church who took care of him and started, gently, to disciple him. Andrey kept growing. For the first time in his life, something that he was working at was actually succeeding. He was no longer a loser, but being used by God to rescue others.

A new chapter of Andrey's life opened up when his pastor suggested that he study at OM Russia's Discipleship Centre for six months. Although he wasn't used to studying at all, Andrey soaked up all the knowledge he could, throwing himself into the practical parts of the course and working with children, teenagers, and young people; preaching, teaching and going on evangelistic trips. Again, Andrey was becoming more and more convinced that not everything he turned his hand to would fail. God could—and would—use him to help build His kingdom, especially if he made his personal relationship with Him a priority over everything else.

At one prayer meeting during the Discipleship course, Andrey listened to a missionary couple from Northern Ireland, Charles and Ann Uprichard, talk about their work with alcoholics. They had moved to Siberia several years before and, after renovating a brick skeleton of a house, started and built a ministry with alcoholics. He was deeply touched by their obedience to God. Charles and Ann had given up everything to serve Him, moving to a foreign country with just a couple of suitcases and the prayers of their church back home.

After graduating from the Discipleship Centre, Andrey married a young lady he had met in one of the Novosibirsk churches. Nina was also a former drug addict and had served as the leader of a rehab centre for women. The couple moved back to Andrey's hometown of Rubsovsk and Andrey started working for his father once again. He was made youth leader in the church and as he considered his new life, Andrey realised that he now had it all: a beautiful new wife, a child on the way, a good job, a respected and responsible ministry at church and the possibility of building a small house on the land by his father's house. What Andrey didn't know was that God was soon to ask him and Nina to give it all up, and to set out on a new direction by faith.

After six months of building their new life together, Andrey and Nina received a phone call from the Northern Irish missionaries, the Uprichards, asking if they would consider moving back to Novosibirsk to help them in their work with alcoholics. After discussing the request with their church and families, Andrey and Nina decided to take the plunge and accept Charles' and Ann's offer. It wasn't an easy step. Andrey and Nina would have to live on very little money and they had a newborn daughter, Angelina. And although they knew a lot about drug addiction and drug addicts, they would have a lot to learn about the particular needs and problems of alcoholics.

After a year of working with Andrey and Nina, the older couple felt it was right to hand over the work and the centre and return to Northern Ireland. Now the Barkovs were responsible for the ministry!

Today, the centre for alcoholics houses up to twenty people and is a source of great blessing to many who have reached the end of their own resources and realise they need God's help, intervention and Lordship in their lives to carry on. With the confidence that Andrey has gained over the last few years, he is brimming with new ideas. He has begun a seminary correspondence course which will equip him to become a preacher and pastor, and he is working out how to make the centre financially self-sustaining. Ideas include everything from breeding rabbits for pies and soups to using a cart and horse to help take the sewage away, instead of paying for a truck! He also dreams about starting a new church in the basement. In the space of a few years, God has taken one of life's losers and turned him into a responsible, hard working visionary. Who knows what the next few years hold in store?

In God's great providence, Georgi has also returned to faith and studied at the OM Russia Discipleship Centre. As part of his practical ministry, he chose to help Andrey and Nina with the centre for alcoholics. Now all of their lives have turned around 180 degrees. And each day is greeted with an optimism that shouts, 'So—*what do you think God has for us today?*'

Resources—Children's Ministry

See also the end of the 'Partnering with the Church' section of this book: 'Resources—Mission Websites for Kids'

▦ Miscellaneous Websites for Kids

▪OSCAR   www.oscar.org.uk/service/children/
                                               scott.pdf
A list of resources for awareness-raising among children and teens (2006-7, slightly dated but worth checking out) has been compiled by Rosie Scott of WEC International.

▪Salvation Challenge (and other games) www.biblicalstrategy.com

▪Torchlighters   www.torchlighters.org
Heroes of the Faith DVD series. Kidzone page has related quizzes, puzzles and colouring pages.

▪WonderZone   www.wonderzone.com/games
Games by Child Evangelism Fellowship.

◼ Websites for Kids Ministry Workers

▪4–14 Window Global Initiative   http://4to14window.com

▪Child Evangelism Fellowship   www.cefonline.com

▪Children in Prayer   www.childreninprayer.org

▪Children's Ministry Magazine   www.childrensministry.com

▪Children's Ministry.net   www.childrensministry.net

▪Children's Ministry Today   www.childrensministry.org

▪Culture for Kids/Asia for Kids   www.cultureforkids.com,
                                     www.asiaforkids.com

▪Family Ministry   www.familyministry.co.uk

▪Hand in Hand   www.familyministry.co.uk

▪Kids Sunday School   www.kidssundayschool.com

▪Kidzana Ministries   www.kidzana.org

▪Kidz At Heart International   www.kidzatheart.org

▪KidsGames   www.kidsgames.com

▪Max7   www.max7.org

▪Ministry-to-Children.com   http://ministry-to-children.com

▪Stand for Kids   www.stand4kids.org

▪Today's Children's Ministry   www.christianitytoday.com/
                                     childrensministry

◼ Other Websites for Information about Children at Risk

▪European Federation for Street Children
                                     http://www.efsc-eu.org/index.php

▪Society for the Protection of Unborn
 Children   www.spuc.org.uk

▪Railway Children   www.railwaychildren.org.uk

- Street Kids International   www.streetkids.org
- Viva   www.viva.org

→ **World Weekend of Prayer for Children at Risk**, first weekend of
   June. Downloadable resources from Viva Network: www.viva.org

   Choose a date to hold an **Orphan Sunday**:
   http://orphansunday.org

Resources—Ministries for Students and Young Adults

◼ Agencies, Opportunities and Networks—A Selection

See also Appendix: 'Missions in Europe—Students and Youth' list and 'Partnering with the Church—Resources—Trips and Opportunities.'

- Changemaker (Norway)   www.changemaker.no
  For Norwegian young people who want to make a difference.

- Dare to be a Daniel   www.DareToBeaDaniel.com
  Billy Graham youth site, for Christian students who want to learn how to share their faith.

- EEA21   www.eea21.eu
  A community of those committed to reaching young Europeans for Christ, part of the European Evangelical Alliance.

- Fusion [UK]   www.fusion.uk.com
  Working with students, serving churches, developing student workers.
  Resources include cell group materials, a student worker handbook and packs for preparing youth for the transition to university.

- International Christian Fellowship (ICF) www.icf.ch
  Church movement aimed at youth and charismatic evangelism and church planting, so far in 5 Western European countries.

- JAM for Friends (Germany)   www.jamforfriends.at/jugendseiten_
                                       37.html

- Jesus Revolution   www.jesusrevolution.com
  Youth reaching European youth. Training school in Norway, an annual
  summer team and group evangelistic and training events for churches in
  European cities through the year.

- Mission Adventures (YWAM)   www.missionadventures.net

- Pray Day (Germany)   www.prayday.de
  How to hold a prayer day in your school.

- Radiate [UK]   www.radiate-uk.com
  Designed and run by students for students.

- Reflex [UK]   www.reflex.org
  Youth for Christ ministry to young offenders and socially marginalised young
  people. Offers accredited training in music, theatre and sport.

- Right Now   www.rightnow.org
  North American agency partnering with 75 other mission organisations to help
  people in their 20s and 30s find their place in reaching the world for Christ.

- Schulbeweger (Germany)   www.schulbeweger.de
  How to start a Bible study group in your school.

- Student Alpha   www.alpha.org/students
  Student version of the Alpha Course. Also Youth Alpha, http://youthalpha.org

- Student Mobilisation   http://stumo.org
  To mobilise North American students to become labourers for Christ.

- Student Mobilization Centre   www.haystack.org
  A ministry of YWAM's University of the Nations 'to serve student
  organisations, mission agencies and local churches by helping ignite a new
  international, broad-structured and inclusive student mobilisation movement
  like that of the Student Volunteer Movement.'

- Students for Christ Europe (Pentecostal network)
                                         www.sfceurope.org

- Teen Q's (Questions and Answers)   www.christiananswers.net/teens/home.
  html

- Teens in Mission (TiM)   www.tim.om.org
  Practical, short-term experiences in mission; a ministry of Operation
  Mobilisation (OM).

- Teen Missions International   www.teenmissions.org
  This agency has 28 bases on six continents, training and sending thousands
  of teens for evangelistic and building projects in Europe and many other
  countries.

- Universities and Colleges Christian Fellowship [UCCF—UK]
                                           www.uccf.org.uk
  Network of Christian Union students, staff and supporters.

- University Ministries Network (AoG)   http://universityministriesnetwork.org/
                                           html/europe.html

■ Events for Youth

Below are some of the excellent, faith-building programmes regularly offered to
young people in Europe.

- ArtCross (Austria)   www.artcross.at
  Arts event hopefully to take place every two years.

- BUJU (Germany)   www.buju.org, www.buju.de
  Annual youth meeting of evangelical free churches.

- CampFest (Slovakia)   www.eng.campfest.sk
  4-day open-air Christian youth music festival.

- *Christaval* (Germany)   www.christaval.de
  The country's biggest congress for young Christians.

- Face to Face (Sweden)   www.equmenia.se/face-to-face
  Autumn youth event.

- Flevo Festival (Netherlands)   www.flevofestival.nl
  4-day event for 15–25 year-olds, organised by Youth for Christ.

- Freakstock Festival (Germany)   http://freakstock.de
  4-day 'Jesus Festival.'

- *Frizon* (Sweden)   www.frizon.se
  Annual August youth event.

- Fusion (UK)   www.fusion.uk.com
  Student weekends, 'Mind and Soul' Day Conference, Student Work
  Conference.

- Go-Fest (Norway)   www.ywam.no
  Youth With A Mission annual conference.

- Greenbelt (UK)   www.greenbelt.org
  Biggest British Christian festival for all ages celebrating arts, faith, justice.

- Gulbranna Festival (Sweden)   www.gullbrannafestivalen.se
  Annual August youth event.

- IFES Europe (International)   www.ifeseurope.org
  Many annual conferences including International Student Work Conference
  and Theological Students Conference.

- IMF UNG (Norway)   www.imf-ung.no
  Annual youth congress organised by Norwegian Inner Mission Federation.

- IMPULS (Norway)   www.impulsweb.no
  Large annual youth conference in January-February, also a small summer
  conference, with outreach.

- JesusHouse (Austria, Germany)   www.jesushouse.at, www.jesushouse.
  de

- Jesus to the Nations (Norway)   www.jtn.no
  Annual missions conference.

- Jongerendag (Netherlands)   www.eo.nl/jongerendag
  EO Youth Day.

- KEN (Greece)   www.k-e-n.gr

- *Korsvei* (Norway)   www.korsvei.no
  For alternative, simple lifestyle; possibly more for families, around 1000 people.

- KRIK (Norway)   www.krik.no
  Several youth camps held year-round, the largest in the summer.

- Mission.ch (Switzerland)   www.mission.ch
  This country's largest biannual youth mission event.

- Mission-Net (International)   www.mission-net.org
  European mission youth mission congress and movement, biannually held in
  Germany, ages 16–30.

- MOBILISE (UK)   http://mobiliseuk.org
  2 major annual events for students and 20's; one in the summertime in
  Brighton, plus a student workers' weekend.

- Pentecost Youth Conference (Austria)   http://2010.pfiju.at

- Pentecost Youth Conference (Germany) www.jugendtreffen-aidlingen.de,
                                                     www.pfijuko.de
  Annual event in two locations, Aidlingen and Bergneustadt.

- *Pinsevennene* (Norway)   www.pinsebevegelsen.no,
                                                     http://www.ufestivalen.no/index.html
  Large Pentecostal annual youth conference.

- Praise Camp (Switzerland)   www.praisecamp.ch
  Biannual teen and youth event attended by several thousand.

- ReachAUT (Reach Out, Austria)   www.reachaut.org

- Salzburger Youth Day (Austria)   www.jugendtag.at

- Schladminger Youth Day (Austria)   www.fontaene.at

- Skjærgårds Music & Mission Festival (Norway)
                                                     www.sginfo.no
  Camping, low key Christian holiday camp with good teaching for those
  interested and many concerts.

- SLOT Arts Festival (Poland)   www.slot.art.pl
  Arts platform where those who don't know God can discuss Him with those
  who do.

- Soul Survivor (UK, Netherlands)   www.soulsurvivor.com
  1-day and 5-day events.

- SOZO International Music & Arts Festival (Hungary)
                                                     www.sozofestival.com
  Training in music, arts, leadership and reconciliation ministry.

- TeenStreet (International)   www.teenstreet.om.org
  Annual summer conference in Europe as well as other continents for ages
  13–17, affiliated with Operation Mobilisation.

- Tenmisjonsfestivalen (Norway)   www.nmsu.no/tmf/
  Norwegian Mission Society's large annual conference.

- Ten-Oase (Norway)   www.oase.no
Oase is for adults, Ten-Oase for teens and Barne-Oase for kids; three Lutheran
Charismatic summer camps in one, totaling around 4000 people.

- The Gathering (UK)   www.serious4god.co.uk
Bands and speakers to 'raise worldchangers.' Run by Elim Pentecostal Churches
national youth department.

- Three Days (*Tre Dagar*, Sweden)   www.tredagar.se
Easter event for youth.

- Trans4mission (Finland)   www.lahetyskonffa.fi

- UPfest (Ukraine)   www.upfest.org.ua
Festival of music and art.

- Young (*Ungdommens landsmøte UL*, Norway)
                                         http://ul.no, www.nlm.no
Norwegian Lutheran Mission's annual youth congress.

▪ Suggested Reading

Boshers, Bo and Judson Poling. *The Be-With Factor: Mentoring Students in Everyday Life*. Zondervan, 2009.

Brown, Lindsay. *Shining Like Stars; The Power of the Gospel in the World's Universities*. IVP, 2006.

Dunn, Richard R. *Shaping the Spiritual Life of Students: A Guide for Youth Workers*. IVP, 2001.

Fields, Doug. *Purpose Driven Youth Ministry*. Zondervan, 1998.

Fields, Doug. *Your First Two Years in Youth Ministry: A Personal and Practical Guide to Starting Right*. Zondervan, 2002.

Johnston, Kurt and Tim LeVert. *9 Best Practices for Youth Ministry*. Simply Youth Ministry, 2010.

Katekaru, James. *Bearing Fruit That Will Last: Making Long Term Friendships with International Students*. Outskirts Press, 2007.

Loveyouruni: Guide to 21st Century Student Mission. Available at http://fusion-org.uk.com/resources

McDowell, Josh and Bob Hostetler. *Handbook on Counseling Youth: A Comprehensive Guide for Equipping Youth Workers.* Thomas Nelson, 1996.

Phillips, Tom and others. *The World at Your Door: Reaching International Students in Your Home, Church and School.* Bethany, 1997.

Pratney, Winkie. *Ultimate CORE: Church on the Radical Edge.* Bethany House, 2004.

Pratney, Winkie. *Youth Aflame: A Manual for Discipleship.* Bethany House, 1983.

West, Liz and Paul Hopkins. *The D Factor: Youth Discipleship, the Hole in Our Thinking?* Monarch, 2002.

■ Videos, Podcasts, etc.

- European Evangelical Alliance   http://www.eea21.eu
  Videos in various European languages.

■ Websites for Youth Ministry Leaders

- Christian Youth Ministry World — www.christianyouthministryworld.com
- Effective Youth Ministry — www.effectiveym.com
- International Christian Youthworks — www.icy.org.uk
- LYFE — www.lyfe.org.uk
- *Para Lideres* ('For Leaders,' Spanish) — www.paralideres.org
- Pray for Young People — http://prayforyoungpeople.info
- Rethinking Youth Ministry — www.rethinkingyouthministry.com
- Simply Youth Ministry — www.simplyyouthministry.com
- The Sophia Network — http://blog.sophianetwork.org.uk
- The Source for Youth Ministry — www.thesourcefym.com
- Youth Ministry.com — http://youthministry.com
- Youth Ministry Ideas — www.youthministryideas.net
- Youth Pastor.com — www.youthpastor.com
- Youth Specialties — www.youthspecialties.com
- Youth Unlimited — www.youthunlimited.org
- Youth Work International — www.youthworkinternational.com/

Section 4

Reaching Neighbours: Secular and Nominal Europeans

Introduction

Who Are Our European Neighbours, and How Can We Reach Them?

The 'neighbourbood' in Europe has changed radically in recent years. A generation ago, we expected our neighbours to have the same skin colour as ours, to be associated with some Christian church or another (if not our own), to speak our language at home, to be heterosexual and married, and to be raising their own biological children. Single parents were the exception. Dads and kids left mums and houses early in the morning with clockwork precision for the office, factory or school, returning home predictably in the afternoon or evening. And to be neighbours, by definition, they lived nearby.

Who are our European neighbours today? That will depend of course on whether we live in the country or the city, in Eastern or Western Europe. But for many of today's city-dwellers in Western Europe, our neighbours could come from virtually any country in the world, speak any language, adhere to any traditional religion or none, or even do-it-yourself spirituality. They could be homosexual, bi-sexual, or heterosexually active with many partners in the contemporary 'celebration of diversity.' Our neighbours' children are less likely to be the biological offspring of both partners of the particular expression of 'family' living in the dwelling next door. And perhaps, if one lives in Hamburg or Luton, our neighbours may have been involved in the 9/11 or 7/7 terrorist attacks ...

Our neighbours no longer simply live next door or across the street or even in the same town or city. Facebook, Twitter and Skype have shrunk the whole world into our mobile phones as we carry on endless conversations simultaneously with neighbours—physical and virtual.

So where do we begin to summarise such diversity and to develop effective ways to reach our neighbours with the love of Jesus? Perhaps it is helpful to identify five types of Europeans today, and then to ask what sort of strategies might speak to each category.

Let's start with Karl from Frankfurt in Germany, a typical *post-Christian European*. Karl now works for a major international bank in the financial district of Frankfurt. He was raised in a good Lutheran family, baptised as a child and confirmed when he became a teenager. But at school, and later at university, doubts about the authenticity of Christianity gave way to outright scepticism. He set his goals on pursuing a bank career and becoming a millionaire before he was 40. He never actually renounced his Christianity. It simply became irrelevant for life in the 21st Century, as far as Karl was concerned. His current girlfriend, his Porsche sports car and yuppie apartment are the realities that interest him the most. Karl is a practising pagan or atheist without necessarily any particular zeal for paganism or atheism as ideologies.

How can people like Karl be reached with the gospel, when they think they have tried it and found it wanting? Missiologist Lesslie Newbigin described the post-Christian pagan as being as different from the pre-Christian pagan as a divorcée is from a virgin. The post-Christian was a much more difficult prospect for evangelism, he argued, and a post-Christian society was the greatest contemporary missiological challenge.

Yet, despite the widespread assumption that the European secular way of life would eventually push religious faith into obscurity, with the rest of the world following, many academics and journalists are waking up to the surprising fact that 'God is back,' to use the title of a book by two editors from The Economist magazine.[35]

Secular materialism cannot meet the deepest human needs. The popular Alpha Course[36] is pitched to the Karls of this world who may be ready to ask, *is there more to life than this*? Alpha, with its personalised, relationship-oriented context of study and discussion around a meal, has proven an effective means for encouraging 'prodigals' to 'come to their senses' and return to 'Father's house.'

A crucial general principle in our contact with secular and nominal neighbours is that there is no substitute for genuine friendship, backed up by a transparent lifestyle of integrity, as preparation for that moment when we may be able to speak encouragement, truth, wisdom or insight into someone's life—as during a bereavement, loss of job, sickness or relationship breakdown.

One extreme form of the post-Christian European is represented by so-called 'New Atheists' like Richard Dawkins, militantly opposed to religion in general and the Christian faith in particular. To the embarrassment of many other scientists, they make grandiose claims for the ability of science to explain mysteries and meaning of life. Others latch on to their arguments about a 'God delusion' as a convenient excuse for ignoring their conscience on moral issues.

Oft-quoted atheistic author Aldous Huxley admitted candidly that the attraction of atheism for him was the permissive lifestyle it allowed. Yet, equally candidly, he conceded that 'science has explained nothing; the more we know the more fantastic the world becomes and the profounder the surrounding darkness.'

To engage with those influenced by these New Atheists, we should familiarise ourselves with both their arguments and the responses from Christian apologists[37]. An invitation to 'post-Christian' friends to watch and discuss the debate between Dawkins and fellow Oxford professor, John Lennox, a Christian mathematician, on DVD[38], could be an attractive way to open dialogue and witness, for example.

Olga, from Kiev in Ukraine, represents our second major category, *the post-Communist European*. In Western Europe we may not rub shoulders often with this sort of European, but in the former Communist countries, post-Communists are the daily reality.

Olga lives in a typical Stalinist-architecture apartment block in Kiev, capital of the Ukraine. She was a young mother when Communism collapsed. Her alcoholic husband abandoned her when her two children, who have now grown to adulthood, were still small. Twenty years after the demise of the Soviet Union she finds herself sometimes wistfully longing for the 'good old days,' when the state claimed to care for citizens from the cradle to the grave. Somehow the hardships of those days have been forgotten.

Millions of post-Communists like Olga now live on both sides of the European Union border, from East Berlin to Moscow. While some quickly converted from *dialectical materialism* to *consumer materialism,* changing their political spots (some even now serve in the European Parliament!), the majority of older Eastern Europeans still live in an ideological vacuum vaguely described as post-Communism. For some, part of that vacuum is being filled by a return to the Orthodox faith of past generations, never totally eradicated by atheistic Marxism. Others are discovering new western expressions of Christianity in American-style megachurches, often preaching a form of prosperity gospel which ignores the deep need for social reformation.

Yet the social needs in Eastern Europe remain great. This region continues to be a major source of women trafficked by the mafia for the sex industry in the West. In Moldova, for example, a small land-locked country sandwiched between Ukraine and Romania, literally half the menfolk have left to work in Moscow and elsewhere in Russia, leaving a lopsided social environment and their womenfolk vulnerable to human traffickers.

Christian witness in Eastern Europe demands engagement with issues of justice and compassion, and a demonstration that the true gospel message will over-flow into social transformation and reformation.

Yes, Jesus Christ can transform the life of an alcoholic like Olga's husband, and give new meaning and motivation for Olga to give herself in service to others. The neighbourhood fellowship of believers she might belong to could have a con-tagious leavening effect if members engaged in community development, spon-soring self-help groups for women, activities for street kids and other teenagers, counselling services, soup-kitchens, community health programmes, awareness campaigns to prevent human trafficking, and other expressions of the two-handed gospel.

Now let's go to Prague in the Czech Republic to meet Katrin and our third category, *the post-modern European*. Like Olga's children, Katrin is too young to remember life under Communism. She has been far more influenced in her lifestyle by Michael Jackson, Madonna and MTV, than by Marxism. She also shares with her peers from Western Europe little faith in modernity's assumption that science, reason and human goodness promise a better future. In her view, all '-isms' are '*was*ms;' ideologies belonging to the past. Ultimate Truth is an il-lusion. What may be true for others like her parents, teachers, priests or pastors is not necessarily true for her. What counts is now, having fun now, living for sensuous gratification and excitement now. Belonging and peer-acceptance is far more important to Katrin than material gain or career advancement. The borders between reality and fantasy are blurred in Katrin's perception; why not just 'mix and match' ideas wherever they come from? Spirituality, whatever its source, is intriguing.

Organised religion, especially of the hierarchical sort, is a definite no-no. She may, however, be open to forms of Christianity offering spiritual experiences but will probably be offended by 'arrogant' claims of Absolute Truth.

Katrin is particularly open to friendship and relationship; to a sense of belong-ing and community; to other peoples' stories and journeying together. This open-ness, also to spiritual reality, offers great opportunity to come alongside Katrin and her peers to 'travel together' in search of a place to belong. While aspects of her post-modern mindset are clearly non-Biblical, others resonate with New Testa-ment Christianity, like community, experiential reality and incarnational living.

In Amsterdam we meet Mustapha, our *post-migrant European*. He was born in Holland to migrant workers from the Mediterranean. He belongs to the majority of urban youth in Holland's capital whose parents are non-indigenous Dutch. Yet he does not feel he fully belongs to his parents' world of Islam in their homeland when the whole family goes there on holiday. Nor does he feel accepted in the white European world. Sometimes he feels blamed for everything going wrong in Dutch society. He has few if any white friends.

Mustapha lives in an identity crisis. His parents and the imam tell him to do one thing. Yet his friends and the attractions of life in the West encourage him to do the other. He doesn't really know who he is or who he wants to be. He knows of a handful who have become radical Islamists. Yet while one third of all European Muslims still attend mosque regularly, another third have become nominal or secularised. A few have even risked everything to become followers of Isa, as Jesus is called in the Quran.

But who does Mustapha want to be? Perhaps if he was befriended by some Isa-followers, he, too, might be open to learn more about this prophet who spoke so much about love, something missing in his parents' faith. But this is a subject for another section of this book ...

Lastly, we meet Celeste in Paris, a *post-secular European*. Like many French, Celeste firmly believes in the reality of the spiritual world, and has dabbled in various forms of the occult. In France there are more spiritist healers than doctors, lawyers and priests combined. Even the Vatican has dubbed France a nation of 'baptised pagans!'

Sadly, the last place Celeste would expect to find spiritual reality is in the church. Her experience is that the church is a patriarchal institution with centuries of suppression of women undermining its moral authority. Yet she knows beyond a shadow of doubt that the spiritual world is real and has had multiple personal encounters with spiritual beings. She's not concerned with issues of morality, sorting right from wrong, doctrinal disputes and all the other things she sees Christians arguing about. She is happy to pursue her own brand of spirituality and let others pursue theirs.

Today across Europe, there are millions of 'Celestes' following pop-stars and films stars who also dabble in do-it-yourself spirituality. In government, business and academic circles, spirituality is being taken seriously, influencing decision-making processes, stress-management, office architecture and corporate philosophies. Far from being part of a lunatic-fringe, they are becoming mainstream in European society.

How then are we, our churches, our organisations and our missions building bridges into the cultures of our European neighbours like Karl, Olga, Katrin, Mustapha and Celeste?

One thing is clear: yesterday's forms of church hold little attraction for most Europeans today. The challenge is for new, fresh expressions which interface culturally with our neighbours' worlds. 'Fresh expressions' is the name of one such effort that you will read more about in the next pages. Other groups are developing incarnational models of outreach, on the streets, in mind-body-spirit fairs, in ethnic neighbourhoods, creating art-cafes or other 'safe places' to build relationships and friendships, or engaging in justice issues to effect social transformation.

The message hasn't changed. But the neighbourhood has. We need to be 'tied to the times, anchored to the Rock' to see these neighbourhoods changed by the love of God.

—Jeff Fountain
Director, The Schuman Centre for European Studies
Chairperson, Hope for Europe

The Majority of Europeans

In this section we consider Europeans who can be regarded as either secular or nominally religious. 'Secular' is defined as a system of political or social philosophy that rejects all forms of religious faith and worship, or religious scepticism or indifference. It is the view that religious considerations should be excluded from civil affairs or public education.

Nominal believers, on the other hand, are those who may identify themselves as Christians or Muslims or followers of another faith, and who may even conform outwardly to it and give it token allegiance. But they do not actually incorporate the teachings of this faith into their daily lives.

Sadly, the vast majority of people living in Europe today fit into one of these two categories, and the resulting impact has been catastrophic. Alexandr Solzhenitsyn put it in very graphic terms: 'If a nation's spiritual energies have been exhausted, it will not be saved from collapse by the most perfect government structure or by any industrial development; a tree with a rotten core cannot stand.'

Let's look at the regional differences in the Nordic countries, the Baltics and Western Europe.

Reaching Europe's Nordic People

—Church-planter Shaun Rossi shares insights into the obstacles and opportunities for introducing a vibrant Christian lifestyle within the region of Sweden, Finland, Iceland, Denmark and Norway.

Walk into my office in Helsinki, Finland, and you may notice a beautiful Yamaha acoustic guitar. The guitar was a gift from my parents-in-law who knew that I had a sincere desire to learn to play the instrument, since it seems groups often have a need for a skilled player. Recently, when a vocalist in our gathering needed accompaniment, I got my chance.

'Shaun, don't you have a guitar? You can help!' This was the moment I had been waiting for. There was just one problem: I had never learned to play. All my sincere desire was no substitute for the actual obedience it takes to master an instrument. The truth is, sincerity is really never a substitute for obedience.

Perhaps there is no place where this is more important than in Christianity, because God who saves us by His grace calls us to a life of joyful obedience. And there is no greater prayer for the Church in the Nordic countries at this time than that it would move from sincerity to sincere obedience.

Sincere Nordic Country Christians

There is no question that the church in Scandinavia is sincere. Statistics in Finland boast around 80% of its approximately five and a half million population are members of the State Church. In the Nordic countries, the Lutheran or Evangelical Lutheran Church is the official or government-endorsed national church (i. e. Church of Norway, Church of Finland, etc.) In Norway, Sweden, Iceland and Denmark (another nineteen and a half million people) the number of members is slightly less, but still high. In virtually every community in the Nordic countries there are beautiful churches or chapels; youth camps are held throughout the summer, and seminaries train no shortage of church workers.

If you were to take a general survey of persons in one of the capital cities, chances are the majority would say they are 'Christian.' Nordic churches and Christians seem to be sincere, so what is the problem? Perhaps we should turn to Jesus for an answer, and a good place to look at is His encounter with a certain rich, young man.

You know the story. The young ruler came to Jesus sincerely wanting to know what was required to have eternal life. Jesus told him for starters to keep the commandments, to which the young man swiftly replied he had already been doing that. But what Jesus said next put his sincerity into perspective.

> Jesus answered, 'If you want to be perfect, go, sell your
> possessions and give to the poor, and you will have treasure in
> heaven. Then come, follow me.' When the young man heard this,
> he went away sad, because he had great wealth.
> —Matt. 19:21–22, NIV)

This man learned that when it comes to following Jesus, sincerity may be a good start but it is no substitute for obedience.

When I think of the Church in the Nordic countries, and specifically the Church in Finland where I live and serve, I am convinced this is a lesson we are learning as well. The sincerity of the Church is unquestionable, but when it comes down to obedience to Christ, sadly, many believers have chosen to walk the same path as the rich young man. In the hope of seeing the Church in the Nordic countries moving in the other direction I will share five prayer challenges.

Prayer Challenges for the Nordic Countries

1. Youth and Young Adults

Almost 20% of the population are aged fourteen or under. A large percentage of young people participate in youth camps run by the state and free churches. While this is encouraging, statistics show that too many of these youth become estranged from the church after high school age. Fortunately there has been a growth in university student ministries in the last decade that have been successful in bridging the gap, but a big proportion of students and young adults who would consider themselves 'Christians' are not obediently following Jesus. Pray that the Church in the Nordic countries will be more committed to the great task of reaching out to youth and young adults, and discipling them.

2. Immigrants

Few churches are equipped or motivated to handle the tens of thousands of immigrants entering the Nordic countries every year. Many of these immigrants are students and guest workers, others are refugees—all of whom need to hear the gospel. An increasing number of groups and churches have ministries among certain ethnic groups, which is encouraging. It is not a surprise that new ethnic and multi-ethnic churches are popping up in virtually every major city. These churches seem to also attract nationals, and for the most part they've had a positive impact on local churches. Like the rest of Europe, Islam is growing in the region and presents new challenges to the Church. Pray that God's people will be obedient in reaching out to immigrants and befriending Muslim neighbours.

3. Theological Training

Some very positive developments have been made in theological education and ministerial training in the Nordic countries over the past decade and a half. A number of degree-granting institutions and short-term training programmes exist in each country, dedicated to training Christians for gospel-centred ministries. Still, a significant portion of state church ministers are trained by theological faculties in universities that do not hold to the same conviction. Pray that theological and ministerial training institutions will be whole-heartedly devoted to their role of training Christians who will take the gospel to the ends of the earth.

4. Missionary Efforts

In order for a much-needed revival to take place in the Nordic countries, missionary efforts are a must. On one hand the Nordic Church needs to see its missional role to reach the people in its communities, training members as missionaries. On the other hand, each country is in need of more foreign missionaries who will stay longer-term. Some of these workers will come through traditional sending agencies and their training and support networks will be a valuable asset. Others will enter the Nordic region informally as students or guest workers. All should seek to serve the Church faithfully alongside local Christians. Pray the Church will be obedient in living up to its missional role, and that potential missionaries to the Nordic countries will obey God's call.

5. A Vision for Church-Planting

The Nordic countries today continue to have a strong need for church-planting efforts. For decades, 'free church' groups (i.e. churches outside the official, national or state-supported churches) such as the Methodists, Baptists, Evangelical Free and Pentecostals have planted new churches. While today many of these churches are flourishing, some have ceased to exist or are in urgent need of revitalisation. New churches must reach new people groups and a new generation. As the population in major cities continue to swell, creative efforts should be made to reach urban populations. Fortunately, a number of new church-planting movements have started in the past decade, particularly in Norway. As new churches take root there, it is important for new and old fellowships to partner together in missions, theological education and community service. Pray that existing churches and church-planting groups will sincerely seek to begin vibrant, culturally-relevant and gospel-centred churches in the Nordic countries.

Heartfelt Evangelism

For the Nordic Church to reach the population it must be in earnest about adopting effective approaches to evangelism.

I began teaching a course on evangelism seven years ago at a Bible college in Finland. On the first day of class I asked my students to share some of their experiences of doing evangelism with their churches. Not long after the discussion started flowing, the tears of a girl named Sara started to flow as well. She began to share the story of her first-ever attempt at outreach. The members of her youth group were given a stack of tracks and told by their leader not to return until they had distributed them all to persons on the street.

Sara is a bit on the shy side, so the idea of walking up to strangers on the street and handing them tracts was absolutely horrifying. After offering a few she had decided to hide the others rather than continue, and until my class she had never shared that experience with anyone. Her tears expressed the guilt she had been holding in for not participating in much 'evangelism' since then.

Every year that I teach this class I find many who have had similar experiences. Their concept of evangelism was handing out literature or going to special meetings, rather than a Biblical process in which every Christian is called to be actively engaged. The tract is still a valid tool, but to the average recipient of one it may not be very convincing evangelism.

In order for the Church to effectively reach residents of the Nordic countries it must seek relevant, up to date, innovative, and non-compromising ways to share the good news of Christ. Perhaps most of all, the Church must be willing to build authentic relationships with its neighbours, which, for many living in the Nordic countries, does not come naturally.

A Sincere Plea

The problem with owning a nice, shiny guitar is that most people who see it just assume that I can play it. Bothered by my recent borderline deception, I began to learn my first few chords. Today I still cannot say I play the guitar but at least I am no longer substituting sincerity for obedience; even if they are small steps of obedience.

While a brief look at the statistics might lead you to believe that the Nordic church is sincere, they do not say much for its obedience to Christ. Fortunately there are many Christians in Finland, Norway, Sweden, Iceland and Denmark who have decided that when it comes to Christianity, sincerity is no substitute for obedience and have taken steps to prove it. It is my prayer—and I plead with you to make it yours—that many others would join them.

The Challenge of Reaching the Baltics

> —Countries released from years of religious repression and persecution
> under Communism present different challenges to faith than those in
> Nordic countries. Rev. Mark E. Krause, the Lutheran Church-Missouri
> Synod Area Facilitator for missions serving in the Baltic region for the
> past three years, explains.

Since the fall of the Soviet Union in the early 1990's, the cultures of Estonia, Latvia and Lithuania that first responded eagerly to religious freedom have become more and more secular and materialistic. Many people now believe the Church is an old institution that is no longer fashionable so they don't, as a result, feel any need for what it has to offer. Some feel the Church is only for established members, mostly older people. Newcomers often don't feel welcomed, especially if they have young children. The challenge for the Church is to proclaim an old, unchanging message in a way that is relevant to a rapidly changing culture; a culture that is distancing itself from spiritual things.

There is a lack of Christian literature and other media, particularly in Baltic languages. The market is small and therefore not productive for most publishers. However, increasing numbers are learning English, especially younger people, and the countries also have a substantial number of Russian speakers. In Latvia, at least 25–30% of the population are Russians.

A huge gap also exists between generations. The older generation has the greatest affection towards the Church, and older women make up the majority of worshippers on Sunday mornings. The middle-aged generation, which grew up in the Soviet times, is the least active segment. An interesting fact is that some post-Soviet youth seem to have more interest in the gospel. Unfortunately, few churches have established dynamic youth and young adult ministries. Congregations need to design outreach ministries that are sensitive to each generation. Alpha courses have become an effective means of outreach for some churches in Latvia and Estonia.

The economic downturn has opened the door for the Baltic Church to serve as a messenger of hope. Many of the seven million people in this region* struggle financially and the government has failed to give hope. Ask the Lord to give the Church His Holy Spirit as well as wisdom and direction to the leadership, to meet this critical challenge.

Estonia

The Lutheran Church is the largest Christian church in Estonia. But Estonia has become the most secular of the three Baltic countries, which presents a difficult challenge for Christians. Most people just ignore the Church; they don't see any reason to attend worship or be involved in its ministry.

The Theological Institute and Mission Centre of the Lutheran Church are working to figure out ways to help pastors and churches connect the gospel of Jesus Christ with the present secular society. Please keep these ministries in your prayers.

Lithuania

Although a very high percentage of the Lithuanian population has been baptised into the Roman Catholic Church, relatively few actually attend worship or are actively involved today in the life of the Church. The Lutheran Church in Lithuania has German historical roots and is very small, with about fifty congregations. The greatest need of the Church is to assimilate into the Lithuanian culture and connect with those who are un-churched, no matter what their cultural

* July 2010 estimate, *CIA World Factbook.*

Christian roots. Many fear that if they talk to an inactive Roman Catholic about Christ they might be accused of taking a member away from that church. This attitude makes it very difficult for Christian outreach.

Many of Lithuania's Lutheran Churches are also in the countryside, where few people live. The population centres have shifted since World War II and the Soviet occupation. Churches need to focus on planting new ministries in towns and cities where the most people are.

Ask the Lord to open up the eyes of the Lithuanian Church so that they may see the harvest field all around them. Pray for believers to have wisdom and courage in finding ways to connect people with the saving gospel of Jesus Christ.

Latvia

Evangelicals do not have a strong presence in Latvia. The four main churches are Lutheran, Russian Orthodox, Roman Catholic and Baptist. There are some charismatic churches, but they are small. Latvia's majority Protestant denomination, the Lutheran Church, has been blessed with an abundance of church buildings and other properties. Members believed that if they could restore their buildings, the people would come. Some did start attending, but many stayed away. Churches in Latvia need to address the need of educating and training its pastors and people for missions—and then encouraging them to get out of their church buildings into their communities, with the message of the gospel.

Many rural pastors serve four or five congregations. In the days of Soviet occupation, the pastor was only allowed to preach on Sunday mornings; it was against the law to have Sunday schools, Bible classes, youth groups and so forth. Today, many rural congregations still operate under this model. The challenge for rural pastors is to develop pastoral relationships with their congregations and the communities they serve.

Before the economic crisis, the central or mother Church was able to sell property whenever it needed cash to support its expenses. During the crisis it has been unable to sell property, forcing church leaders to make very deep cuts in their budget. A priority for the Church today is to develop a stewardship programme; teaching and encouraging members that giving is a natural response to God's grace.

St. Gregor's School of Christian Ministry, the only in-residence training centre for lay believers in Latvia, has an excellent opportunity to play a major role in creating a more missional understanding of ministry. Awareness-raising and training is also needed in the area of other faiths. The Mormons, for instance, have a strong presence in Latvia through the American Embassy.—A number of the embassy staff are Mormons. It is essential for the school to promote itself more to congregations so they will send and support students, and provide the funding needed for the school to develop its ministry.

If the Church is to survive, it is imperative that it figures out how to reach young people with the gospel. The ways of the past don't always work in our post-modern times. Let's ask the Lord to provide pastoral leadership with a passion for creating new and exciting ways to reach the youth and young adults of Latvia. Pray also for a new vision for the Church that will unify and encourage believers to be more missional in reaching the lost in this country.

Western Europe: The Search for Spiritual Reality

—By Frank Hinkelmann, European Director for Operation Mobilisation and Lecturer in Modern Church History at the MBS Seminary in Austria.

When we speak of Western Europe we refer to two main groupings of countries: On the one hand there are those countries which once formed the heartland of reformation, like Germany, Switzerland, the Netherlands and United Kingdom, which have remained predominantly Protestant. The other grouping of countries has traditionally been the heartland of Roman Catholicism, including Italy, France, Belgium, Austria, Ireland and the Iberian Peninsula. Smaller countries like San Marino, Luxemburg, Monaco, and Andorra also need to be remembered in this group.

What characterises these diverse and unique nations? What do they have in common? All of them look back to a centuries-long Christian heritage, be it Lutheran, Reformed or Roman Catholic. Yet in all of them we have also seen a dramatic decrease in church membership, church attendance and traditional Christianity in general.

Let's look at only two examples; first, church membership developments in the Reformed Church of Switzerland for the city of Zürich. In 1970, 53% of Zurich's population belonged to the Reformed Church; in the year 2000 this was only true of 20.3%. Most likely the numbers will drop to 14.2% by the year 2020.[39]

UK statistics tell us that more than one million people stopped going to church over the last nine years. One thousand youth under the age of fifteen leave church each week, and one million believers don't attend any church at all.[40] The attitude of people all across Western Europe seems to be a reflection of the statement Peter Stephenson wrote in his book, *Christian Mission in the Postmodern World*:

'Christianity is seen to offer no answers because it has been one of the main purveyors of the Modernist myth, and has legitimated the abuse of global resources with its insistence that the World is essentially evil (or at least, unimportant), and that the only thing that really matters is the soul and heaven.'[41]

We live in a time of cultural overlap and transition. Especially in Western Europe, modernity (belief in rationality and progress) is still very much alive and remains part of our mission context. At the same time, post-modernity (wherein all reality is relative) is rapidly challenging and changing vast parts of our culture and already has great impact on many Western Europeans, especially young adults and youth in urban areas. In many ways Western Europe seems to be not only post-modern, but even post-Christian.

If we look back into Church history, we see that within less than three hundred years the Roman Empire was turned upside down. A pagan empire had turned to Christianity. What were some of the reasons for this dramatic transformation? First of all, Christians were deeply convinced of their faith. They didn't just give intellectual agreement to some theological doctrine. The affirmation of Peter and John in Acts 4:20 was true for all committed followers of Christ: *'For we cannot help speaking about what we have seen and heard.'*

However, there is a second reason for the vast spread of Christianity during the first centuries AD. The message given by Christians was welcomed by the people of their time because it gave an answer to their deepest needs. And, thirdly, the ethical lifestyle of the Christian community was a message in itself. Christians practised fellowship at a level unknown to most people; they lived up to their own (strict) ethical standards, and they practised charity by caring for the needy.

What do our neighbours see when they watch our daily living? Are we in any way different from others around us who don't have a personal relationship with Jesus Christ? Is what Peter and John said true for us, today, that 'we cannot help speaking about what we have seen and heard?'

It should not surprise us that the largest evangelical churches in Western Europe are either African or led by people with African descent. The Nigerian-led Kingsway International Christian Centre has the largest congregation in the entire United Kingdom with over 10,000 men, women and children. Another

Nigerian-based movement, the Redeemed Christian Church of God, established its first church in Britain in 1989 and by 2005 grew to 141 churches with a total of 18,000 members.[42] Why does the African Church seem to be far more attractive to Europeans than many of our traditional European churches?

Each Sunday in Vienna, Austria, more than 3,000 evangelical believers meet for services in foreign languages, among them Iranian, Chinese, Brazilian and English-speaking congregations. These foreign language church services might well outnumber those of evangelical believers in Vienna's Austrian churches. Since the beginning of the late 1980s, the number of Romanian churches in Austria has grown to around 40 congregations in a number of denominations, with approximately 10,000 believers attending church regularly. African churches are also on the rise: in Linz, capital city of Upper Austria, at least nine churches were planted within the last couple of years.

Jehu Hanziles comments, 'In Western Europe, the rise of African immigrant churches and other non-Western Christian congregations has been dramatically visible because of the stark contrast between the dynamism of new immigrant Christian groups and the often moribund tone of the traditional churches.'[43] Again, it seems that the key in being a transformational witness is the relevancy of our faith: our relationship with God.

Yes, there is great spiritual hunger in Western Europe. Just take a look at the frequent appearance of articles in newspapers and journals on the subject of spirituality and other faith issues. Try doing a Google search on the words 'spirituality Europe.'—You will get over four million hits. Notice the interest in the occult and supernatural escalating as individuals sense there is more to life than materialism. Think about how many people—even those with hardly any affinity to Christianity—join religious pilgrimages. German comedian Hape Kerkeling was one such 'pilgrim' who travelled 'the way of St. James' to Santiago de Compostela in Spain, and wrote a book about his experience.[44]

A few years ago a campaign was initiated by a number of atheist movements. Trains and buses across major European cities were plastered with posters reading, 'There's probably no god. Now stop worrying and enjoy your life.'[45] The campaign only underlined the deep frustration of atheists over what a German newspaper called a widely felt 'resurgence of spiritual needs.'[46]

People today are searching for answers to their lives' tough questions. They are striving for deep spiritual experiences. They are longing for real meaning and fulfilment. And they are crying out for healing of their often-broken worlds. *What do we have to offer?*

Unreached People Groups in Europe

Most Christians would be surprised to learn of the number of people groups in Europe that are as yet unreached by the gospel message. A 'people group' can be loosely defined as an ethnic community with a common name, language similarity and cultural identity. The Joshua Project lists 192 such unreached groups in Western Europe alone—and a total of 333 in all of Europe. According to their scale, over 22 million men, women and children can be considered unreached or least-reached, having less than 2% evangelicals or 5% Christian adherents. These include people as diverse as:

- Northern Norway's reindeer herders, the Sami people, who only just recently received the New Testament in their modern-day language after twenty-two years of work by the Bible Society.
- Ukraine's mostly-Muslim Crimean Tartars, who became bitter towards Christianity when the Orthodox Church attempted to force their conversion in the 19th Century, burning their mosques.
- Italy's Han Chinese residents, who have only one known church among 50,000. Most of them continue to adhere to traditional beliefs and superstitions.
- France's Khmer or Cambodian people, whose lives still revolve around Buddhism. Few of these 69,000 have been introduced to Jesus.

Keep in mind, however, that the Joshua Project's list of 51 European countries does not (as we do in this book) include Russia, which they list as part of Eurasia. Russia alone has 162 diverse ethnic people groups—32 of them considered unreached with the good news of Christ! This puts Russia near the top of the list of countries with unreached people groups.

Because of its history and cultural orientation we also include the small Caucasian nation of Georgia in this book. While we cannot detail every people group, we have chosen Georgia's unreached Svan people as a case study, below. Also see the note about the Yakut people in the 'Touching Hearts Through the Arts'— 'Heartsounds International' page in this section. Readers should take advantage of the excellent information given in websites like the Joshua Project [www.joshuaproject.net], Peoplegroups.org and the Adoptapeople.com Clearinghouse. As individuals and churches we need to be part of efforts to reach these largely-neglected peoples.

Georgia: On Top of the World

Few readers will be familiar with the tiny country lying in the shadow of the Caucasus Mountains, surrounded by Russia, Turkey, Armenia and Azerbaijan. This narrow stretch of land between the Black and Caspian Seas belonged to Russia for a hundred years before winning independence in 1991. Georgia, the former 'fruit basket of the USSR,' is only now beginning to recover from a collapsed economy. Civil wars among the ethnic Abkhazians and South Ossetian peoples gave Russia the excuse to maintain military bases in the country, adding to the instability.

John Crawford's* interest in the Caucasus region led him to pioneer a one-man team in Georgia in 1999, following seven years of service in St. Petersburg with OM Russia. He explains that since Georgia is the second country in the world (after Armenia) to officially adopt Christianity, most people don't think of it in terms of missionary work.

'Orthodoxy still reigns here, giving other branches of Christianity and any other religions a hard time. I know there are plenty of real believers among the Orthodox. But I also know plenty of Georgians whose Orthodoxy is just part of their nationality, a keeping of traditions without an understanding of doctrine or a relationship with a living God.—It doesn't touch their daily lives at all. Once they understand that I'm not here to drag them off into some other church, and that I believe in the same core doctrines that are found in Orthodoxy, we have a chance to read the Bible together and bring it into everyday experience.'

Out of a population of 5 million, only 3 million of the country's residents are Georgians. Another half million are Mingrelians, and nearly half a million more are Armenians. Georgia's border with war-devastated Chechnya also means that about 10,000 Chechens have sought refuge with its neighbour. John spent five months helping to oversee medical projects funded by World Concern, looking for opportunities to show the Jesus film in the Chechen language. 'These people are crying out for attention and salvation,' he affirms, 'devastated by war but not giving up.' So far there is no church among them.

Later, while living in Tbilisi, John was walking home one day when he spotted a man preparing to throw himself into a river. He listened to an all-too-com-

---

* Names of workers have been changed to protect their security.

mon tale of seven mouths to feed and no income. Then he asked the man if he was a Christian.

Of course, he replied. He was an Armenian and all Armenians were Christians!

'In that case,' said John, 'please believe that God sent me here to you now to save your life, and to say that your family would suffer much more without you than with you. And while I can't give you work, here's enough money to show you that He cares for you.'' John stuffed the bills into the man's bag and left before he could refuse them.

But even before he moved to Georgia, it was the Svan people, out of the country's 36 people groups, that most captured John's heart. During his first eight years in Georgia he made twenty-four explorations into the western mountains where the 35,000 Svan people live. Although the Svaneti mountains were not considered very safe for foreigners, with a reputation for kidnappings and robberies, John persevered. On a trip in 2007, he and a friend travelled 111 kilometres by horseback through Svaneti's alpine meadows and forests, praying for every village they rode through. As far as he knows it was the first prayer journey ever made in the area.

Later that same year John moved to a tiny Svan community with only 220 to 250 residents. The name of his mountain village meant 'Fearless Heart.'—With good reason. At 2,200 metres, villagers live at the highest altitude in Europe, and winter blizzards and avalanches sometimes keep them snowed in for weeks at a time.

'I picked this village because it's the end of the road, literally. Its location makes it one of the hardest places in Georgia to live. The people don't even have a doctor. In 1987, one of the worst winters in history destroyed part of the village in an avalanche. These people are sometimes seen as the purest Svans, so it's like a stronghold.—A good place for me to learn about them. And if God's love can transform the highest and hardest place, he can do it anywhere!'

John agreed with the villagers to teach English without payment in exchange for room and board. The Svans are typically bilingual, speaking Georgian and their own unwritten Svan language, but they know that English is a key to the future. While living in this community, John identified with it as much as he could, feeding the cows, sawing wood for the fire and playing football with the young people.

Among the Svans live just a handful of evangelicals. As small as it was, John's village had seven tiny Orthodox churches, most belonging to families. Like the majority of Georgians the Svans consider the ritual of toasting with wine at meals to be a form of prayer. These toasts must always include three persons: 'the big God,' the virgin Mary and St George, their patron saint. Jesus isn't nearly as important a part of their religion as He is of Orthodox Christianity. Superstitions are common, so is alcohol abuse, and blood feuds can exist for generations all over the Caucasus. The Svans have a strong sense of honour and shame, fear and power. If you're a guest, you're under your host's protection.

John said he told the people, ' "I'm here because God knows who you are!" I knew I was there to pray, to bless them, to find out how God could break through and reveal himself in Spirit and truth, and give them hope.—Because that's one thing they need. The Svan are a people in decline, losing their culture. They have many more funerals than weddings. They are also very focused on tradition, and even to suggest change is threatening. So they have to be the ones to start it.'

John Crawford has no regrets about falling in love with Georgia. In fact, he also gave his heart to a Georgian girl named Nia,* and as a married couple they continue to make Jesus known, working towards the establishment of a church from their home in upper Svaneti.

But a lot remains to be done throughout Georgia. Ministries to children are scarce, and little or no outreach exists to some of the other ethnic groups, such as the country's 15,000 Jews and 500,000 Mingrel people. Relationships between churches need to be developed, and much more Christian literature needs translation. The republic has ten indigenous languages, but only one of these has a translation of the whole Bible, and only one has the New Testament. The Georgian language is a challenge of its own—definitely harder to learn than Russian, according to John. But the people are hospitable, the markets with their variety of foods a treat and the mountain scenery is spectacular.

High above the old city of Tbililsi stands a giant 'Mother of Georgia' statue. One of her hands brandishes a sword to defend herself from enemies; in her other hand a cup waits to welcome friends. This small country has suffered much from cruel invasions through its 1,500-year history.—The capital has been completely destroyed twenty-nine times. Perhaps the day has arrived for Georgia's people to welcome those who come in the name of the Lord.

New Church-Planting Initiatives

It's no secret that Europe's church attendance has been steadily shrinking for some time. It is now estimated that less than 10% of the entire population attends church regularly. And only 5% or fewer people living in Denmark, Latvia, Norway, Sweden, Finland, Estonia, Iceland and Russia, attend a service one or more times a week.[47]

A Gallup 2009 survey of 114 countries showed that five European Union countries are in the top ten 'least-religious' list. Only 14% of Estonians agreed that religion was important to their daily life. Sweden was next-lowest with 17%, then Denmark (18%) and Norway (20%). Large majorities in the Czech Republic, Finland, France, UK and Russia also indicated that faith was not a major issue for them.[48]

The fact is, more churches are closing than are opening in Europe. Hundreds if not thousands have already been turned into restaurants, shops or accommodation. Many of the largest and healthiest congregations are composed of migrants. In a sort of 'reverse mission' movement, Africans and Asians coming to the continent are evangelising and starting thousands of fellowships. According to an Assist News Service report, Germany alone has at least 1,100 foreign language Protestant churches with more than 80,000 members. The UK has over 3,000 black-led African churches, and four out of ten of Britain's largest mega-churches are led by Nigerians. The Protestant Church in the Netherlands freely admits to working with migrant churches in the hope of evangelising their increasingly secular society.

In addition to the un-churched are the disturbing numbers of people who once had a relationship with God, but who have dropped out of churches. The Centre for European Church-Planting found that in the UK, church attendance has plummeted 34% over the last 16 years. Two-thirds of people in Britain currently have no church connection.[49] Similarly, less than two-thirds of all Germans are still members of a Christian religious community,[50] and a great percentage do not attend regularly. Disillusionment with the State Church in Iceland has led to a massive wave of resignation by members.

How then can we interest our nominally Christian or secular neighbours in embracing a vibrant faith? A number of new initiatives in the last few years have had encouraging success. While we cannot consider all of them here, we've chosen the 'Fresh Expressions of Church' movement in Britain and Multi-Site Church concept in Switzerland as positive examples. By some estimates, Fresh Expressions has already birthed several hundred new congregations with thousands of members. The movement's goal is to create many more new worshipping communities across the country within the next decade, by resourcing innovative mission through fresh expressions of church life.

Fresh Expressions of Church

—The following introduction comes from former OMer Reverend Katryn Leclézio of the Halas Team Ministry in England's West Midlands.

You can't stop the work of the Holy Spirit! Fresh Expressions within the traditional Anglican Church is a way in which the Church is making room for fresh works of the Holy Spirit in our local communities. It is a wonderfully freeing innovation for those of us who minister in ancient liturgical traditions but who want to reach out to people who would never relate to traditional liturgical worship. The Anglican and Methodist Churches in the UK wanted to respond to Britain's changing culture in a post-modern, increasingly post-Christian society. Fresh Expressions was the result of the deliberations of what it would take to reach non-churched peoples. De-churched people (who once attended but dropped out) had initiatives like 'Back to Church Sunday' and other more mainstream ministries; but the un-churched, who form the bulk of our Parishes, seemed to have no means of connecting with the Christian faith with the gospel about Jesus Christ.

Mainline, traditional church activities didn't appeal to the un-churched, so freedom was given within the discipline and authority of the Anglican Church to take the church to where people were and remain there. This is a fundamental concept to Fresh Expressions, in my view. You go to where the people are and you stay there.—You don't plan to bring them back to the Parish church building. The intention from the start of any Fresh Expression of church is to create a worshipping community in whatever locality to which you (individual or team) are called by God to share the gospel. So, if you are sharing the gospel with skaters in a skate park, you find a space in the skate park for being church. There you form a community of believers who meet together to worship, pray, break bread, engage with the Bible and reach out and serve their communities.

Dioceses around Great Britain have made space for Fresh Expressions of church alongside the traditional Parish churches. There are special Bishop's Mission Orders which allow for experimentation of all sorts, with and without liturgy, in an accountable way. The Archbishops have encouraged Fresh Expressions in what they have called a 'mixed economy' of church; that is, a mix of traditional and fresh expression.

In my little village the old, eleventh century church building is situated one and a quarter miles out of the village. It is a wonderfully intimate worship space much loved by its members. But it has no plumbing and no space. People with small children did not feel comfortable there on Sundays, especially when their children were at the wriggly, run-around phase of life. Though the congregation didn't mind the noise and movement, the parents did.

Our village also has a thriving Church of England Primary School. The unchurched newcomers to the village have families who go to school there.

We have begun a Fresh Expression of church in the church hall, which is in the centre of the village. This is the only meeting place available at present, and though it is a church hall, it is perceived and called the 'village hall.' The building has recently been refurbished and is now a wonderful space for all sorts of activities, including all-age worship. Several families in the village come to Worship4All because they want to worship with their children in a space that is safe and comfortable for children.

The life of this new congregation will centre around the hall rather than the church. This is a source of some sadness for older members who love the old church. Recently I was asked by the church wardens whether I could encourage the parents to come to the church for communion in the weeks between the Worship4All services because, since it began a year ago, they no longer come to church, especially for communion. This is where the church sometimes takes a while to understand Fresh Expressions: the solution is not for families or individual members to come to the old church in the weeks between Worship4All. The Fresh Expression solution is to begin a communion service that is all-age-friendly in the hall. We go to where the people are, and we stay there.

Of course in the reality of Parish life there are compromises, and the Worship4All team are happy to share festivals and important services in the old church. In this way we integrate our history—where we've come from—and share it with the children. They love the old church too, but when Worship4All is in the old church, we do a Worship4All style service, we don't expect the families to suddenly, inexplicably fit into the traditional Anglican form of the old church. We had a wonderful, child-friendly Easter Communion in the church with *vuvuzela* horns (before the World Cup popularised them!), bells, rattles, and flinging water around to accompany the great Alleluia shouts; and then a communion prayer with all participating in the actions. The traditional congregation loved it, too!

Worship4All is a good example of a mixed economy of church. Fresh Expressions thinking and practice have given the freedom for totally innovative ministries, like church in a skate park. But because they are in the centre of most communities, traditional parishes also have the freedom to use their facilities for different ways of being church and different ways of worship, which reach out to particular communities like families and the de-churched.

As a Fresh Expression of church we are still within the disciplines and authority of the Anglican Church, which provides a great security and great resources. Though our worship doesn't use a set form of liturgy, it is shaped by liturgy. Our worship has the elements of good Anglican liturgy providing balance and a sense of direction. The Bible is central, but the disciplines of prayer for the global and the local within the service, of confession, of fellowship, which are intrinsic to Anglican liturgy, are preserved in creative, interactive and worshipful ways. Fresh Expression worship may not look and feel Anglican or Methodist at all, but it is shaped by those traditions in important ways.

The other great strength of the Fresh Expression initiative is that it is a genuine way of attempting to be church in a relevant and acculturated way. Its motivation is love for those who do not know Jesus Christ. Because this love compels us we are prepared to go to where the people are, whether it is geographical locality, or style of worship, and stay there. This 'staying' is what I believe gives Fresh Expressions of church its integrity. There isn't going to come a point when people are 'tricked' into joining the mainstream, as it were. Of course, life isn't neat and easy, Fresh Expressions are experimental and not all experiments work. If a pioneer minister moves on, sometimes the Fresh Expression cannot be sustained, whereas the mainline church which gave birth to it and supported it may continue. But the genuine intention is to become all things to all people in order to win some; and, when they are won, not to then make them into something other than what they were. The aim is to enable all who have come to faith in Jesus to become more like Him, and to reflect Jesus to those around them.

Some Fresh Expressions of church have a lot of work to do in working out what it means for their project, especially if it is independent of any local Parish church, to truly be a mature church within the Anglican Communion. This process is being addressed by some of the best theologians in the Anglican Church who are also involved in the Fresh Expressions movement. The joy is that the church is recognising and following the Holy Spirit's lead in reaching out to those who do not know Jesus Christ—where they are—and staying there.

※※※※※

Fresh expressions of church can be found in rural or urban settings, and they can target children or older people or even special groups like the learning disabled. Many take the form of café or workplace churches. One man ran an Alpha Course and built a new fellowship from those who attended. Community projects like charity shops or youth drop-in centres have developed into churches. So has a play centre for under-5s, with their parents and carers.

Café churches have started up in church premises or community centres, and Christians have rented commercial cafés when they aren't normally open. The Whitehaven, England, caféchurch started one Sunday afternoon each month in 2009 through an arrangement with the local Costa Coffee management. The Emmanuel Café Church is on the University of Leeds campus, attracting healthy numbers of students.

A good example of fresh expressions in the workplace is 'Riverforce,' in the UK's Merseyside Police Force. This started with a lay person, Peter Owens, who wanted to be more missional in the workplace. Supported by his local church and diocese, he began meeting with three other colleagues who no longer went to church. Other groups formed, meeting at lunchtime or after work. These have linked up to become a missional network that has been effective in swiftly connecting with large numbers of people who have dropped out of church.

Riverforce is structured around several cell groups, and gathers together about eighty people for worship in the central refectory area of the police headquarters. The network has a three-pronged focus: supporting Christians in the workplace; reconnecting people who have left church; and engaging with people who have hardly ever been to church through a mixture of pastoral welfare programmes and seeker events.

These and other inspiring examples of fresh expressions of church can be found on the movement's websites. Check them out!*

* Information reproduced above with permission from www.sharetheguide.org.uk
© Church Army and Fresh Expressions 2010 freshexpressions.org.uk.

The International Christian Fellowship and Multi-Site Churches

—This report about the multi-site church movement comes from Heinz W. Strupler, President of *Bund Evangelischer Gemeinden (BEG)-Newlife,* in Switzerland

I have seen many changes in the spiritual climate as I look back at forty-five years of ministry, mainly in Switzerland, Europe and Africa. During the late Sixties, my wife Annelies and I were part of the Jesus People movement, and through our contact with OM we were inspired to reach other people for Christ. We then started Newlife,* a partner organisation of OM, and beginning with summer outreaches we planted churches and Bible Colleges. We saw hundreds of young people give their lives to full time ministry.

From the mid-'60s to mid-'80s there was a strong movement among youth towards evangelism and missions. All the churches that got involved in this experienced growth and many other churches were planted, mainly through the traditional Evangelical Free Churches.

In the mid-1980s, unfortunately, the interest in missions and passion to reach un-churched people gradually decreased. The mentality of believers changed from being mission-orientated to event-orientated.

Inter-denominational youth churches were started during the '90s, usually in co-operation with several churches. When our International Christian Fellowship (ICF) began holding international services in 1990, we pioneered a new kind of worship. Our founding team was composed of Mathai and Doris Matthew and my wife Annelies and myself, all of us former OMers, with fifteen teenagers. The goal of ICF in those days was to reach the international community with a service in two languages: English and German. A group of Korean Christians helped us with street meetings and we handed out over forty thousand flyers, preaching to hundreds of passing people. On the very first Sunday almost four hundred people gathered, representing over thirty nations.

During the next years ICF grew and helped start churches in different language groups including English, French for Africans, a Tamil-speaking church in Zurich and even an Arabic fellowship for Muslim-background believers.

* www.beg-nli.ch

In 1996 ICF and *Limmatgemeinde*, a church we had started earlier, merged into the International Christian Fellowship Church under the leadership of Leo Bigger. This began speeding ahead like a rocket. Attendance has shot to over two thousand and dozens of new churches are being planted worldwide.

The idea of becoming a multi-site church was experimental. ICF had forty church-plants across nine countries when one of the churches decided to take the multi-site route in 2007, and launched a fellowship in Rapperswill, near Zurich.

We drew a circle around a thirty-minute travel distance from our central meeting place, and asked what would happen if we drew another thirty-minute distance around the outside of that. Zurich is the biggest city in Switzerland, with not even 400,000 people; but if we planted seven campuses, each thirty minutes travel distance from the centre, we could reach a population of around 1.5 million people.

The concept of 'One Church—Many Campuses' is still in the beginning stage and the sites are still small, finding their own ways to grow. There is still un-certainty if this model will work.—Only time will show if this strategy will reach more un-churched people. However, another large church in Zurich with over two thousand members (*Christliches Zentrum Buchegg*) divided into two campuses under two good leaders in 2007. Both sites work closely together and they offer courses during the week that complement each other. They also follow the idea of 'One Church—Many Campuses,' and their model seems to have worked very well for years.

While in the 1970s and '80s it was mainly evangelical churches that did church-planting, the majority of church plants from the late 90's to date have been spearheaded by the Vineyard and ICF Movements. This development has been supported by new types of in-service theological education, like the International Seminary of Theology and Leadership (ISTL.net). The leadership has dedicated it-self to training their students not only in the classroom but in practical evangelism on the streets and other places, in order to raise up a new generation of pastors who have a heart for un-churched people. They believe it is important that the students see their leaders in action, participating up front in outreaches.

I look forward to the future with mixed feelings, unsure where the journey will end unless we as a Church get on our feet again and reach out to un-churched people as never before. Over the last twenty to thirty years a new mission field has opened up in our country, from a population of twenty thousand Muslims thirty years ago to over four hundred thousand today. What an opportunity on our doorstep! If we do not reach these people for Christ—as well as our secular, next-door neighbours—our society will change dramatically. It's time to do what Jesus told us to do: *Go into all the world and preach the gospel!*

Traditional Evangelism

Many Christians would argue that the old, time-honoured strategies like open-air evangelism and door-to-door literature distribution have had their day. 21st Century Europeans, they insist, are too caught up with busy lives and tight schedules to pause long enough to listen to a gospel pitch on streets or doorsteps, no matter how creatively presented.

We invited Chris Mathieson, Chairman of Open Air Campaigners (OAC) Europe, along with other members of the OAC staff, to share from their experience. After this we'll consider the personal profile of a man who has made open air evangelism part of his lifestyle.

Open Air Ministry—A Valid Strategy for Post-Modern Europe?

During Spain's transition from dictatorship to democracy at the end of the 1970s, the streets of Spain were an exciting, if occasionally hairy place to be. Once I was in a café on Barcelona's Ramblas when police led a charge against communist agitators. Another evening in Madrid, a young foreigner named Farid was walking disconsolately along the street after being turned down by Madrid's School of Performing Art. What would he do now? Where could he go next? Perhaps he could do some clowning on the street to earn his supper.

Then Farid noticed a man painting on a board and speaking to the crowd. He stopped to see this street performer and was amazed to hear him talking about what Christ had done for him. Farid realised he needed a new start in more than one way, gave his life to the Lord and from that day on has been serving him. We brought Farid to Britain to study at a Bible School; he married and returned to his home country Colombia, where he has been involved ever since in church-planting and evangelism. As I write thirty years on, he is working on the streets of Cartagena, doing what he learned that spring evening in Madrid.

The world has certainly changed. Fantastic new evangelistic methods using the latest technology are now available. But in many cases they are little more effective and a lot more expensive. Friendship can reach the few who live or mix with us closely on a regular basis, but most people will never read our blog or share a chat over the garden fence. They will, however, be out in the street at some time or other.

Meanwhile, Europe is in many ways becoming an easier place in which to preach in the open air. Across Western Europe forty years ago the car was king. City centres were blocked by traffic and the High Street was a nightmare for shoppers. Now shopping centres may be pedestrianised, former inner-city industrial areas and docks have been renovated and opened to the public and people are looking for 'greener' ways to move around. Meanwhile, in countless areas of Southern and Eastern Europe, high-rise estates are still crowded with young people and families in the afternoons, enjoying time outside their cramped homes. The shared gardens that these estates afford are great places to reach locals.

Madrid's Puerta del Sol is the heart valve of Spain. Some two million people pass through every afternoon, although many are merely changing trains on the metro system. At any moment thousands can be found milling around the square, heading to or from the underground station, the shops or theatres. Our Open Air Campaigners (OAC) ministry began there on a weekly basis in the mid 1980s, and even before that we occasionally had programmes, like the time we met Farid. Now there is ministry in the square every day.

Leicester Square is the centre of London's night life. Weekly teams there and at nearby Oxford Circus have resulted in many people coming to Christ. Numerous other locations across the United Kingdom regularly see similar outreaches.

Stefansplatz is the very centre of Vienna. Every summer our teams run a week of evangelism and training, reaching thousands with the gospel. But one of the main objectives is to train local people and others from across Europe in evangelistic skills. As a result of 'Reach The City' outreaches, teams have continued regular open air activity in Vienna, across Austria and into Eastern Europe.

Training seminars are enabling churches to take their teams out of their four walls to where the people are. Men, women and children who would never cross the threshold of a church building are hearing the gospel and turning to Christ. One pastor once told me, 'The great thing about open air preaching with a sketchboard is that I can go alone and people will stop and listen, but I can also go out with the church and everyone has a job to do, whether preaching, singing, giving a testimony, holding the board, praying, being part of the listening crowd, or speaking with contacts after the presentation.'

So why do we do open air evangelism in Europe?

1. Because the apostles successfully used it to reach the world in their generation. Veteran OACer Korky Davey [www.korky.info] writes: 'The Apostolic Ministry outlined in the New Testament, beginning with the hugely successful ministry of Jesus to the population of Israel, was based on the prophetic pattern commanded by Moses (Deuteronomy 31:12). The disciples who were commissioned as Apostles to preach the Gospel to every human being went far beyond Israel to the Gentile world. Historians reckon that the Gospel went across the world in around 22 years through public preaching. They had learned from the Master how this was done.'

2. Because every revival since the Reformation and even before has employed open air preaching as key to multitudes hearing the gospel. Wesley and Whitefield, Booth and many others saw thousands coming to Christ through open air appeals.

3. Because it still works. OAC has been following this age-old tradition—using new, age-appropriate ways—across Europe for over forty years; almost 120 years around the globe. Through these efforts we can point to people who have found a transformed life through Jesus Christ, and churches which have released members into ministry. We have also had the joy of knowing we are following in the footsteps of the Master himself.

→   OAC is an international, interdenominational society, and outreaches are church-based. For more information about specialist training and other resources and opportunities see www.oaci.org

In the Steps of Saint Patrick

Several days a week he can be found in the centre of Dublin, setting up his sketchboard in the busy pedestrian shopping area at the corner of North Earl and O'Connell Streets. Tourists and Irish alike who pause to look at the famous James Joyce sculpture nearby eye him curiously, hoping he will prove to be one of Dublin's live attractions. With his twinkling blue eyes and thatch of greyish white hair and beard, Mickey Walker rarely disappoints.

'Hello, my name is Mickey!' he introduces himself with a grin. 'I'm a refugee from California who came to Ireland to escape sunburn. Here we all look like mayonnaise!'

The crowd—a cross-section of young and old shoppers, sightseers, mainland Chinese students, Bosnian or Nigerian refugees—warms to his humour. A Muslim woman wearing a veil stands on the edge of the crowd, taking flight only when Mickey mentions the name of Jesus Christ. Others walk away at the mention of sin. But when the sketch and accompanying story are finished, a number of listeners linger long enough to take tracts and/or talk with Mickey and his team of Irish believers. Two members of his team were won to Christ the same way.

Mickey Walker is one of OM's best-known and most-loved open-air evangelists. After trusting Christ while he was studying psychology in college, Mickey enrolled in Moody Bible Institute to study theology and spent a summer with OM in Turkey. Graduating from Azusa Pacific College in '69, he and Kathleen were married and went on to serve together in Nepal, India, Lebanon, Belgium, Iran, and aboard OM Ships. For the last 26 years they have made their home in Ireland, raising six great kids and continuing to motivate and train many other would-be evangelists all over the world. Mickey produces his own tracts and has written a creative training manual called 'The Cross and the Sketchboard.' * But he is happiest when he is on the streets himself, sharing the Good News.

'I've preached on the same street on this very corner since the day we arrived in Dublin,' Micky confirms. 'It's said to be the most traversed crossroads in Ireland on any given day. I had large crowds when I started doing open-airs because what I was doing was new and novel. People used to be much more entrenched in traditional religion, offering severe opposition to many of those who preached on the streets. The Roman Catholic Church could do no wrong in the eyes of most people. But many things have happened to change their attitude, including numerous substantiated allegations of abuse by the clergy and religious orders that have come to light after years of secrecy. This has resulted in widespread cynicism, with many people feeling utterly deceived. Today on the street most opposition is born of anti-religious secularism, with more and more Muslims challenging what I'm saying.' He adds, 'I've always been challenged about one thing or another, but I try to "keep the main thing the main thing." That is: exalt Jesus!'

Mickey is ready to do whatever it takes to see his listeners—whether in the

* Available by e-mail from: walker.mickey@gmail.com. By post: Mickey Walker, 59 Glenbrook Park, Rathfarnham, Dublin 14, Ireland.

crowd or talking to him one-on-one after each message—turn to Christ. For instance, after giving Chinese mainland students Mandarin tracts, he might walk them over to where the Chinese church meets to make sure they'll be able to find the place on Sunday.

'The fact is, no laborious sowing, no glorious reaping! There are no shortcuts to a harvest,' he warns. 'But when the fruit comes, it's worth it all.'

Mickey sees men and women find faith in Christ and go on well, even serving God full-time. At least two more evangelistic ministries have been birthed by men who came to faith through his open-air ministry. He's been especially encouraged by several who have returned years later to confirm that those first contacts on the street had led them to the Lord.

Mickey and his motorcycle have become a familiar sight around Dublin. At one of the annual St. Patrick's Day celebrations he gained recognition doubling as the saint himself atop a float themed 'Light the Fire Again!' The two missionaries actually have a lot in common. Neither was born in Ireland, but both are sons of Ireland by adoption. And each of them were totally convinced of the effectiveness of open-air evangelism. Thanks to Mickey, the determined words of the preacher who walked the emerald isle fifteen hundred years ago can still be heard on streets today: 'Let those who will, laugh and scorn.—I shall not be silent!'

Non-traditional or Creative Evangelism

Older evangelism techniques are often most effective when combined with some of the dozens of new ways that exist to reach into the lives of today's Europeans. Although the Church has traditionally employed writing, music, painting and sculpture in worship, for instance, it is only in comparatively recent times that it has taken advantage of many other powerful art forms. In the next pages we examine a few of these.

Touching Hearts through the Arts

OM Arts International* is a pioneering initiative that facilitates short mission trips and long term mission activities with the goal of establishing arts ministry models in Europe, the Middle East, Asia, South America and Africa. The

* http://omartslink.org

ministries it encompasses are ArtsLink, DanceLink, the Bill Drake Band, Heart Sounds International, Jon Simpson (songwriter, singer and multi-instrumentalist) and UniShow (Dustin Kelm, unicyclist tours).

ArtsLink

OM's ArtsLink* ministry is expressed as 'a passion to see visual artists get involved in the Great Commission by uniquely impacting communities around the globe.' This desire has fueled the development of radical overseas opportunities for visual artists to serve the Church and engage the world.

One 2010 initiative was the establishment an art studio and gallery in southern Spain. After years of praying, dreaming and hard work the opening night drew Spanish, Latinos, North Americans and North Africans, young and old, rich and poor to marvel at the transformation of the former warehouse. Artwork from a mixture of local artists and immigrants graced the walls of the brightly coloured space. Some guests sat on modern couches sipping glasses of hot mint tea and talking about the work while others milled about and chatted with artists.

Several children, paintbrushes in hand, added their personal touches to a mural in progress. The images in the mural illustrated life, love, community and freedom. Lively hues and a splash of graffiti lettering reminded guests that art is for everyone. The place heated up as the varied company savoured the art and toured the new space.

One believing artist whose work was exhibited noted that interest in her art spawned several conversations about birth and rebirth, loss and second chances. She found a natural way to connect with viewers and plant seeds of hope.

The team in Spain is overjoyed by the first fruit of their dreams. Their goal is that workers at the art studio will provide a positive spiritual influence in the city as they live as a community with Kingdom values.

Another project during the summer of 2010 allowed art to communicate hope in L'Aquila, Italy, a city that was devastated by a massive earthquake in April 2009. The tremor not only destroyed the city centre but took hundreds of lives, displacing thousands of others.

The Transform 2010 Travelling Prayer and Creative Arts Team was the first in what is hoped will become an ongoing series of teams in Italy's key cities, softening the ground so that seeds of truth will germinate and take root. Those with

* www.arts.om.org, http://arts-missions-trips-mv.blogspot.com

a creative aptitude were encouraged to respond through drawing, painting, writing, photography, and so forth. The goal was to flood the streets and piazzas with prayer and to experience the hand of God at work. The writing and artwork that was created will be used to develop a prayer guide book for future prayer teams.

Bill Drake Band

'Are you stealing from Jesus? Did Jesus get what he paid for? Is what you're living for, worth dying for?'

About 10,000 people were confronted with these three pivotal questions during concerts by the Bill Drake Band during one of their many European tours. Audiences in 12 cities and towns in Germany, Austria and Switzerland responded, many turning their lives over to Christ. Others dedicated themselves to more uncompromising Christian service.

'I don't see myself as a musician with a message,' says Bill Drake. 'Rather, I am a preacher who happens to use music.' Bill and his team's international multimedia concerts present a unique focus. Not only are these events about music, but about God and experiencing His reality in life. The team ministers through worship and teaching in church services and at missions conferences, schools, colleges and camps.

A typical story took place during the summer of 2010. The team arrived in Tatabanya, a town outside of Budapest, Hungary, and began setting up their sound system in a skate park. There amidst the half-pipes, graffiti, and broken lives that congregated there for various types of cheap thrills Bill started to share his own story. A young man named Dobsi stood on the edge of the pavement, hanging on every word. Bill's broken home, the child abuse, the deaths of his mother and best friend were parallels to his own life. But what really struck him was the peace and joy that radiated from Bill as he related these tragedies. Dobsi was drawn to the message of life—resurrected from the depths of destruction—like a man dying of thirst drawn to water.

Dobsi told Bill that he used to be 'king of the hill' in the skate park—it was his heaven. But younger kids had pushed him out, and his reasons for living were getting less compelling. He had contemplated suicide as Bill had so many years ago. Dobsi wanted to know if Christ could rescue him, too.

When Bill asked Dobsi if he was ready to surrender his life to Jesus, he said yes, and with a trembling voice prayed alongside Bill. There in that dingy skate park in Hungary, a young man's broken life was transformed by the gospel.

DanceLink

Before Linda Wells became a Christian she was a professional dancer in England. The woman who led her to Christ told Linda that she would have to give up dancing. She went to Bible College and began singing in a gospel group and sharing her testimony, but for eighteen years she did not dance a single step. After marriage and the birth of her second child, Linda fell into a deep depression. Her minister one day presented her with a key and said, 'I hear you used to be a professional dancer. In this church we believe that God uses the arts in worship. Take this key to the church and come and dance here alone whenever you want.'

Linda did so and found that as she danced, the depression lifted. She experienced complete healing and at last felt released to dance in worship. She began by spontaneously dancing in church, then as she learned Sign Language she began to incorporate signing into her dancing. She has since received requests from all over to teach signed worship dance. With the founding of OM DanceLink, teams have also travelled for ministry in Europe.

Recalls Linda, 'Albania was amazing. In spite of no water or electricity for eight hours each day and temps over 38 degrees Centigrade, we had some divine connections. Dance grabs a crowd instantly, and the people were wide open to talk about God, faith, and their desperate need for Him in their culture, economics and personal circumstances.'

Team member Jen Devoe, adds, 'Dance can communicate so much more than words. A middle-aged woman named Mariska came up to me and told me how much she enjoyed the dancing. I asked her if she was from the church, and she said yes. The church in her city was very discouraged. Many of the members thought that if no one was open to hearing about God, then why should they even try? Mariska was tearful, and I told her that we were in prayer for the church, and we wanted them to feel encouraged to learn, study the Bible, and reach out to their community. She leaned in and whispered, "The dancing encouraged me to love God more. I want to be closer to Him." That is a serious praise!'

During a dance workshop held in Birmingham, England, one of the ladies who came to the church revealed her devastation over her husband's recent suicide. Remembers Linda, 'I shared with her how dance had helped me get through a deep period of depression. She said to me: "God told me to come to this church today, and now I know why. I believe God is calling me to teach dance to Muslim women, using Christian music."'

Linda has repeatedly seen the Lord using music and dance to break the chains of darkness. *'The enemy will attack and interfere in believers' lives if they let him,'* she testifies. *'His power is real, but the power God has given believers through the work of Jesus is greater! … Sadly, we rarely use it.'*

UniShow

UniShow is a one-of-a-kind performance incorporating a motivational and inspirational message illustrated with world-class unicycling set to high-energy music. World champion unicyclist Dustin Kelm demonstrates a variety of unicycles: freestyle, mountain, racing, ultimate wheel, double wheel, six-footer; and for the grand finale, he juggles on his ten-footer! Dustin's unique skill and presentation captivates people of all ages in youth and family events, school assemblies, camps, festivals, outreaches and most any open-air gathering. Dustin has presented the UniShow in over 30 countries including festivals in Germany, Spain, Switzerland and Eastern Europe where he has seen the creative arts truly building bridges for the gospel.

Using unicycling as a metaphor, he gives a vivid demonstration of persistence and dedication, challenging youth to have the character to accomplish anything they put their minds to. He shares from his own experience dealing with rejection, his parents' divorce, suicide, relationships, purity, perseverance and becoming a world champion. His ultimate challenge is to live a life surrendered to Jesus Christ and to use God-given gifts and talents to make an eternal difference. UniShows often lead to serious conversations with individuals searching for the truth.

Jon Simpson

A few years ago Jon Simpson took the step of joining his faith to his passion and became a full-time musician, working alongside OM. Helping to fulfill the Great Commission through his music and touring other countries has had a strong impact on the songwriter, singer and multi-instrumentalist:

"What I've seen in other places in the world has made me rethink and reconsider many of the things I hold dear in my life. It's strengthened some of my convictions and caused me to jettison others."

Jon's song 'Olivia' in his album, *'Dark Gives Way,'* has led to the making of a short film called 'Olivia's Song,' highlighting the menace of human trafficking.

Heart Sounds International

The vision of Heart Sounds International (HSI) is to help ignite biblically appropriate and culturally relevant heart worship, in places where Christ-followers are restricted, persecuted or unknown. Partnering with churches, missions and other organisations, a volunteer team carries out audio and visual recordings and even, on occasion, provides modest studios for ongoing productions. In addition HSI teams equip local people with basic, entry-level instruction in audio or video techniques, and help to facilitate the process of composing indigenous, biblically-based songs along with their distribution. When requested, HSI teams also provide teaching on the fundamentals of Western music notation or offer seminars on biblical worship.

While the majority of their work is in Asia, Africa or the Middle East, HSI's specialised services are also very much appreciated in some places in Europe.

The Turkish-speaking Millet communities in *Bulgaria,* for instance, have faced much discrimination over many decades, and live in poverty and unemployment. Despite the hardships, and no doubt in part due to them, thousands of Millet in Bulgaria have come to Christ in recent years. The Jesus film has played a major part in the harvest, along with a recently published New Testament that also included hundreds of song lyrics.

To continue the spiritual harvesting, Christian leaders in Bulgaria recognised the need for a worship recording. This would have the double aim of strengthening Turkish believers as well as providing a tool to proclaim the greatness of Jesus to nonbelievers. HSI took the challenge and thanks to seasoned engineers, produced a recording that is now being greatly used of God.

As recently as the 1990s, the thought of a New Song Festival put on entirely through the efforts of Sahka (or Yakut) Christians in *Siberia, Russia,* was so preposterous it wasn't even a dream. At that time, the first few Sakha Christians were only beginning to come to the Lord. They had no thought of using music and art genres from their own culture to worship the Lord and to spread the gospel to their own people.

The Sakha people have for centuries considered their traditional religion, shamanism, to be the only true Sakha religion. The first evangelical believers came to the Lord after the fall of the Iron Curtain in the 1990s. The number of Sakha Christians in 2007 was estimated at about 400, out of a 400,000-plus population, and was growing slowly. Unfortunately at that time the vast majority of published Sakha-language songs were ones that had been translated from a Russian hymn-book.—Many indigenous Christian poets and songwriters had not been able to see their works recorded and published.

HSI became convinced that culturally-appropriate recorded music would make a huge difference to this people group. They encouraged the formation of an arts fellowship with Sakha men and women gifted in music, writing and art. Out of this grew the idea of a New Song Festival that would encourage Christians but also show non-believers that Christianity was not just a Russian or 'foreign' religion.

HSI produced a DVD to document the historic first New Song Festival, which opened the floodgates for creative cultural expressions of worship and sharing of the gospel in this part of Siberia. Repeat festivals were held, and as a result other indigenous groups in Siberia have been inspired to put on Christian "Ethno" festivals in their regions. HSI participates in these festivals by offering short-term trips for interns in which the team provides video, audio, and worship training support at the discretion of the local organisers.

Even the Sakha songbook has grown. In addition to the original translated hymns, it now contains seventy new Sakha songs, with many more being created each month. HSI workers are thrilled that Sakha indigenous creative expression in worship and witness is providing a model for other people groups around Siberia.

Austria's HEART*beat*

An altogether separate arts initiative was born in 2006 with four young Austrian musicians offering their gifts to God. They decided the emphasis of their group would be on training church worship leaders and offering seminars of interest to Christians in Austria. But only a year after they started 'HEART*beat*,' circumstances forced one of them to drop out.

Leaders Richard and Melanie Schmidt attended a vocal training school in Germany called Powervoice Academy, inspiring a change of focus for the ministry. The couple decided to re-launch HEART*beat* in October that year with the goal of reaching secular musicians with the gospel.

But then, without any warning, gifted songwriter and pianist Richard Schmidt collapsed from an unsuspected heart defect at the age of 31. The dream almost died with him.

Just two days before, he and Melanie and team member Andi Heusser had been thrilled to find the right location to start their own training school. What better place could there be than Vienna, in the heart of a land renowned for music? And what more appropriate use for a former candle factory, than to multiply the influence of God's life-giving light?

Now Richard's widow and Andi were at a crossroads. States Melanie, 'It was always our goal to live for God, whether that be 20, 30, 40 years or more. So I accept that Richard's time on earth had run its course and he had fulfilled his ministry.'

Yet along with this acceptance came the conviction that HEART*beat*'s ministry was not finished. And if God meant it to keep going, he would provide the ways and means. 'Richard was the businessman, the "front man,"' she admits. 'I never felt like a businesswoman! But that's what I am now. It's always a risk. You don't always know the answers. But each of us takes a share, and we are learning to "walk on water."'

God proved his faithfulness over and over and the '*Stimmfabrik*'* or 'Voice Factory' is now one of the most modern music training schools in Austria. 'We've seen so many miracles! A lot of personal friends helped to get the building ready. A sound engineer, friend of team member Dominik Travnik, loaned us equipment. One family donated ten thousand Euros towards lighting. Another person gave money for a recording studio. And we finally found a marketing executive who was willing to help us for free! Roland gives so much enthusiasm.'

The school currently has five coaches and 150 singers. 'It's unique because of the personalised style we have of coaching each student,' CEO Melanie explains. 'Our speciality is rock-pop. Most vocal teachers have a classical education, so we have an advantage. Students can come for a single weekend or every week.

'It's a point where musicians meet—both Christians and non-Christians. Our goal, as we go about our work, is to influence society through Christian values. We don't preach, but those who come sense the Spirit in us.'

Public performance programmes are held every few months and sometimes include guest artists like the top Austrian Christian band, '*Menschensohn*.' Other groups use the facility for concerts. The team also offers workshops, both at the school and on the road as far afield as Germany and Switzerland.

'There are still days when I feel as if the rug has been pulled out from under my feet, and the pain of my loss is almost too much to bear,' admits Melanie. 'Yet I am experiencing that God is carrying me, and that He won't allow anything more than I can bear.'

* www.stimmfabrik.at

On a spiritual level, she continues, the team wants to encourage Christian musicians not only to play in churches, but to practice performing outside the church, at a level capable of competing. 'We have to learn how to write songs—and sing songs—for non-Christians.'

'We want to set people free,' agrees co-worker Dominik. 'Some Christians are locked up inside. We want to see them bloom. And we want non-Christians to see God in us, and begin to ask questions.'

Although for various reasons the Voice Factory is not an OM entity, Melanie and Andi still count themselves as OMers. 'They're very creative, and very professional,' says Austria leader Philipp Eschbach, 'and we want to give them the freedom to develop. Quite a few worship leaders and Christian performers are now going to them [for training], which is helping to equip the church and mobilise people for ministry. We want to be carriers of hope at the heart of society—where the people are. It's a real business for transformation.'

'When you work with someone on their voice, you go much deeper than just their vocal chords,' observes the *Stimmfabrik* coaches. 'The whole personality is involved, and if there are emotional blockages which hinder them from putting their "heart" into the interpretation of a song, that soon becomes obvious. We are often able to engage in deep conversations about problems or hurts from the past, and often have an open door to share about God's help and healing power.'

Affirms Corinna, a student at *Stimmfabrik*, 'This place is like a church for me—more than most church buildings I know!'

With God's enablement and the prayers of his people, HEART*beat* will continue to bring light and life in Austria through the sound of music.

Other Examples of Creative and Non-Traditional Evangelism

Mobile phone users around the world now total well over three billion. Two billion people regularly access the internet. 500 million alone—speaking nearly 100 languages—use the social networking site Facebook, making it (in population terms) the planet's third largest country. Many read and update their Facebook pages through mobile phones.

The Christian world has just scratched the surface when it comes to harnessing digital media for evangelism and discipleship. Radio and TV stations with corresponding website links are receiving extraordinary responses. In one year alone Global Media Outreach (GMO), a ministry of Campus Crusade for Christ International, presented the gospel to over 66 million people around the world through its 100-plus websites. Ten million listeners indicated a decision for Jesus, and over 4,100 GMO online missionaries respond to emails requesting follow-up. And just one radio network in Poland, CCM, launched an evangelistic website that received over a million hits within the first two years of operating. Of these, some 112,000 visitors filled out a form saying they had prayed to commit their lives to Christ.

Non-profit agency Galcom International is partnering with evangelicals internationally to facilitate spreading the gospel through technology. One project has been distributing over 800,000 radios in 125 countries, fix-tuned to evangelistic programmes. Through Trans World Radio more than 2,000 of their specially-made solar panel radios have also been provided to Roma (gypsy) people living in remote areas of Romania, and 4,000 to people in the Balkans. Galcom's other communication devices include radio transmitters (AM, FM and SW) for the setting up of local Christian radio stations, low power FM speech transmitter systems for translating at bi-lingual conferences or equipping churches with hard of hearing apparatus, and MegaVoice Audio Bibles.

Of course, most of us are aware that the best way to make friends and influence them for the Kingdom is by meeting their felt needs. Medical missions, humanitarian aid and development projects, education—encompassing everything from children's homework help groups to adult language, sewing and computer classes—have all effectively opened European hearts. On the other end of the scale are sports and recreational activities, even adventure holidays in informal settings where a spiritual message can be introduced. Since we obviously cannot cover all of these possibilities in the remaining pages, we have chosen to give an example of a small 'niche' recreational ministry in Britain, followed by a very much broader initiative that is making a profound difference in several countries across Europe.

Mission Afloat

The Seventh Wave is no ordinary sailboat. The elegant 49-foot yacht belongs to the Christian trust Quest for Life and is a part of OM. While focusing especially on youth, this charity also offers cruises for the disadvantaged plus spiritual retreats, adventure training and evangelism outreaches for all ages.

Skipper Andrew Thompson has been sailing ever since acquiring his first small yacht in the 1970s, during nine years in the Royal Navy. His involvement with the present ministry began about twenty years ago, with a different boat and different name—Westward Quest. Andrew was at that point establishing OM's UK base (then called LUKE, 'Love UK Evangelism;' now Lifehope), and was convinced that sailing would make great adventure training for young people. The work developed until Quest for Life became an official part of OM's ministry in 1999.

Up to two hundred people enjoy *Seventh Wave* cruises off Sweden and Scotland's Western Isles each season, which lasts from March through October. The boat can accommodate up to ten persons and is bookable for any length of time, usually from a weekend to up to two weeks.

Christians often bring along non-believing friends, says Andrew. 'Once some men from my church invited members of a really tough road-building crew. We've even had bikers on board. A vicar organised a sail for a group of nominal believers, business and professional men. They did a "Discovering Christianity" course over the weekend, and the interest of these men was amazing.'

Andrew calls the ministry 'very much personal work' and is always ready to speak for his Captain whenever the opportunity arises. Once, invited onto a boat off Iona, he met an Oxford professor who announced he was an atheist.

'How can an intelligent man like you believe such a load of nonsense?' Andrew challenged him. 'We had a good chat. He finally admitted that he'd been searching seventeen years for God.'

OM short-term teams sometimes use the boat to reach islanders with the good news of Christ. Other groups opt for a walking and sailing or golf and sailing combination trip, and many simply go to explore new places, enjoy the wildlife, or just chill out. Those who wish can learn basic sailing skills such as steering and hoisting sails. But whether gliding by rolling green hills dotted with sheep and white stone crofts or being chased by dolphins, Quest for Life participants are seldom disappointed. As one young person exclaimed of his experience, 'This was the best day of my life!'

→   For more details contact Andrew Thompson, 14, Lismore St., Carlisle, Cumbria CA1 2AH. TEL/FAX 01228-535831. Email: info@questforlife.co.uk, Website: www.questforlife.co.uk

business4transformation

The heart of the spiritual battleground is the workplace; it is also at the centre of economic structures and systems. 'business4transformation' (b4t), also called Business as Mission in some circles, is about real, 'for profit' businesses that are not only profitable, but intentional about effecting social, economic, environmental and spiritual transformation (4t's) in their communities. This goes quite a bit beyond the more traditional development approach of helping people achieve financial stability. The financial scale involved in OM projects also differentiates b4t from similar things happening around the world.

Participants are believers, usually business people or those who are gifted or inclined to business, who want to engage in missions. Their ministry flows out of the very act of doing business. Although OM was initially thinking of engaging primarily in the 10/40 and creative access (CAN) nations, God opened the leaders' minds when an increasing number of business people in Europe (and America) asked why they couldn't also become b4t businesses.

Read about one exciting project in the pages above, in the 'Touching Hearts with the Arts' section: *Austria's HEARTbeat*. The Voice Factory (*Stimmfabrik*) currently has a clientele of some 200 students.

As of this writing, starting a private kindergarten aimed especially at foreign (immigrant) children, is in the planning stages. If this one takes off it could be the beginning of a whole chain of kindergartens that will employ staff, charge fees and enjoy tremendous opportunities to speak into the lives of little ones, as well as their extended families.

A third project is also still very much in the fledgling stage: a hotel in a strategic part of a large city that will engage the community, especially giving youth alternatives to the drug and alcohol culture clubs they normally frequent. This project will be working very closely with local churches.

Ten Reasons Why b4t Works

1. It transforms people and communities through an encounter with Jesus. As people move towards a Biblical worldview they discover that loving and being loved by God is the root of all blessing.
2. It decreases dependency and encourages the mobilisation of the church to reach unreached people groups.

3. It models Kingdom values, especially to influential people, and demonstrates an alternative to corruption. It is effective in opening doors to the upper middle class in urban cities.

4. It may create employment for new believers (Galatians 6:10) and profits from the business can help resource the local church.

5. Good business teaches good management and accountability skills that are greatly needed in churches.

6. It can provide training and skills for the poorest of the poor.

7. It allows entry into the more developed, least evangelised peoples. The reality of missions from the western world is that fewer people are going and they are going for a shorter time. They are finding it harder to get funding and they are restricted from 'key' areas.

8. It can be a blessing to a nation, developing trade instead of reliance upon aid.

9. It is a response to the massive rural to urban shift in the world, and the resulting search by many for work in slums and depressed areas.

10. It is addressing the issue of human trafficking. Trafficking people usually ends in sexual exploitation and forced labour. People are held in captivity and forced to work for little or no wages. What is the cause of modern-day slavery? It is largely unemployment, insufficient income and no jobs at home. The cure is job creation: viable, sustainable and profitable business. b4t not only deals with the root cause of trafficking, it is a cure for the victims!

Successful businesses initiatives vary widely, from travel and tourism, education, handcrafts and consultancies to medical services. The following case study shows how business4transformation is working in the tiny country of Moldova.

Finding Solutions for Survival

30% of the Eastern Europe country of Moldova's population lives below the poverty line. Unemployment is high and economic and social conditions continue to deteriorate, especially in the villages. The situation is the legacy of seventy years of oppression as a member of the former Soviet Union, where private enterprise was forbidden.

However, Moldova has significant human and natural resources, and OM has proven that showing God's love in a practical way can do much to change attitudes and hearts. The mission hosts at least four business courses each year for people from small towns and villages. Although participants need a reference from a pastor they don't necessarily have to be Christians.

Eugen Tcaci, who heads the team, once ran his own successful apple export business but gave it up to attend Bible School and plant churches. He still serves an assistant pastor, but considers his OM work just as much of a ministry.

The five days of training offered to each group of twenty men and women are extremely practical. Materials are furnished by the International Labour Office, and local business people are invited to share. Along with learning about planning, stock control, costing, buying and marketing, entrepreneurs learn how to write a business plan. Twelve projects are then selected and contracts drawn up. Individuals receive start-up loans of six to twelve hundred Euros, provided at a very low interest rate by the Christian relief and development organisation, Dorcas International.

'Over the next two years we visit, monitor and counsel clients,' Eugen explains, adding that during the second year, entrepreneurs may attend a level two business course to further their knowledge and skills. 'When loans are repaid, the money is recycled to fund other micro-enterprises.'

Natalia is just one of the success stories. After she took the business training in 2008, OM helped her rent a room and buy supplies for a hairdressing salon. The salon thrived. The next year Natalia and her husband took level two training and opened a second business together, selling car parts!

So far, 133 families—ten belonging to pastors—have managed to achieve financial stability through the project, and thirty-four have fully repaid their loans. Income-generating schemes range from breeding cows, goats, and other livestock to greenhouses for growing vegetables and fruits, or shops selling construction materials and electrical supplies. In 2010 Dorcas sponsored a new agricultural project, funding ten individuals in a single village to receive training and form an association.

Moldova's Communist government was ousted several years ago, but the party remains strong and few outside businesses are ready to invest in a less-than-stable country. Investing in individuals, however, is the option God taught us. By giving hope to people in His name, we can't go wrong.

Resources

■ 'business4transformation' or Business as Mission— Selected Reading

Baer, Michael R. *Business as Mission; The Power of Business in the Kingdom of God.* YWAM Publishing, 2006.

Danker, William J. *Profit for the Lord; Economic Activities in Moravian Missions and the Basel MissionTrading Company.* Wipf and Stock Publishers, 2002.

Lai, Patrick. *Tent-Making; Business as Missions.* Authentic Media, 2005.

Steve Rundle and Tom Steffen. *Great Commission Companies—The Emerging Role of Business in Mission.* IVP, 2003.

Suter, Heinz and Marco Gmur. *Business Power for God's Purpose.* Switzerland, 1997.

Swarr, Sharon B. and Dwight Nordstrom. *Transform the World; Biblical Vision and Purpose for Business.* Centre for Entrepreneurship and Economic Development, University of the Nations, 1999.

Yamamori, T. and K. A. Eldred, editors. *On Kingdom Business; Transforming Missions through Entrepreneurial Strategies.* Crossway Books, 2003.

■ b4t—Selected Websites

- Bizplan — www.bizplan.com
- Business as Mission — www.businessasmission.com
- Business as Mission Network — www.businessasmissionnetwork.com
- Global Opportunities — www.globalopps.org
- Scruples — www.scruples.org/bizetmiz
- Tentmakernet — www.tentmakernet.com
- Tentmaking—Business as Mission — www.tentmaking.org

▪ Evangelism—Recommended Reading

'Biblical Patterns of Evangelism Today' and *'Jesus—Faith and Fact,'* (articles) by
veteran Open Air Campaigner Korky Davey, are both available online at
www.korky.info.

Brookes, Andrew. *The Alpha Phenomenon*. Churches Together in Britain &
Ireland, 2008.

Clancy, Dawn, editor. *Child's Play; How to Use Sketchboard Talks Effectively*.
Kevin Mayhew, 2004.

Croft, Steven and others. Evangelism in a Spiritual Age: Communicating Faith
in a Changing Culture (Explorations). Church House Publishing, 2005.

Howe, Mark. *Open Air Evangelism*. CLC, 1991.

McLaren, Brian D. *More Ready Than You Realize: Evangelism in a Post-Modern
Matrix*. Zondervan, 2002.

The New Faces of Europe (Unreached People Group Booklet). Caleb Resources,
2003.

'Reaching Neighbours; Some Practical Steps for House-to-House Visiting.' (Article)
http://www.e-n.org.uk/p-1871-Reaching-neighbours.htm

Sanders, J. Oswald and George Verwer. *Effective Evangelism/Literature
Evangelism*. Authentic, 1999.

Sutherland, Arthur A. *I Was a Stranger: A Christian Theology of Hospitality*.
Abingdon, 2006.

Tennens, Terry, editor. Journey Into Growth: The Seven Core Values of a
Mission Church. Churches Together in Britain & Ireland, 2007.

▪ Evangelism and Church-Planting—Websites

▪ACTS 29 Network   www.acts29network.org
All about churches planting churches, started in USA but has spread to Western
Europe.

▪Alliance for Saturation Church Planting

www.alliancescp.org/resources/
index.html

Although this formal partnership has now dissolved, resources are still available.

- The Alpha Course   http://alpha.org/home
  Opportunity for unchurched to explore Christianity through weekly sessions.

- Alternative Worship   www.alternativeworship.org
  Information about and links to worldwide alternative worship sites and resources.

- Back to Church Sunday   www.backtochurch.co.uk
  Initiative to encourage church drop-outs to return. Free resources.

- Bethinking.org   www.bethinking.org
  Resources to stimulate thinking about and communicating the Christian faith.

- Blah   http://blahonline.wetpaint.com
  Conversations hosted by the Church Mission Society on mission, worship, church and Christianity in contemporary culture.

- CellUK   www.celluk.org.uk
  Training and support for Cell Churches, both denominational and non-denominational.

- Christianity Explored   www.christianityexplored.org
  Informal evangelistic course series based on Mark's Gospel, similar to Alpha.

- Church Army Research Unit   http://encountersontheedge.org.uk
  Publications about emerging forms of church crossing to non-churched people.

- Church Growth International   www.churchgrowthinternational.com
  Books and videos to encourage individual believers as well as churches that want to grow.

- Church in New Housing Areas   www.cinha.net
  Churches Together in England site sharing information and networks for church-planting on new housing estates.

- Dynamic Church Planting International
                                   www.dcpi.org
  Training ministry in many countries.

- Emergingchurch.info   www.emergingchurch.info/
  Research, stories, discussion and links about the emerging church.

▪ Encounters on the Edge   www.encountersontheedge.org.uk

The Sheffield Centre's series of quarterly investigations, written by George Lings, looking at emerging forms of church and crossing the widening gap to the non-churched.

▪ Fresh Expressions   www.freshexpressions.org.uk

Church-planting and new expressions of church in a changing culture, linked to several denominations. Offers booklet guides, a 'Mission-Shaped Ministry Course' and DVD: Stories of Church for a Changing Culture. Although this is UK-based, the concept has spread to other parts including Northern Europe. Links to website with more how-to-do-it advice: www.sharetheguide.org

▪ Image Bank   www.newchristian.org.uk/
                                       churchresources.html

Free resource for churches seeking to explore how images can help in fresh expressions of worship.

▪ Incarnate Network   http://incarnate-network.eu

Grass roots Baptist-run network for church-planting, emerging and fresh expressions of church, open to all. Training events and database of stories and resources. Some of the regional networks are in mainland Europe.

▪ Interface   www.theinterface.org.uk

'Where Christianity meets culture.' Methodist website that invites discussion on contemporary issues from a faith-based perspective.

▪ Internet Evangelism Day   www.internetevangelismday.com

How your church can reach out online.

▪ The Mark Drama   http://themarkdrama.com

▪ Networks of Fresh Expressions   http://freshexpressions.org.uk/networks

Information and help for various types of new churches.

▪ New Churches   www.newchurches.com

Online tutorial on church-planting, connecting with other people and events.

▪ New Way of Being Church   www.newway.org.uk

Building small Christian communities through training, research and resources.

▪ Proost   http://proost.co.uk/

Creative worship resources which have come from alternative worship in fresh expressions of church.

- Purpose Driven UK   www.church-growth.co.uk
Church health model that provides a pastoral team with a unique, biblically-based approach to establishing and growing congregations. ReSource trains people with a vision to engage in mission and start churches in the emerging culture.

- Reaching the Unchurched Network (RUN)
www.run.org.uk/
RUN's goal is to envision, provide resources and network with others concerning emerging forms of church in our changing culture. Includes conference and workshop events and online magazine.

- Schuman Centre for European Studies www.schumancentre.eu
'Promoting Biblical perspectives on Europe's past, present and future.'

- Together in Mission   http://togetherinmission.co.uk
Works with denominations, networks and local UK churches to encourage emerging church plants with a mission focus, and leadership development.

- WebEvangelism.com   www.webevangelism.com

■ Fresh Expressions and Church-Planting—More Reading

Atkins, Martyn. Resourcing Renewal: Shaping Churches for the Emerging Future. Inspire, 2007.

Bayes, Paul and others. Mission-shaped Parish: Traditional Church in a Changing World. Church House Publishing, 2006.

Bossingham, Mike. Building Family Friendly Churches. Epworth, 2004.

Collyer, Michael and others. A Mission-Shaped Church for Older People? The Salvation Army and The Leveson Centre, 2008.

Cuthbert, Nick and Chris Stoddard. Church on the Edge: Principles and Real Life Stories of 21st Century Mission. RUN, 2006.

Gaze, Sally. Mission Shaped and Rural; Growing Churches in the Countryside. Church House Publishing, 2006.

Gibbs, Eddie and Ryan Bolger. Emerging Churches; Creating Christian Communities in Postmodern Cultures. SPCK, 2006.

Glasson, Barbara. Mixed Up Blessings: A New Encounter with Being Church. Inspire, 2006.

Hope, Susan. Mission-shaped Spirituality: The Transforming Power of Mission. Church House Publishing, 2006.

Jones, Tom, editor. *Church Planting from the Ground Up.* College Press Pub. Co., 2004.

Male, Dave. Church Unplugged: Remodelling Church Without Losing Your Soul. Authentic, 2008.

Moore, Lucy. *Messy Church; Fresh Ideas for Building a Christ-Centred Community.* Bible Reading Fellowship, 2006.

Moynagh, Michael. emergingchurch.intro. Monarch, 2004.

Percy, Martyn and Louise Nelstrop, editors. Evaluating Fresh Expressions: Explorations in Emerging Church: Emerging Theological and Practical Models. Canterbury Press Norwich, 2008.

Robinson, Stuart. *Starting Mission-Shaped Churches.* St. Paul's Chatwood Parish Council, 2007.

Stetzer, Ed. *Planting Missional Churches.* B&H Academic, 2006.

Stetzer, Ed and Warren Bird. *Viral Churches: Helping Church Planters Become Movement Makers.* Jossey-Bass, 2010.

Strauch, Alexander. *Hospitality Commands.* Lewis & Roth, 1993.

Sudworth, Tim and others. Mission-shaped Youth: Rethinking Young People and Church. Church House Publishing, 2007.

Stuckey, Tom. Beyond the Box: Mission Challenges from John's Gospel. Inspire, 2005.

Stuckey. Tom. On the Edge of Pentecost: What Is the Spirit Saying to the Churches? Inspire, 2007.

Wagner, C. Peter and Francis A. Sullivan. *Church Planting for a Greater Harvest: A Comprehensive Guide.* Regal, 1990.

Williams, Rowan. *Mission-Shaped Church.* Church House Publishing, 2004.

Williams, Stuart Murray. Changing Mission: Learning from the Newer Churches. Churches Together in Britain & Ireland, 2006.

Williams, Stuart Murray. Church after Christendom. Paternoster, 2005.

Withers, Margaret. Mission-shaped Children: Moving Towards a Child-Centred Church. Church House Publishing, 2006.

■ Miscellaneous Outreach Tools

- Back to Church Sunday (UK)   www.backtochurch.co.uk
  Campaign materials.

- EvangeCube, EvangeBall (soccer) for sports outreach and other useful tools
  from   http://store.e3resources.org/
                                                Evangelism/EvangeCube-Products

- Evangelism Toolbox   www.evangelismtoolbox.com
  A large data base offering multi-lingual, multi-format resources.

- Evangelism Tools (OM)   www.lifehope.om.org/index.php/
                                       Evangelism-Tools

  Sketchboard talks, paper or rope illustrations, puppeteering, open air
  evangelism and more.

- Open Air Evangelism   www.oaci.org/aids
  Boards and other supplies from Open Air Campaigners.

- Sketchboard Talks—Free scripts online from
                                       www.grassroots.org.uk/home/about/
                                       other-people/130
  Also from Open Air Mission   www.oamission.com/resources.html

Section 5

Partnering with the Church

Introduction

The Multiplication Factor

I have always loved the pictures of the 'body' given in Ephesians 4:14–16 and Romans 12:3–8, and the vision of shared life those metaphors present. They are powerful reminders that not only is it a Biblical mandate that we work together, it is a practical necessity. The situation in Europe since the end of WWII has been a great proving ground for this Biblical truth, as opinions of the 'body' have turned increasingly negative. Indeed, for evangelical Christians, life in post-war Europe has not been so comfortable.

The nations of Europe, impoverished by years of fighting, sought to deal with the aftermath of the massive conflict. Not least were questions raised against God, against belief, and against faith. Once the Cold War began there were serious ideological issues facing the Church and her beliefs: a public whose faith had been exposed to unspeakable horrors; an intellectual elite alienated from the very notion of Christianity; and a mood of doubt and scepticism which pervaded so much of life that it made any truth claims appear ridiculous.

Though circumstances were grim it was not all bad news, as agencies like Greater Europe Mission were born in this setting. They launched a vision for church planting, evangelism and theological education in many needy areas. Youth for Christ swung into action, as did many other groups. Francis and Edith Schaeffer founded L'Abri to provide space and opportunity to speak to some of Europe's disillusioned young people.

For many the 1960s brought the renewal of passion, vision for mission, and evangelism. The birth of OM, YWAM, the work of Campus Crusade as well as InterVarsity Fellowship, the Navigators and others, showed that much could still be accomplished, despite the sceptical climate. Many faithful churches continued in mission as new fellowships were born. However, all was not easy, and the mood and attitude of the times often kept believers and churches confined to their own denominations, their own context, and limited to a local or smaller vision.

The 1980s seemed to bring a greater surge of cooperation between churches and missions. During the Cold War years most evangelical missions worked well with one another, coordinating literature production, transport, and teaching opportunities. As is often the case, the success in mission, along with the mutual benefits of shared prayer, focus and fellowship encouraged all; often leading to a desire for more. Could we do bigger or better things, together?

In the late '80s many across Europe sensed the need for increased efforts and effectiveness in mission on a broader front. The Lausanne movement provided excellent data on the needs of Europe and many of the underlying reasons for the weaknesses of mission. Younger leaders who attended these consultations were often left restless by an insufficient emphasis on planning and action. The information was powerful, the picture somewhat clear, but the challenge remained of what was to be done, and by whom?

I personally felt led to contact many of the European directors of various missions to see what God might be saying to us all. I have to admit that this turned out to be one of the richest experiences in my Christian journey. Getting together with other leaders and those with a passion for mission, for the Church and for Europe, was a deep inspiration. As we shared stories, history and insights as well as personal and mission-specific visions, it became clear there was a bigger picture; there were common threads; and there was huge potential for further joint efforts.

These conversations led to years of working together to establish offices in Brussels that could interact at the same level with Europe's needs. Many local and national campaigns resulted and increased consultation on shared efforts appeared at a pan-European level. The vision of 'Hope for Europe' was nurtured in the cradle of ongoing conversations, prayer and reflection about needs and challenges. The idea was to target an issue essential to the human condition, something begging for attention, and yet an answer that was undeniably Christian and grounded in the gospel (Romans 15:13, 8:24–25).

Now let me fast-forward to the present. We can now identify many exciting initiatives and strategies underway across Europe. The European Leadership Forum (ELF) that meets annually in Eger, Hungary, is a great model of shared and cooperative vision. The leadership team is drawn from Norway, Sweden, Holland, England and the United States. The annual event is anchored in a serious focus on truth applied in various networks to specific target areas. These include university work, politics, apologetics, reaching Muslims, helping businessmen and women to be effective as believers in the marketplace, church planting and counseling. Even more areas are covered in forums before and after the main event that aim for issue-specific seminars on topics which address the felt needs of many. In addition, ELF speakers visit a number of countries for specially arranged debates, lectures or seminars. When we also consider the associated website [http://www.euroleadershipresources.org] and its resources, the Leadership Forum is a tremendous boost to mission in Europe.

My own organisation, Ravi Zacharias International Ministries (RZIM), has its European office in Oxford, and we actively partner with Wycliffe Hall in the Oxford Centre for Christian Apologetics. This is an exciting initiative, involving dynamic teaching from speakers like Michael Green, John Lennox, Amy-Orr Ewing, Michael Ramsden, Ravi Zacharias and many others. The focus is on a serious engagement with unbelievers in Europe's pluralistic milieu. Students not only study the 'hard' issues like violence in the Old Testament and sexual ethics, but learn to discuss those questions with others, compassionately and truthfully. Participants do many mission outreaches throughout the study year so they get opportunities across the UK to engage with sceptics of all stripes. Students are encouraged to enter the most challenging arenas and to take on the most serious questions.

One of the fruits of the partnership in Oxford has been invitations from across Europe, the U.S. and Hong Kong for missions and training. Students are applying from all over the world, and especially encouraging are the testimonies of changed lives: of men and women responding to Christ and overcoming internal fears and doubts.

In Norway, Lars Dahle heads up the Gimlekollen Media School in Bergen. Lars is an active believer and heavily involved in the Lutheran Church in his country and beyond. He and his colleagues are working creatively to engage seekers and sceptics in Norway and across Europe. Lars has studied apologetics and has deep roots in the local church, so he understands the need to equip local congregations to stand strong in their faith. But he also sees the need for the Church to publicly confront the challenges, threats, attacks, or counter claims against the gospel.

In Sweden, Stephan Gustafson heads up the Credo Institute that offers seminars, training and events which also seek to engage the issues of their society. In the last few years the institute has identified Sweden's key atheists and organised public debates which were then televised and broadcast. Stephan is part of the leadership team of the European Leadership Forum, so he combines local vision with Europe-wide and, indeed, global vision.

So what do all of these initiatives have in common? They are all from conservative, Biblical Christians with a deep commitment to the local church. They also reflect a belief in the mandate to be involved in mission and the need to publically proclaim the gospel. They are not afraid of the social/political mood of the age, but rather embrace it as an opportunity to educate and inform their neighbours about Christianity. They also stress co-operation, partnership and dialogue. Why waste resources, duplicating efforts or competing, when so much more can be gained by intentional sharing and working together?

Examples of such co-operative efforts are everywhere, and they highlight the ongoing passion for Christ and real possibilities of embracing His call. Once individuals mobilise and link with others they can dramatically impact a whole area, a people group, or a specific context with the gospel.

Over recent weeks I have seen other fruits from a common vision. Polish people are being reached with fresh and relevant ways of evangelism. In Dziengelow, a small village in the south, large crowds attend an annual camp with large-scale public evangelistic meetings. It is amazing to see 1,000 to 1,200 people show up every day to listen to messages in the searing heat or even occasional downpours. The spark has not gone out, and the vitality, vision and passion of Polish leaders are an encouragement that God still has His purposes for Europe.

As I left this country filled with joy at the changes that have taken place in the last twenty years—and at all that God is still doing—I plunged into yet another stream of God's activity in this continent and beyond. The International Baptist Association (IBA) was holding its annual gathering in Interlaken, Switzerland. Those who attended represented English-speaking expatriate congregations from all across Europe, the Middle East, Latin America, Africa and elsewhere. The IBA also includes military chaplains serving in posts worldwide. In today's highly diverse societies, English-speaking churches are often well attended. They draw people from different backgrounds, including nationals who like to practice their English and who may prefer the 'feel' and focus of an international congregation.

As I listened to stories from Germany, France, Holland, Italy and other countries, it was encouraging to see what God was doing; not only in a local way but across Europe. Once again, an active network provided resources, coordination, support and input that no church or mission in isolation could supply or receive alone. The multiplication effect and its increased benefits are clear. Does this mean it is all easy or that it involves no struggles, pains or difficulties? Of course not, but the gains truly outweigh the costs.

As I reflect upon what remains to be done in Europe, I still feel there is a serious lack in several important areas:

- *At the strategic level.* There is little or no active cooperation of an intentional kind that effectively targets nations or regions within Europe.

- *At the informational level.* There is an appalling lack of awareness of existing resources, ideas or materials that can aid local churches in mission, education and growth.
- *At the supply level.* Lacking any system, personnel, vision or intent, there seems to be no one whose job or calling is to traverse Europe, join the dots, link hands and help foster connections to people, resources, events and support.
- *In terms of research and development.* Within industry, leaders know the importance of continually researching trends, knowing their markets, designing new products and improving service, quality and delivery. In the church and mission, we seem to give only token approval to this kind of analysis, and suffer as a result.

God's people have great resources and potential at their disposal, yet they are often fragmented, isolated or segregated through various forms of protectionism. Perhaps it is a desire to jealously guard a unique 'donor' stream; perhaps it is an attitude of holding to the high ground of 'relevance;' perhaps it is the fear of theological or philosophical 'contamination;' or perhaps it is just a desire to protect our own turf. I believe that though these issues have practical ramifications, some people and agencies have answered the challenges effectively, and they can and must be addressed. The kingdom impact of self-denial, shared vision, and costly obedience is worth the effort!

The 'us versus them' language needs to be dropped as we all seek to find one another, listen and learn from one another; and, where possible, engage one another.

David Robertson is the minister of St. Peter's Church in Dundee, once the home of the famous preacher Robert Murray McCheyne and scene of a major revival. Today's Dundee is a different place with rampant signs of decay and social problems. The community is vastly different as well. Thousands of international students attend the local universities and Europeans from across the continent now work in Scotland. These are all people in search of hope, relationships, work and security.

In a climate of intense agnosticism and scepticism towards religion, David and his church team are reaching out to the community, the nation and beyond. David has sought out partnerships with RZIM and others in order to enhance this mission and increase the fruit of all involved. We have great expectations about the upcoming launch of a 'Centre for Public Christianity,' based on a model founded in Sydney, Australia, that is a direct result.

We need more fresh ideas like this, new and bold initiatives. We must also have the courage and conviction that Scripture is relevant to every age, and that God is definitely speaking to ours. We need to embrace His vision, and also His way. The 'body' as used in Scripture is not a mere metaphor; it is the agent of Christ in this world and works as an instrument and servant of His will, His way and His hope for all those around us. My prayer for myself, for Europe, for the gospel, is that we as God's people will truly embrace His wisdom. And that 'by that which every joint supplies, according to the proper working of each individual part ... [we may see] the growth for the building up of itself in love.' *

—Stuart McAllister
Vice-President for Training & Special Projects
Ravi Zacharias International Ministries

Linking with the Body of Christ

Partnering with the Church, equipping and empowering believers to live out Christ's calling in their own community and nation and to the ends of the earth, is a fundamental, Biblical strategy. Under this umbrella comes envisioning and mobilising churches for local, national and international ministries, advocacy and prayer.

From its earliest days OM has sought to link with local evangelical fellowships during outreaches and follow-up activities. It has also gratefully supported and cooperated with like-minded missions.

In some countries, where churches have not had a history of working together, OM has acted as a catalyst to strengthen those ties. In 2008, for instance, the mission instigated a 'Year of Prayer for Bosnia-Herzegovina' that united churches across the country and between many denominations—a first for this severely divided Balkan nation. The team ran a website during that year in five different languages and local pastors wrote daily prayer points for each day as well as a prayer focus for each month. People around the world used the website to pray for Bosnia. Three big prayer conferences concentrating on different parts of the country were also organised in January, June and December, each drawing about

* Ephesians 4:16, NASB

two hundred participants.—Not bad, considering Bosnia-Herzegovina had only about one thousand evangelical believers in total! By the end of the year, all major towns as well as all churches and church-plants had benefited from their own special times of prayer.

Continent-wide mission conferences such as Mission-Net and TeenStreet, described in the 'Empowering Kids and Youth' section of this book, have also been founded on the joint participation of hundreds of churches and mission groups. So is Transform 2010 and 2011, OM's most recent summer evangelism initiative, focusing on the twenty-one countries around the Mediterranean Sea.

Obviously, projects that result in equipping and mobilising believers come in many shapes and sizes. The next pages demonstrate just a few ministries that continue to need your prayers and involvement.

> There are different kinds of gifts, but the same Spirit. There are
> different kinds of service, but the same Lord. There are different
> kinds of working, but the same God works all of them in all men
> ... Now you are the body of Christ, and each one of you is a part
> of it.—I Corinthians 12:4–6, 27, NIV

Partnering to Resource the Church

The Lifeline of Literature

Between the early 1970s to late '90s, specially-prepared OM vehicles and trained OMers smuggled over four million Bibles, Christian books and evangelistic tracts into Communist countries. The story of this amazing convoy of hope and salvation would take a book in itself. Yet during this period a particular gap became evident: the lack of study and issue-oriented books to support the leadership of the persecuted church. This situation led to a joint effort by OM and the International Fellowship of Evangelical Students (IFES) to found the East European Literature Advisory Committee, or EELAC. The vision of this entity was not only to encourage the publication of books of enduring worth in East European languages, but in the long term to establish national publishing houses within that region.

Thankfully, even in those days it was possible for individuals from countries like Hungary, Poland and the former Yugoslavia to travel to the UK for training. Gerry Davey had been seconded half-time to EELAC as General Secretary after serving eighteen years as Director of OM's literature ministry, Send The Light (STL). He was also a founder and the Chairman of the British Christian Book-sellers' Convention. In this capacity he was able to find sponsors for occasional visitors from Eastern Europe.

EELAC did a great deal of fundraising for the book publishing process, but the Advisory Committee members were keen not to overstep their role as advisors. They felt it was essential for national pastors and students themselves to select which books to translate.

'I never chose a title,' affirms Gerry. 'I would gather a group of representative pastors and ask questions that would help them determine the most critical issues that needed to be addressed in their area. Once they came to an agreement I sent them three or four books to evaluate for their suitability. It took hundreds of hours in each country to go through this process.'

Another difficulty was finding the funds to publish within each country. The Greater Europe team had given their evangelistic books away free. But because EELAC wanted to see publishing houses established, it insisted on working with individuals who could come up with a sensible price-setting system. Since Communist authorities had hugely subsidised the cost of publishing, people really had no realistic idea of the costs of running a business.

When the Berlin Wall fell and one country after another declared independence from the Soviet Union, EELAC found itself trying to help start publishing houses in five or six countries almost simultaneously. It was a hectic time, recalls Gerry.

'Of course, a lot of Christians and organisations rushed into the East and offered to give money to publishers who would print their books. Our goal was to make these fledgling Christian publishers self-supporting. So I told them, "You can be forever dependent on subsidies from the West, or you can develop products that people will be willing to pay for."

'Putting it another way he suggested, "I am the midwife, but you are the mother, and the baby will be your responsibility!" '

Gerry admitted that this was a scary proposition to men and women who had always been told what to do and when to do it. But EELAC was determined that they take ownership, both economically and emotionally. And their insistence paid off.

Today, out of the ten Christian publishing houses EELAC helped to start, nine—in Russia, Romania, Bulgaria, Poland, Hungary, Albania, the Czech Republic, Serbia and Croatia—are still in business. Some of them are totally self-supporting, others are 70–80% self-supporting, with links to outside groups that they've developed on their own. Between them all they have produced over two thousand quality titles since 1990: a total of four to five million books.

EELAC ceased as a separate entity a few years ago when it became part of the Langham Partnership International. Langham's literature programmes continue to address the lack of reference books and Bible commentaries in over ninety countries; resourcing pastors, theological faculty, students and libraries; writers and publishers. Although Gerry is now retired he is still frequently called upon as a consultant.

The value of partnerships that build God's Kingdom through print are immeasurable. As writer Helen Exley noted, 'Books can be dangerous. The best ones should be labelled: "*This could change your life!*"'

Books for Europe's Forgotten Peoples

In the previous section of this book, 'Reaching out to Neighbours,' we looked at just a few of the dozens of ethnic groups in Europe that are still unreached in Europe and Central Asia—thirty-two in Russia alone. OM EAST—or the Eurasia Support Team, formerly known as Greater Europe and based in Vienna, has published a phenomenal six hundred-plus titles in more than thirty languages since it began in 1983. New impetus came after the Iron Curtain fell in the 1990s and it became possible to openly transport and distribute Christian media in the spiritually-famished Eastern bloc.

As more Christian publishing started up within Russia, Romania, Bulgaria and other countries, OM EAST's focus moved to where the greatest needs remained.

'We want to fill the gaps where there's still little or no literature,' asserts Field Leader Steve.* 'It's important to concentrate on people groups that are forgotten.'

Surveys help to pinpoint which books are most urgently needed. Contacts with mature believers in many countries also offer helpful insights when making selections. Usually the first books focus on evangelism, then discipleship, children, family and social issues.

'Our emphasis is not so much on theological titles, but books for the man on the street,' Steve explains. To facilitate this goal the team has forged partnerships with at least twenty other Christian organisations like Josh McDowell Ministries, Tyndale, CLC and Bethany House. Some of these partners provide copyrights for the books they want to publish; some help with printing and distribution costs.

A total of sixty projects may be in the pipeline at the same time. Each book can take up to several years to complete, and some of the team work remotely. It's up to Simon* to oversee each phase of production until the book is ready for the printer. Asked why he and his wife joined the EAST team, Simon responds that they looked into many options. 'We were surprised at how many Christian organisations need people with graphics skills. It's a privilege to use my profession to build God's Kingdom!'

During his many trips to Eastern Europe Simon has been able to witness some the results firsthand. One of his most thrilling visits, he says, was to a small community in Croatia.

'People ask if it's really worth it to produce a book for a language group with less than a few hundred thousand people. A few years ago we went to visit the Bayash, a despised and rejected minority group who are descended from Roma (gypsies). These people are living in destitution inside cold and dirty hovels with only plastic to cover the windows. Together with our Roma Bible Union partners in this project, we started giving out a children's Bible at each house. They looked at it—and us—and couldn't believe it was in their own language. They were the outcasts! Why would anybody take the trouble to do this for them? … It was a powerful experience.'

The reality is, however, that few publishers are willing to produce books in minority languages because they won't make money. That makes companies more open to giving copyright permission to a non-profit ministry like OM EAST. Electronic and multimedia options are also being developed: electronic materials for places where computers are readily available, and DVDs which can be made and distributed at a fraction of the cost of printed media. Still, books continue to be in demand, especially in places without adequate supplies of electricity!

My First Bible has been one of OM EAST's most significant publications over the years, introducing God's Good News to hundreds of thousands of people in thirty different languages. In the Crimea, authorities wanted to use this book as a

---

* Surnames omitted to protect security.

language text in schools. The first 15,000 copies printed were snapped up within weeks.

The team is also publishing and distributing Christian comic books with impressive results. Their first experiment, illustrating the real-life story of orphaned 'Dorie,' brought countless grateful letters from individuals who, like the real-life Dorie, had given up hope that anyone cared about them. Demand for this comic has led to translation into fourteen languages. And the Crimean Tatar comic 'Light in the Darkness,' based on Patricia St. John's book, *Star of Light,* is being eagerly received by scores of individuals in the Crimean Peninsula who had little previous knowledge of Jesus.

Local churches benefit at least two ways by OM EAST's publications. The discipleship and study books they provide may be the only ones available in their heart languages; they are a huge contribution to Christian life and growth in places where believers are few. But evangelistic literature for reaching their neighbours is also vital. Churches play an essential role in distributing these resources, and they are often rewarded by seeing more people come to faith because of them.

Regretfully, finance and staff shortages too often restrict this fruitful ministry. OM EAST's sales cover only about 15% of actual costs and books are often distributed free to children in schools, for instance. So along with missionary pioneer Adoniram Judson's assertion that 'the future is as bright as the promises of God,' we might also reasonably add, 'and the faithful teamwork of His people!'

Just as partnerships were needed to sustain and grow the church during the years of Communism, the urgency remains to reach each man, woman and child in places forgotten by the rest of the world. After all, God's Son died for them. Isn't that a good enough reason to ensure that we 'get the word out?'

Filling the Gaps: Special Projects

George Verwer has maintained a 'Special Projects' fund ever since he began OM, although it's only been officially titled as such for the last twenty-five years. Many of the donations given to Special Projects have been channelled into supplying key media through partnerships with churches, publishers and other Christian organisations, to virtually every country in Europe.

'The very first project on the continent, back in the 1960s, was a Bible Bus in France,' recalls George. 'Later we also had a Christian bookmobile in Spain, and then a bookshop. Part of our vision from the very first was to mobilise the Church, and we believed that if we could encourage the Church through literature it would lead to mobilisation.'

Since then OM literature projects have led to partnerships with about fifty publishers throughout Europe; the mission has helped to start some publishing houses where they were needed, and coordinate publishers' conferences. This strategy has made possible a number of projects, including printing and distributing thousands of gift packs with important books, CDs and DVDs to pastors and leaders in every major language. Bible Schools and even prison libraries have also benefited from free media.

Asserts George, 'We want to continue working with the Church to produce media that will stir believers to a deeper walk with God and to a greater vision for world evangelisation, as well as reach the unconverted.

'We have so much available in English; we long to see more material translated into all languages. In recent years, for instance, we've sponsored European-language translations of books about HIV/AIDS. We want to raise awareness in the Church and try to get her to reach out to those who are affected by this disease. Another one of my passions is partnering for the cause of the unborn, flooding out pro-life material to help people understand the danger and complexity of abortion.

'There are tens of thousands of "micro ministries" around the world,' he concludes. Most of these are small and often unnoticed, and I have noticed how hard it is for such groups to get funds for their projects. Over the years I have been trying to release finance and mobilise prayer for such ministries.'

Thanks to Special Project donors, the dream is coming true.

Mobile Resourcing

Central Europe: The Bus4Life*

Weighing in at twelve tonnes, OM's Bus4Life is a twelve metre-long multimedia ministry on wheels that attracts attention wherever it goes. Based in Finland, most of the time the bus is on the road in the Central European countries of Hungary, Romania, Moldova, Slovakia and Bosnia.

* www.bus4life.org

OMer Luminita Dragusin spends an average of one to two months to line up each visit in Romania. She reports that it is a real privilege to minister alongside the national churches, which eagerly take ownership long before the colourful red, white and blue vehicle is set up in parks, festivals, conference venues and village greens. Volunteers must be on hand to invite curious people inside to watch films and peruse the books on sale, or to relax at tables and chairs outside enjoying free coffee, snacks and chat.

As the bus team effectively engages youth with sports, games, face-painting and singing, various local church groups present dramas, concerts and short messages for the crowds that gather. The possibilities for creative interaction are endless.—Even blood sugar and blood-pressure check-ups are sometimes offered. And not waiting for people to come to them the team often shares their good news with local schools, elderly homes and refugee camps along the way.

Church volunteers in each town or city often hand out New Testaments, tracts and magazines on the streets, missing no opportunities to draw people of all ages into discussions. For many Romanians this may be their first encounter with evangelical Christians; it's a surprise to learn that *pocaiti,* the Romanian term for born-again Christians, are not a sect but normal folks, living out their faith with all their hearts.

Volunteers, too, are surprised as they learn how easy it is to reach out. Declared Christian worker Valentin Bita in the town of Calarasi, 'I saw something that made me very happy.—Members of my own church came to make coffee and talk to people. It's easy for Romanians—even Christians—to lose their focus and passion. But this event has brought all the Christians together. Even the pastor from a very traditional church came and sang with us. It's a beginning! We want the bus to come again, for sure!'

OM began in Hungary in the early 1970s by smuggling in and distributing Christian literature. After the fall of Communism in '89, evangelism teams began to develop relationships with churches and encourage a mission vision. By the '90s OM Hungary was placing church-planting helper teams into several needy areas. It also provided a facility for church retreats and church-planting training.

Today the team continues mission mobilisation through church presentations, preparation weekends and facilitating a large annual Mission Expo event. Short and longer-term teams also work alongside churches for evangelism outreaches. The Bus4Life has proven a valuable tool in helping Hungarian churches fulfil their mission vision for their community and neighbouring communities.

Affirmed Pastor Agoston Dobos, who has headed the Reformed Church's mission activities in one region of Hungary and hosted the Bus4Life in Bekes, 'I think this [bus ministry] is a key for the revitalisation of our denomination, that we would feel the call for missions.' He added that he hoped the Church would no longer wait for richer countries to take up the work of the cross.

Many of the country's villages and smaller towns, in particular, have had relatively little exposure to the gospel. OM Hungary encourages ownership of what they call 'Operation Village Mobilisation' by requesting hosting churches to take financial responsibility for outreaches. Since most of them struggle to even pay their pastor, OM often subsidises the cost.

An outreach usually consists of English classes and sport activities, highlighting baseball as a unique sport to attract Hungarian children. The team also offers children's programmes and film clubs in the evening, and sells Christian and educational English and Hungarian literature from the bus. As in other Central European countries, there is often no Christian bookshop for miles.

But the Bus4Life is not meant to be simply a hit-and-run ministry. As short-term volunteer Kristi from the United States noted, 'It's one thing to have a team come for a week or two and do all this great stuff, but then they leave! By partnering with local Christians we can provide them with tools to impact their own community, we can encourage and equip them to be their own "missionaries" to their neighbours, family, colleagues and friends.'

In 2010, inspired by the success of the Bus4Life, Slovak partners decided to reconstruct another vehicle as a mobile mission centre. The Slovakian Baptist Union and Creativepress launched the ministry of 'Van4Life' in co-operation with local Baptist churches in Slovakia. So more believers are catching the vision, and the work is being multiplied.

Ireland: The Big Red Bus

While serving on board Operation Mobilisation's ship MV Doulos for four years, Irishman Mike Mullins saw first hand how effective the vessel was in spreading the good news of Christ around the world. At that time God gave Mike a vision for a double-decker bus ministry in his home country—much like a ship on wheels!

When he returned home Mike gathered together a group of like-minded people who began to pray and plan. In 1998, the team borrowed a single-decker bus from a ministry in Northern Ireland to help with an outreach in Donegal. They were amazed at the doors this opened for the gospel message.

The following May, Mike and his wife Aster were invited to the Associated Bus Ministry convention in the UK and were offered a double-decker bus. By December 1999 Mike had passed his PSV bus driving test and launched the Big Red Bus ministry together with a small team of friends and supporters. They began running children's clubs and other programmes alongside different churches around Ireland.

In 2002, when Mike was asked to become OM Ireland's field leader, the Big Red Bus became an essential part of the mission's evangelistic ministry. His team's vision is to see people across Ireland transformed by the gospel and added to the local church; and to see churches mobilised, equipped, strengthened and encouraged to reach out into their local communities.

The vintage double-decker bus travels throughout the country providing a range of activities for all ages, in co-operation with local churches and communities. On housing estates, in parks and shore-fronts, the Big Red Bus has served as an ideal venue for children's holiday clubs, craft workshops and family fun events. Bus teams also make a point of benefitting the local community through litter collection and other social projects.

The bus invariably proves a popular attraction at St. Patrick's Day parades, vintage car rallies and festivals. Teams provide face painting and balloon modelling for children, free teas and coffees and a range of programmes on board. On one occasion the bus even served as a mobile art gallery!

Special programmes designed for different age groups are popular in primary schools throughout the country. Puppet shows, crafts and games are perfect for younger children while older ones enjoy creative and interactive lessons exploring social and religious issues. The Big Red Bus team also produces theatre presentations for schools based on the major Christian festivals of Christmas and Easter.

Wrote one school principal, 'We at Ayr Hill National School, Ramelton, were absolutely delighted with the visit of the Big Red Bus. The whole team was enthusiastic, friendly and organised and fantastic with the children … We wholeheartedly recommend the Big Red Bus and its wonderful team as a spiritually enriching, fun-filled and educational experience for children of all ages.'

The problem of anti-social behaviour and under-age drinking is challenging authorities in towns and cities across Ireland. The Big Red Bus provides a safe, mobile drop-in centre and coffee bar for teens with interactive games and activities on board—a positive alternative for bored youngsters.

Children's Work & Bus Ministry Coordinator Junior De Larina, from Brazil, recalls one of the times he shared the gospel message using a modeling balloon:

'We had a lot of children upstairs on the bus that evening and one boy kept asking me for a balloon, interrupting the story. My first reaction was to tell him to be
quiet, but when he got closer I could smell alcohol on his breath. I realised he was
drunk. That shocked and saddened me, because he was just ten years old. The boy
was just asking for a balloon because he is a child ... and yet he was also drunk.
For him, this was normal.'

Wherever the bus travels, training and equipping Christians to share their
faith is integral to the ministry. As local churches get involved, believers have
opportunities to gain practical mission experience they can use in Ireland or anywhere else.

'Partnering with OM and the Big Red Bus Team has really transformed our
church's approach to evangelism and ministry,' confirmed Pastor Dominic Mont-
gomery of the Cherith Athlone Baptist Church. 'Through OM we have had training to help our people share their faith, and then our folk worked on and off the
Big Red Bus doing kids' clubs and street evangelism. During the summer months
we had Saturday bus programmes, with one kids' club in a local housing estate in
the morning and another in the afternoon. Our combined OM and church team
met for prayer, went out to serve, came in for lunch, fellowship and more prayer,
went out to serve again and finally came back to close the day in prayer. What
blessed days these were for all concerned! The Lord was exalted, His people were
challenged and blessed and much seed was sown. To Him alone be the glory,
honour and praise.'

Resourcing Church Facilities

Providing venues for ministry and sharing building facilities are extremely
practical ways to further the work of God's Kingdom, especially in these times
of financial shortages. OM Austria's office in Linz is a good example, purpose-
built to accommodate several missions under the same roof. Meeting rooms in
the building are also put to good use by African and Romanian churches, an
evening Bible School and a weekend theological seminary. A mission library is
jointly available as well. In Germany, OM's 'old mill' is often used by churches as a
meeting place or retreat centre, and in co-operation with other missions they host
an annual weekend seminar on reaching Muslims. However, at least two other
countries take facility-sharing to a further level.

Belgium: Serving at the Hub of the European Union

The office, garage and accommodation complex of OM's Zaventem,* Belgium, base was once the hub of vehicle maintenance, finance and deployment of teams throughout Europe and beyond. In the last decade, however, the century-old former paper mill in this Brussels suburb has slowly but surely undergone a dramatic metamorphosis. When the building ceased functioning as the mission's Central Accounting Office in the 1990s, some of the building was converted into conference facilities. The property's key location—only minutes from Belgium's international airport—makes ZavCentre a convenient venue for not only OM but many other groups wanting to hold smaller training events and meetings. As the need for more space became apparent, more rooms were converted for guests. At the same time, OM Belgium's operations continued to grow to the point where it was necessary to rebuild a large part of the garage, creating ten new offices and two small meeting rooms.

ZavCentre, the new name for this facility, provides twenty bedrooms which can expand to accommodate from two to four people each if necessary. The building also offers a 140-seat conference room (currently being used on Sundays by a local church), a half dozen smaller meeting rooms and dining room.

What makes ZavCentre unique is that it isn't run for profit, but as a resource and service to facilitate God's work. The volunteer team who run the place not only provide hospitality to visiting groups, but assist local churches and engage in friendship evangelism, literature distribution and prison evangelism in the surrounding area.

Italy: Valley Vision

The mountainous northwest of Italy occupies a special place in Christian history. Long before the Reformation swept Europe, a group of people called the Waldensians fled to those mountains and valleys to escape persecution. Their determination to study, preach and even translate the Bible into the language of the common people had attracted the wrath of the Church of Rome. For three centuries they lived in hiding.

In his sonnet, 'On the Late Massacre in Piedmont,' the famous poet John Milton lamented the brutal torture and death of thousands of Waldensian men, women and children in 1655:

* www.zavcentre.be

Avenge O Lord thy slaughter'd Saints, whose bones
Lie scatter'd on the Alpine mountains cold,
Ev'n them who kept thy truth so pure of old …

Much later, during World War II, the Waldensians saved the lives of many
Jews by hiding them in their mountain valley. Sergio and Anna Gastaldo-Brac are
very conscious of the spiritual heritage of this area. Anna's own family experienced
tragedy in nearby Turin, when her father and grandfather were shot by the Nazis.
The Bible that her father was holding—a bullet scoring its pages—remains as
evidence.

During their years with OM on the ships and leading the Italy field, the couple had seen a need to help churches grow their missionary vision. Italian congregations were also struggling with how to attract and disciple the next generation.
They required a place to train young people. It was while they were visiting the
historic Waldensian valley in the year 2000 that Sergio and Anna found exactly
the right property. Others had doubts about the state of the derelict army barracks
nestled on this land in the mountains of Bobbio Pellice. But when the property
was auctioned in 2002 the pair prayerfully put in a bid—and won. By March '04
they had enough money to start building. And after much hard work and several
setbacks 'Forterocca' opened its doors to the first visitors in March 2008.*

The name 'Forterocca' is meant to refer to God as our fortress or stronghold.
The facility offers quality accommodation for 147 persons with the possibility of
expanding to 200. 25 beds are suitable for disabled persons (or, as Italians prefer to
put it, the 'differently abled'). Conference rooms are available and a dining room,
kitchen facilities and 240-seat auditorium are also planned.

The evangelical Church of Italy has given warm support to the OM initiative
in this 'Valley of Light.' A wide variety of fellowships and organisations are already
making use of the facility. The Gastaldo-Bracs would love to see Christians from
all over the world using Forterocca as a base while reaching out to Italy's growing
population of Chinese, Filipinos, Albanians and Africans.

The majestic scenery is a magnet for tourism and already attracts many thousands of holiday visitors. An Ice Palace, built for the 2006 Winter Olympics just
down the road from Forterocca, is used for international ice skating and hockey
events. Hiking and mountain biking on the surrounding Alps are major summer
activities. All of this action makes the place an ideal base for OM SportsLink
and their partner agency, the Fellowship of Christian Athletes, who regularly use

* www.forterocca.com

the Bobbio facility for training coaches and encouraging sports ministries across Europe.

Thanks to the vision of one couple and their partnership with scores of churches and organisations, God is doing a new thing in this famous valley. Pray with them that the rocks of Forterocca—surrounded by peaks once stained by the blood of the martyrs—will again be the foundation for transformed lives, and a revitalised witness in Italy.

Partnering to Mobilise the Church

The principle of working alongside existing churches wherever possible has proven particularly important when pioneering in countries that achieved independence from the Soviet Union. Moldova, Poland, and the Czech Republic, below, are good examples of what can happen through mutual efforts.

Moldova: Sowing and Harvesting

Sandwiched between Romania and Ukraine, Moldova is the second smallest of the former Soviet republics. It is also said to be the poorest country in Europe. 30% of residents, approximately one million men, women and children, live in absolute poverty.

But Moldova has at least one important asset: its fertile soil. Claiming one of the highest percentages of arable land in the world, the country's rich, black earth supports a wide range of crops and vineyards.

On a spiritual level, this republic has also opened itself to the good seed of the gospel after 70 years of a repressive Communist regime. Although Russian Orthodox traditions retain a firm grip and the domes of Orthodox churches are prominent in every town and village, many Moldovans hunger to know what it is to have the joy of the Lord in their everyday lives.

In 1996 OMers Matthew and Helen Skirton led the first international outreach team into Moldova. Among the hundreds of young people they visited in schools was 15-year-old Tamara. She listened, prayed, and believed. The seed fell into fertile soil.

When the teenager announced that she'd become a Christian, her family threw her out. In 2000 Tamara joined OM's first "Challenge into Mission" training and stayed on to serve in other parts of her country. But as time passed she felt increasingly certain that God's mission for her was at home. Tamara obeyed, and in the years that followed started ministries to destitute children and old people not only in her own village but surrounding villages. In the process she planted the first church. A white building now stands in the isolated countryside like a lighthouse, a community centre drawing both young and old to the Source of life.

Tamara's is only one of many harvest stories. 'Living in a local village mission situation when we first came helped to establish a relationship and trust,' reflects Matthew about those pioneering years. 'I can remember walking into the bishop's office with mud-covered boots. He laughed and said, "Matthew, you're more Moldovan that I am, look at you!"'

OM was careful from the first to earn the confidence of the country's leading evangelical denominations. 'Every single ministry is under the authority of the church,' Matthew confirms. 'We have top people from both of both Baptist and Pentecostal Unions on our board.'

Honouring relationships with leaders has resulted in firm partnerships with local churches which, in turn, are willing to send their young people to OM for training and service. The team is currently comprised of twenty-four Moldovans and fourteen foreigners; seventy percent of field workers are Moldovans and they oversee relief and development, micro-business projects, transformational ministries and next-generation sports departments.

Churches are also working with OM to provide day centres for children from broken families and hot meals for the elderly. Many old people live alone on tiny pensions if they get one at all, and they aren't enough to cover food and medicine. A nutritious meal at the church may be their only one that day, and their only social interaction. Homebound folks are visited at home and receive parcels containing food, hygiene products and other necessities like soap powder and socks.

Snejana Ursu, who oversees this ministry, notes that the goal is to see it become locally self-sufficient. 'Right now the centres are dependent on outside resources, with churches supplying 5% of the budget—a big amount for them. The mayors in the towns are happy for this work and sometimes offer help. But the church "owns" the project. They decide on what facility to use, come up with a proposal and select the workers.'

But it is the 'Challenge into Missions' (CiM) programme that lies at the heart of OM Moldova. Twice a year, forty-five to fifty men and women recommended by their pastors arrive at the mission base in Chisenau for ten weeks of intensive mission exposure. Six of those weeks are actually spent on outreach teams, working alongside local fellowships in all sorts of ministries. Participants who take the level two course become team leaders; others may elect to stay for a year of service, called the "Delta" plan. Over 300 Moldovans have benefited from this excellent training, some later choosing to join OM more permanently or else serve in their home churches.

In addition to equipping Moldovans for ministry inside Moldova, OM has kept an average of four national workers on other fields each year. Matthew Skirton reckons they've just scratched the surface.

To boost awareness and encourage churches to send missionaries, the mission makes good books available through CiM teams and conferences, and sends out a free monthly prayer bulletin. The bulletins are in Russian and Romanian, and reach over 550 church groups, pastors and other individuals. Interceding for other nations is a relatively new concept for Moldovan Christians who have so long been burdened by their own problems, but more and more are catching the vision.

OM Moldova abounds with creative ideas for increasing the future harvest. The number of hands available and funds to carry out all the work are limited, true. But as long as the rich soil of Moldova continues to bear much fruit, how can they stop planting? As Matthew and Helen maintain, with a smile, 'To help the churches make a difference in their communities, we need to dream big dreams!'

Poland: Making an Impact in the Community

95% of Poles claim to be Roman Catholics and many are deeply religious. Yet an ever-increasing number do not feel their everyday needs are being met by their church, and live in a spiritual vacuum. Only 0.4% of the population are regarded as evangelical Christians. This tiny minority find themselves facing constant discrimination; even intolerance. Thousands of towns and villages have no evangelical presence at all.

OM's work in Poland centres on a church-planting project in Kutno, initiated by the Polish Pentecostal Union in 1999. OM Country Leader Arek Delik is a Pole himself and serves as the church's pastor. He believes that while the country is economically better off than it used to be, materialism hasn't satisfied. His goal is to restore hope to disillusioned Poles of all ages through holistic ministries, partnering with other organisations.

Arek's church identified alcoholism as one of their country's—and city's—urgent social problems. In 2005 a group of believers took the initiative to start a community project that would make a difference, and 'New Life Association' was officially registered as a Christian charity. The main aim of New Life is to see those who have problems with alcohol set free by the power of Jesus Christ, and to help them and their families integrate into a normal Christian fellowship where they can find support.

New Life's activities include two weekly support group meetings, a bi-monthly gospel concert, and six weekend outreaches in Kutno during the year. The outreaches include free meals and target not only alcoholics, former alcoholics and their families, but anyone who is interested in learning more about the impact of alcohol on the community.

Every two months a meeting is held for patients in Zgierz hospital who are addicted to alcohol. Multimedia drug and alcohol awareness programmes are also presented in local schools. And in co-operation with Teen Challenge, a team brings food and hot drinks for the homeless at the train station and surrounding poor area of Kutno, setting up a 'coffee house' in the street!

A retreat is also organised every two months in Wisla, a mountain area three hundred kilometres south of Kutno. This weekend evangelistic outreach for alcoholics (which includes patients from Zgierz hospital) is co-partnered with Elim Christian Foundation, which also focuses on ministry among alcoholics.

130 people attended one such weekend event last year, and when Arek Delik shared the story of Lazarus and invited his audience to 'come out' from their bondage to alcohol, more than ten decided to give their lives to Jesus. During the following week seven of these men and women joined a home group meeting. As Arek's wife Donna noted, 'These are the very first steps for them. Like babies they need a lot of care. We need to lift them up in our prayers as it is God who makes things grow.'

Janek and Zosia Jedrzejczak lead the church's New Life work. Janek was himself delivered from twenty-seven years of alcoholism and crime through an encounter with Christ.

'Probably the biggest cause of alcoholism in Poland is the fact that it is so interwoven into the social fabric of our culture,' he observes. 'It is common to hear people say, "It was a good party—there was plenty of free alcohol!" From the day you are born, alcohol is part of life: at your baptism, communion, wedding and even funeral; a sign of blessing and a good life. Business, holidays and social life all co-exist with alcohol, so much so that most people are not even aware of the affect until it is too late.

'But what really concerns me is that people are drinking at an ever-younger age these days. Many parents offer their children soft alcohol such as beer at home, and think that it's okay. What they don't realise is that their children will face serious problems with addiction later in life.'

When he is asked why Catholic churches do not do more about the situation, Janek smiles ruefully. 'Many of the priests have an alcohol problem, too. There are special rehabilitation centres for priests in Poland. Without Jesus, an alcoholic is powerless to change his destiny. "Religion" might have the right answers, but it has no power to change lives. Only Jesus is able to set us free, if only we will let Him!'

Janek's friend Jacek Rylko, who is doing a similar work in the south of the country, adds, 'Poland is a Christian country, but on the streets I feel there is no God. 90% of the population claims to be Christian, but how many have experienced God in their hearts?'

In addition to the ministry for alcoholics the church shows its concern for the community's poor through children's programmes and an annual distribution of Samaritan's Purse Christmas shoebox gifts in needy areas. Realising that many teens find it difficult to understand how Jesus is relevant to their daily lives, they have offered an English language school for several years and run a youth club.

The team are excited about the possibility of expanding their ministries in the near future. They have won the bid for a suitable property that was up for auction. Arek and Donna Delik and their church members have prayed a lot for God's leading in this and they are confident He will help them meet the financial challenge. 'The property has plenty of space for church activities, work among alcoholics, and a real coffee house for weekend outreach,' they enthuse. 'We are also dreaming of new ministries among poor children and providing a youth centre.'

The Deliks and their small team are keen to encourage mission awareness and involvement in other churches. OM is a member of the Biblical Mission Association (BSM) of Poland, which aims to mobilise churches for world mission. Each year the team organises numerous mission events like Missions Sunday, seminars in the church and weekend conferences. BSM publishes a quarterly mission magazine that is distributed to over 1500 believers. 'IDZCIE' or 'GO' serves as a valuable aid in widening the vision of the Polish church.

Arek and Donna stress that they don't want OM to be seen as a 'foreign mission' in Poland that tries to impose its values and ideals on Polish churches, without fully understanding them or their surroundings. 'Our desire is to partner with God's people to bring His hope and healing to society through holistic ministries.'

Czech Republic: Changing Times

—Hans Koebele, who has lived and worked in this area of Central Europe for nineteen years, explains why he feels co-operation is essential, and how OM is helping local churches fulfil their God-given purpose in the Czech Republic and beyond.

In November 1989, the Velvet Revolution started the transformation process of the area then known as Czechoslovakia. Those first years after the fall of Communism were unique. They offered tremendous opportunities to freely share the gospel on the streets and in schools, mainly because Czechs were very ready to see and hear *anything* that was new.

We partnered with local churches throughout the country, usually arriving several days before an evangelistic outreach in order to train church members in open-air evangelism. The biggest challenge during those days was to convince the churches that we were there to support *their* evangelistic endeavours, meaning active involvement on their part. We didn't want to be seen simply as a group hired to do the evangelism for them.

During the outreach week we visited one or two local schools each morning. Usually we had the whole of the class time to share the gospel message without restrictions, using music, drama and sketchboard talks followed by question and answer sessions. We used the same basic methods to share the good news of Christ on the streets or town squares, often using a 'Tea Bus' as the backdrop. After the programmes we invited people onto the bus for further conversation. During those years, many thousands of people had the opportunity to hear and respond to God's plan of salvation, and a good number professed faith in Christ. It was quite easy in those days to immediately strike up spiritual conversations, even with complete strangers.

That incredible responsiveness changed quite drastically during the mid-1990s. Materialism became the dominant goal, and the influence of modern European secularism also began to take hold, revealing people's true attitudes toward spiritual things. There were even times when we seemed only to be 'preaching to the choir' as we shared a sketchboard message on the streets, since only our own teammates were listening.

The Czech Republic has a rich spiritual heritage. The names of martyrs and reformers like John Huss and Jan Komensky are known around the world. The modern missionary movement was actually started by the Moravians of Bohemia (now part of the Czech Republic), who formed a Christian community under Count Zinzendorf. Moravian missionaries went all over the world, taking the gospel to some of the most inhospitable places imaginable. The Moravian church had an average of one missionary in every sixty members, compared to one in 5,000 within other Protestant denominations. The Moravians had a significant influence on John Wesley, and were at the roots of the Great Awakening in North America and the Methodist Revival in England.

Today it's a different story. Despite its heritage the Czech Republic has been occupied by foreign powers throughout its more recent history, from the Austro-Hungarian Empire to Nazi Germany to the Communists. As a result, the Czechs are generally a very sceptical people. A very high percentage would say that God doesn't exist. Even though most of the people hated Communism, the teaching that God is not real is still very much a part of their worldview. In fact, the Czech Republic is considered to be one of the most atheistic countries in the world today. Less than one-third of one percent of Czechs are born-again believers. The key to reaching them is to make long-term relationships, really getting to know individuals on a deeper level in order to break down the mistrust and scepticism.

Partnership in more recent years has meant that expat workers must learn the Czech language and culture. They must also become actively involved longer-term in the life of local churches, seeking to support them in fulfilling their vision.

My own family works with a church that shares the common vision of wanting to evangelise and see new churches planted in the most unreached, southwest region of the country. This region (South Bohemia) covers an area of over 17,600 square kilometres and has only about a dozen small, evangelical churches. Most residents have no access to a church and little means of hearing the Gospel.

We have been using English as a great bridge-building tool in establishing relationships. Our overall ministry in South Bohemia involves various means of evangelism and discipleship, including small group ministry, preaching, friendship evangelism, teaching English and helping with sports camps (specifically football and basketball).

Though it's quite rare to see much spiritual fruit in South Bohemia, we as a church-plant team have been very encouraged that over the last couple years in the town of Strakonice, several individuals have either trusted in Christ or are actively seeking God's truth. A number of our students who have been to English camps during the summer have actually become part of small fellowship groups, and have either come to faith in Christ or have grown significantly as believers. Other young people have started attending an English club and a youth Bible study. These English-teaching ministries have been instrumental in building trust relationships, and providing us with a real impetus in our current church-planting ministry.

Another thing we are really excited about is how God is motivating Czechs to participate in missions. A few years ago a young Czech woman shared with me how she had a real desire to serve among the Tibetan people. It wasn't possible for her to go to Tibet at the time, but God worked it out for her to join our OM team in nearby Nepal, where she has now served for several years. Through her influence several other Czechs have since participated in short-term mission trips to Nepal, and one couple hopes to serve there longer-term. As a result, Nepal has spontaneously become an adopted field of our OM team in the Czech Republic. We're really thankful about this development because one of the major thrusts of our team's vision is to motivate and resource the sending of Czechs into missions.

The most obvious barrier to the overall ministry is the spiritual apathy among the Czech population. In the realm of the Church there is a real lack of leadership training or even potential leaders to train. Many regions and church-planting situations exist where pastors and leaders are desperately needed.

However, although the Czech Republic is a very challenging field, we are grateful for what God has done and is continuing to do, especially in terms of changing people's lives. It's a true privilege to partner with the Czech Church in these exciting days!

Global Focus: The Changing Paradigm of Partnership

It is one thing to partner with the church to help mobilise its mission potential. It is quite another to help the local church retake ownership of the responsibility for mission itself, especially in European countries with a strong historic church.

In 1995, an American pastor/evangelist who recognised that the local church was God's primary instrument to fulfil the Great Commission began a ministry called Global Focus [see http://www.globalfocus.info/]. His aim was to change the paradigm of the church regarding mission. Rather than seeing mission as just another programme of the church that it supported, in the new paradigm, Global Mission became *the* mission of the church.

For churches which totally accepted this new paradigm it changed everything from their ownership of mission, through their leadership structure, to their level of involvement. No longer could mission be delegated to an enthusiastic few on the fringes of the church on the missionary committee; mission became the whole focus of the whole church.

The relationship between the mission agency and the church changed from a 'support paradigm' to a 'personal ownership paradigm.' The church defined their mission strategy within an Acts 1:8 concept to own ministries in their personally defined Jerusalem, Judea, Samaria and the ends of the earth. In doing so they took ownership of these ministries and redefined the partnership with mission agencies working in these areas, becoming equal partners rather than just supporters.

In the same way within congregations individuals were encouraged to personally own the church mission strategy, and, within their giftedness, to find and own their role in that strategy. The church leadership took the lead in not only defining the strategy but in providing a myriad of opportunities for involvement and personal ownership by each member.

In 2003 OM in the Netherlands and the United Kingdom signed a partnership agreement with Global Focus to contextualise the material and bring it into their countries. Since then the concept has also been introduced to Switzerland and Austria. Other counties are also investigating the idea.

Developments in the United Kingdom

In the UK the strategy has made a big impact on churches that have embraced it. However, probably the most significant impact has been on OM. The much greater degree of flexibility has resulted in tailor-made mission opportunities to link with churches' needs, as well as new levels of partnership between OM and local churches. In addition, OM UK has been instrumental in forging direct partnerships between the local church and partner churches overseas, especially within India. The most significant case in this new paradigm has resulted in an equal partnership between OM and a local church in the setting up of a new ministry, where members from both partners have been seconded to the new enterprise.

Gradually, progressive churches around the UK are seeing the benefits of this new mission partnership paradigm—and the role of mission agencies like OM is slowly changing as a result.

Developments in Switzerland

By the late '90s in the last century it became very clear to OM Switzerland that many churches were looking for a new paradigm for missions. On the one hand, churches realised that mission was no longer confined to the needs of other countries. Many Swiss had left the church disappointed and were looking elsewhere for satisfaction. And with a population of over 20% immigrants, the world had come to Switzerland. On the other hand, churches wanted to be involved in mission in a different way. They were not content with simply giving their people, money and blessing to outside organisations and letting them do the job. This kind of delegation was becoming less and less attractive.

In 2004, OM Switzerland got involved with the Global Focus model. The mission felt strongly that this should not be just another programme to be delivered to churches. And although OM would act as a catalyst in getting this initiative started, it should not be limited to OM. Therefore, among others, the Chairman of the Evangelical Alliance of Switzerland (Thomas Bucher, who was also an OMer) and the General Secretary of the Evangelical Missionary Alliance (Martin Voegelin) became part of the founding committee. OM Switzerland's leader Markus Flückiger and long serving head of PR Michelle Krauss were also among the founding members. Later on, the former director of *Chrischona* churches, Karl Albietz, joined in as well.

Everyone, of course, hoped that things would take off quickly. However, the group soon realised that it was trying to climb a steep slope. Getting the idea established meant wrestling with terms and making sure they resonated with the local situation. It also meant informing and educating the organisations involved about local and global missions. And last but not least it meant helping churches understand what the Global Focus concept was all about.

As a result, members of the Global Focus committee realised their understanding of the local church and what partnering really meant was being progressively and positively shaped. Global Focus has increasingly become a more effective tool in this group's hands.

Over the past six years many churches have attended Global Focus seminars. Some of them have embarked on the journey of consciously defining their paradigm. Because of this their involvement in missions has become much more focused and has gained momentum. A 'same size fits all' approach was never possible. Every church was and is in a different situation, and coaching has been individually tailored.

In 2010 Global Focus became its own association, and in August that year Martin Voegelin began to dedicate 60% of his working time to Global Focus. The process has been much slower than anticipated, but the people driving this initiative are convinced of its potential. This is why they dared to step up to the plate and assign someone to work on the Global Focus programme three days a week. They have seen the positive results of Global Focus on their own ministries, the churches and the entire mission scene. They believe Global Focus to be an integral part of mission, from a local to global perspective, in all its facets.

Global Focus has also been started in Austria and it is hoped that this model will continue to influence and touch many more countries in Europe. Thomas Bucher, heading up Partnering with the Church for OM Europe, is actively working to see this change of paradigm established across the continent.

For more information see www.globalfocus.org.uk, www.globalfocus.ch, www.globalfocus.at.

Partnering for Advocacy

Advocacy can be defined as the active support of an idea or cause. It is defending the rights and welfare of disadvantaged people and promoting justice. It is serving as a voice for the voiceless.

The advocate role needs to be part of the DNA of committed 21st Century Christians, just as it belonged to Jesus Christ when he walked among us. William Faulkner put it succinctly: 'Never be afraid to raise your voice for honesty and truth and compassion against injustice and lying and greed. If people all over the world … would do this, it would change the earth.'

Advocacy may involve us in speaking out, writing letters, signing petitions or raising awareness. It certainly requires our faithful intercession before God. It makes sense that the more of us in the body of Christ who are willing to act as salt and light in our society, the greater our impact. Think of the awesome potential of two billion believers across the world uniting against for a cause!

It's the aim of a number of organisations to facilitate advocacy on behalf of victims of poverty, war, human trafficking, abused women and children, persecuted Christians, and the many others in society who need our hands and hearts. The global network of Advocates International (AI) informally links 30,000 lawyers, law professors, jurists, law students and other law professionals and their colleagues in 700 cities, towns and law schools, in 150 nations on six continents.

AI has also organised over one hundred national fellowships. Their motto, 'doing justice with compassion,' comes from Jesus' admonitions to the lawyers of his day (see Matthew 23:23) and from His parable about the Good Samaritan.

Groups like International Christian Concern and Christian Solidarity Worldwide (CSW) specialise in religious freedom, working to help Christians suffering for their faith including believers in Belarus and Bulgaria. The CSW team documents what is happening around the world through fact-finding visits; then they raise awareness, influence legislation and offer support and solidarity to affected believers. Updates about the situation in each country can be found on their website (see resource list below).

Want to do something about global poverty? Join one of the campaigns launched in forty countries by the Micah Challenge. Assist the efforts to give dignity and hope to India's 250 million 'Untouchables' or 'Dalits' through the Dalit Freedom Network in several countries.* Or if you think it's time to stop the trafficking of women and children across borders, check out the resources offered by Stop the Traffik or CHASTE (Churches Alert to Sex Trafficking Across Europe) or one of the other agencies listed in this book's 'Caring for the Marginalised' section. Find out about current campaigns and learn how you and your church can take practical action.

The options are exciting, and the Lord's mandate is clear. He is waiting for us to step away from the sidelines.

> Do not withhold good from those who deserve it, when it is in
> your power to act.—Proverbs 3:27, NIV

* See www.daliteducation.org, www.dfn.org.uk, or www.dalitfreedomnetwork.de

Partnering In Prayer

—Perhaps it is stating the obvious to say that we cannot hope to see the transformation of Europe without fervent and concerted intercession before God. What could be more appropriate, then, to end this book—and particularly this focus on Partnering with the Church—with the following challenge from a respected prayer co-ordinator?*

A number of years ago, 24/7 Prayer Founder Pete Greig was visiting Cape St. Vincent, the westernmost point of Europe. He was awakened in the middle of the night to see a red moon rising,[51] and as he began to pray he received a picture from God. Europe stretched out before him and an army was rising up all around the continent, awaiting orders. Interestingly, it was a younger generation of soldiers that he saw.

As a prayer co-ordinator I had previously had questions about how the mantle of prayer would be passed to a younger generation. Would there be a rising wave of prayer for Europe and for the world? Now, looking back, not only is a great increase of prayer evident, but leading the charge is a new generation; and there seems to be a greater surge of oneness, of unity, of doing things together. It seems to be less and less about denominations and organisations, and more about God's Body and His Kingdom. Pete Greig's 'army' is moving forward!

This became clear to me during a recent summer outreach throughout the Mediterranean with OM. I was in a prayer room in Malta where a team of sixteen of us had committed to pray 24/7 for the two weeks of the outreach. Two key intercessors had joined us from a few global prayer networks, and others came from the national prayer house. This was not a corporate project but a relational move of God. We all wanted to see God's Kingdom move forward in the region: not just the name of an organisation

After Malta we went to North Africa for almost two weeks to pray with different workers from many organisations for their cities and country. Together we were seeking the Lord's will for His work. It felt prophetic that as we were praying down walls that hinder the local people from knowing Jesus, we were also demonstrating that walls can come down between individuals, organisations, mission agencies and churches. We could work together as one for His Kingdom

* Name withheld for security reasons.

and glory; the glory of the One who 'has destroyed the barrier, the dividing wall of hostility' (Ephesians 2:14).

In the book *God is Still Speaking*,[52] Brian Mills, who is considered the father of the British Prayer Movement, writes, 'When God's people pray things happen. Nations change, the enemy is held back, the Kingdom of God advances. If the glory of God is to be revealed, then there needs to be a huge increase in believing prayer. Every expression of God's glory is associated with an unusual level of prayer.'

We are seeing this unusual level of prayer right now in many places like Korea, China and India. We see young people sowing a tremendous harvest, and it is my prayer that this will overflow into Europe! For this is a shift toward relationships and away from traditional ministry forms. Friendship is now more important than membership. And this is encouraging, particularly in the area of prayer and mobilisation. I believe partnership and friendship are the way forward in prayer.

Key European Christian prayer leaders have indicated that they see the same importance of partnering in prayer. Says Ian Nicholson, European Director of 24-7 Prayer, 'The groundwork for a transformed Europe takes place on our knees in prayer, and the Spirit who inspires prayer doesn't respect organisational boundaries! He is calling us to co-operate and work together in this great gospel adventure.'

Recently I spent a day with Roy Godwin of the Ffald-Y-Brenin Retreat Centre in Wales, who told me about 'TransMed,' a growing partnership of people, churches and agencies who have a passion to see missional houses of prayer planted all around the Mediterranean: houses dedicated to worship, loving the poor, winning the lost and asking the Lord to reign in their nation.

Ben and Eve Passmores of the Malta 24/7 Prayer House remind us, 'When we listen to Jesus tell us what He wants to do, and then we corporately ask Him to do it, there is power released beyond our greatest expectations. We've seen bitter feuds healed, sudden awareness arise in churches to repent and seek His face, and nations shaken after a few saints gathered continually to pray with fervour and Holy Spirit conviction.'

'Celebration for the Nations' is a gathering of worshippers in Wales from the countries touched by the 1904 Welsh Revival. It includes intercessors from South Korea and is partnering with Global Day of Prayer London for "500 days of prayer for Britain." Already the response to get involved in this 500-day prayer chain has been overwhelming.' Jonathan Oloyede, Convener of Global Day of Prayer London, says their target is to have 1,000 churches, groups and networks linked in prayer across the whole of the British Isles.[53]

Ian Cole, founder of the World Prayer Centre in Birmingham, England, believes that as Europe struggles with its financial, social and spiritual needs, the oneness of the followers of Jesus in their prayer, mission and action will demonstrate something very profound to the peoples of this great continent: that God sent His Son (John 17:23); that He still loves every individual (John 3:16); and that through our united praying His Kingdom will come and His will be done in Europe, as it is in heaven.

These leaders are seeing what Mike Bickle of the International House of Prayer in Kansas, USA, describes as a convergence of three movements: mission, prayer and church-planting. In God's eyes these are all one movement, fulfilling the words of Jesus to his Father in John 17:21, *'that they may all be one, that the world may believe that you sent me.'*

Earlier this year I travelled to the European side of Istanbul to attend a gathering brought together by a single mission agency. A host of different agencies had been invited to pray together for God's Kingdom to come. The move to join forces for His sake *is* happening!

Partnering is not competing but collaborating with others for the common good and common outcome. In prayer partnerships we are not looking for programmes, performance and procedures but passion stemming from humility and desperation. As British Prayer Minstrel Godfrey Birtill sings, 'Just one touch from the King changes everything.' As I look around Europe there is hope because His people are praying as never before, partnering as never before and seeking together for His Kingdom to come. We are receiving that touch from the King and He is changing everything. *The walls are coming down!*

> Look at the nations and watch—and be utterly amazed. For I am
> going to do something in your days that you would not believe,
> even if you were told.—Habakkuk 1:5, NIV

Resources

The following list represents some of the excellent materials and organisations available to help you and your church move out effectively. Resources below are for general mobilisation; also see the Resource Lists following each of the focus areas of this book for help in addressing particular ministries or issues.

■ General Helps for Mobilising and Equipping

■ Antioch Network   www.antioch network.org
Dedicated to 'empowering churches to reach the nations.' Hosts numerous events throughout the year including the 'Unhindered Conference,' 'designed for the emerging leader by emerging leaders.'

■ Caleb Resources   www.cartpioneers.org
Mission mobilisation resources for church and home (merged with Pioneers products).

■ Catalyst Ministries (UK)   www.catalystministriesuk.org
Raising cross-cultural mission awareness and action among UK Christians … leading to a specific focus on reaching and training Chinese in the UK.

■ Catalyst Services   www.catalystservices.org
Aiding agencies and churches to fulfill Jesus' global mandate.

■ *Developing a Missions Strategy that Fits Your Church*
                                           http://www.davidmays.org/Strategy/
                                           Contents.html
Website by David Mays offering documents and other media, some free and others for purchase.

■ Disciple Nations Alliance   www.disciplenations.org
Equipping churches to transform communities.

■ Every Nation, One Location (E1)   http://everynationonelocation.com
Greater Europe Mission's network invites you to connect with different ministry focuses in various countries.

■ Faithworks Movement (UK)   www.faithworks.info
Exists to 'empower and inspire individual Christians and every local church to develop their role at the hub of their community.'

- The Finishers Project   http://finishers.org
Connecting mid-life adults in North America with global impact opportunities
for God.

- Global Focus   http://www.globalfocus.info,
                                           www.globalfocus.org.uk
Helping church leaders to become more effective in mobilising congregations
for mission.

- Global Harvest Ministries   www.globalharvest.org
Strengthening global networks in order to fulfill the Great Commission.

- Hope for Europe   www.hfe.org
Pan-European network of leaders to promote local and national evangelistic
strategies and mobilise Europeans for world evangelism.

- Lausanne Committee for World Evangelisation paper, "The Local Church in
Mission …"   http://www.lausanne.org/
                                           documents/2004forum/LOP39_IG10.pdf

- Max7   www.max7.org
Online library of free resources for all ages.

- Mission Alive   www.missionalive.org
USA-based organisation that equips and nurtures church-planting leaders and
helps churches plant other churches. Useful articles.

- Mission Mobilisers International   www.mobilise.org.au
Consulting, resourcing and facilitating. Associated with Assemblies of God.

- Mission Prep   www.missionprep.ca
Preparing Christians for effective intercultural service. Geared towards
Canadians.

- Missionary Resources   www.missionaryresources.org
Library of materials, ideas, events and news.

- Missions Help for Church Leaders   http://DavidMays.org/Strategy/
                                           Contents.html
Free materials to help your church develop or rethink their mission strategy.

- New Wine (UK)   www.new-wine.org
Non-denominational network equipping churches and believers to change the
nation.

- North American Mission Board   www.namb.net
  Mission resources for children, youth, families and adults.

- OSCAR—UK Information Service for World Mission
                                      www.oscar.org.uk
  UK-based service providing a wealth of information, advice and resources for
  those interested or involved in Christian mission overseas.

- Schloss Mittersill   www.schlossmittersill.org
  A conference centre where established and emerging leaders are developing
  answers for a post-secular Europe.

- Short-Term Mission Network   http://stmnetwork.ca/mtm
  Canadian-based short-and mid-term network of Pentecostal Assemblies of
  Canada, assisting in training and facilitating mission workers.

- Starfish Partnership   http://en.starfishportal.net
  Informal global network dedicated to the multiplication of simple house
  churches.

- Street Pastors   www.streetpastors.co.uk
  A UK initiative of Christians mobilising to help young people on the streets.

- Tearfund International Learning Zone http://tilz.tearfund.org/Churches
  Assessment Tools, facilitator manuals and practical advice in 4 languages.

- The Upstream Collective   http://theupstreamcollective.
                                      wordpress.com
  'Seeking to create a missions movement uniquely focused on Europe, mobilising
  missional churches and church plants in North America to engage Europeans
  (both indigenous and immigrant) with the Gospel in relevant ways.'

- UrbanMinistry.org   www.urbanministries.org
  Resources for serving urban communities.

- World Christian Database   www.worldchristiandatabase.org/wcd
  Comprehensive statistical information on world religions, Christian
  denominations and people groups.

- World Christian Missionary Resources www.missionaryresources.com
  Information on resources in many different languages.

- World Mission Consultancy   www.worldmission.co.uk
  Aiding churches to plan and implement their world mission involvement.

▪World Thrust   www.worldthrust.org
International ministry serving as 'a catalyst to help pastors and church leaders mobilise the local church toward a more effective, personal involvement' in world mission.

■ Advocacy and Human Rights—Selected Reading

Note: also see resource list after 'Immigrants, Refugees and Trafficking Victims' in the 'Caring for the Marginalised' section of this book.

Catford, Cheryl. Following Fire. Urban Neighbors of Hope, 2007.

Gordon, Graham. Understanding Advocacy. Teddington: Tearfund, 2002.

Gordon, Graham. What if You Got Involved? Taking a Stand Against Social Injustice. Paternoster Press, 2003.

■ Advocacy and Human Rights—Websites

▪24-7 Prayer UK   http://uk.24-7prayer.com
Prayer, mission and justice.

▪Advocates International   www.advocatesinternational.org

▪Amnesty International   www.amnesty.org

▪Anglicans in World Mission   www.uspg.org.uk/article.php?article_
                                                  id=238

▪Christian Solidarity Worldwide [CSW]
                                                  www.csw.org.uk

▪Youth and student programme   www.outcry-uk.org

▪International Christian Concern   www.persecution.org/suffering/
                                                  index.php#

▪International Justice Mission   www.ijmuk.org/contribute/church
Advocacy, volunteering, internships.

▪The Micah Challenge   www.micahchallenge.org
A global voice on poverty for Christians, encouraging them to learn about the issues, find ways to reach out and help the poor, and to fight for justice.

▪Mother's Union   www.themothersunion.org

- Release International   www.releaseinternational.org
  Free, downloadable 'Advocates Pack' by Release International provides guidance in how to write to support persecuted Christians around the world; also other materials.

- Viva (Network)   www.viva.org
  Supports organisations helping children at risk and encourages advocacy.

■ Mission Websites for Kids

Excite your children about changing the world!

- Caleb Resources.   http://store.calebresources.org

- Caravan Friends (IMB)   www.caravanfriends.org

- Children's Missions (WMU)   www.childrensmissions.com

- Children's Prayer Network   www.kidspray.org.au

- Christian Aid   www.christianaid.org.uk/resources/games

- Compassion Explorer (magazine)   http://issuu.com/creativeblueagency/docs/ci_explorer_winter_2010_issuu

- G. C. Kidz Club (CMA)   www.cmalliance.org/kidz

- Global Eye   www.globaleye.org.uk

- Global Kids (OM)   www.globalkids.om.org

- Global Xpress Kids Club (U. S. Center for World Mission)   www.uscwm.org

- Great Commission Kids (magazine—World Team)   www.elinoryoung.info/gckids.html

- Impact KIDS (Kids in Dire Situations) www.impactkids.org

- Kids of Courage (Voice of the Martyrs) www.kidsofcourage.com

- Kids Prayer Network   www.kidsprayer.com

- Kidstuff (New Tribes Mission)   www.ntm.org/kidstuff

- Kids Web (Wycliffe)   www.wycliffe.org/Resources/Kids/Kidssite.aspx

- Kidzone (Open Doors)   kidzone@opendoorsuk.org
- Leprosy Mission   www.leprosymission.org.uk/kids_place
- One Mission Kids   www.onemissionkids.org
- Oxfam   www.oxfam.org.uk/education
- Tearfund   http://actionpack.tearfund.org/
- The Owl and the Pussycat   www.owlandpussycat.org/ourworld/
                                    index.htm
- Quest for Compassion (game)   www.questforcompassion.org/learn
- Red Card Kids   www.redcardkids.org
- SIM Kids   www.simkids.org
- Window Kids   http://www.windowkids.com
- World Champions for God (OM)   www.omnz.org.nz/kids

▉ More Recommended Reading to Encourage Involvement

Behnken, Kenneth W. Planting Missions Across Cultures. Concordia Publishing House,1999.

Borthwick, Paul. *How to Be a World Class Christian.* Gabriel Publishing, 1999.

Borthwick, Paul. *Six Dangerous Questions to Transform Your View of the World.* Intervarsity Press, 1997.

Engel, James F. and William A. Dyrness. *Changing the Mind of Missions: Where Have We Gone Wrong?* Intervarsity Press, 2000.

Foth, Sylvia. *Daddy, Are We There Yet? A Global Check-in on the World of Mission and Kids.* Kidzana Ministries, 2009.

Fountain, Jeff. *Living as People of Hope; Faith, Hope & Vision for 21ˢᵗ Century Europe.* Initialmedia, 2004.

Greenway, Roger S. and Timothy M.Monsma. *Cities: Missions' New Frontier.* Baker Academic, 2000.

Jeffery, Tim and Steve Chalke. *Connect! Your Place in a Globalised World.* Authentic, 2002.

Jenkins, Philip. *God's Continent: Christianity, Islam and Europe's Religious Crisis.* Oxford, 2007.

Mandryk, Jason, editor. *Operation World, 7ᵗʰ ed.* Authentic, 2010.
    *** Indispensable, country-by-country guide with facts and prayer targets

Mays, David. *Building Global Vision; 6 Steps To Discovering God's Mission Vision for Your Church.* ACMC, 2005.

McQuilkin, Robertson. *The Great Omission.* Gabriel Publishing, 2002.

Miley, George. *Loving the Church ... Blessing the Nations: Pursuing the Role of Local Churches in Global Missions.* Authentic, 2005.

Nyquist, J. Paul. *There is No Time.* Avant Ministries, 2007.

Piper, John. *Let the nations be glad! The Supremacy of God in Missions.* 3ʳᵈ ed. Baker, 2010.

Piper, Joy. *Bringing the World to Your Church.* WEC, 2001.

Pippert, Rebecca Manley. *Out of the Saltshaker & Into the World: Evangelism as a Way of Life.* IVP, 1999.

Pirolo, Neal. *Serving As Senders: How to Care for Your Missionaries While They Are Preparing to Go, While They Are on the Field, When They Return Home.* Emmaus Road Intl., 1991.

Pirolo, Neal. *The Re-Entry Team: Caring for Your Returning Missionaries.* Emmaus Road Intl., 2000.

Roxburgh, Alan J. and M. Scott Boren. *Introducing the Missional Church.* Jossey-Bass, 2006.

Roxburgh, Alan and Fred Romanuk. *The Missional Leader: Equipping Your Church to Reach a Changing World.* Jossey-Bass, 2006.

Rusaw, Rich and Eric Swanson. *The Externally Focused Church.* Group Publishing, 2004.

Simson, Wolfgang. *Houses That Change the World; The Return of the House Churches.* Authentic, 1999.

Spraggett, Daphne and Jill Johnstone. *Window on the World.* Authentic, 2007.

Spraggett, Daphne and Jill Johnstone. *You Can Change the World.* Zondervan, 1996.

Telford, Tom and Lois Shaw. *Missions in the Twenty-First Century.* Shaw, 2000.

Warren, Rick. The Purpose-Driven Church. Grand Rapids: Zondervan, 1996.

Winter, Ralph D., editor. *Perspectives on the World Christian Movement: A Reader. rev.ed.* William Carey Library Publishers, 1999

■ See also:

■William Carey Library   http://missionbooks.org
Hundreds of missions-related titles from over seventy-five publishers, all at discount prices.

■World Evangelical Alliance Resources   www.wearesources.org
Books and articles to download free in English and Spanish, including some great titles on missionary care and support.

■ Courses, Seminars, and Other (non-residential) for Envisioning and Training to Reach the Nations

Note: Resources specifically geared toward reaching Muslims are listed in the 'Loving Muslims' section of this book.

■Emmaus Road International   http://www.eri.org
ACTS 29 Training Course, 10-week total immersion in a second culture; a mini 4-week course; or ACT Team Orientation for groups going on a brief weekend or up to a 3 to 4-week trip (USA). Also offers seminars and audio-tape library.

■AIMS Seminars   http://aims.org
Over 7 seminars to equip churches to engage in missions. 'The Harvest Connection,' an introduction to missions for church leaders, is available in 7 languages.

■Caleb Resources   http://store.calebresources.org
A number of courses and Bible Studies, including "Eternal Impact," "Encountering the World of Islam," and a new one for children about children at risk, "Red Card: Standing Against Oppression, Providing Hope." DVDs, workbooks, kits, booklets, prayer cards

■Christian Life & Global Mission   www.christianlifeand.com
6-week home or church group study course.

- Christian Courses   http://christiancourses.com
  Non-certificate (free) and certificate (paid) courses offered, the latter including
  world religions and encountering Islam.

- Facing the Challenge   www.facingthechallenge.org/quotes.php
  Free downloadable courses include: 'Facing the Challenge of our Times,'
  'Facing the Challenge of a Hostile World,' 'Facing the Challenge of Other
  Faiths,' 'What Muslims Believe,' 'What Hindus Believe.'

- Global Purpose & Study Booklet   http://missionbooks.org/
                                        williamcarelibrary/home.php
  DVD that gives an overview of God's plan through history and how we can
  join Him now to help fulfill it.

- Globally@Home   www.janzteamuk.org/Globally%40
                                        Home/Globally%40Home.html
  Modules devised by Janz Team International to help people adapt to foreign
  cultures, whether home or abroad.

- International Christian Mission   www.icmission.net
  Church-planting training, 'Bible School in a Briefcase.'

- The Kairos Course   www.wouk.org/courses/mission_
                                        course.php
  8-lesson curriculum formerly known as the Condensed World Mission Course.

- The Missionary Training Service   www.missionarytraining.org
  Online training of missionaries and help for churches.

- On The Box Mission   www.ontheboxmission.com/training.htm
  Cultural orientation training videos for groups or individuals, manual,
  simulation activities.

- Perspectives on the World Christian Movement
                                        www.perspectives.org
  Complementary courses on Islam (see resources in the 'Loving Muslims'
  section of this book) and 'God's Heart for the Nations;' an 8-lesson Bible study
  designed to walk believers through the Bible to discover God's global purpose
  for themselves.

▪SIM Global Outreach   www.simusa.org/index.php/category/
                                    training-steps
    Mission mobilisation training seminar. For European office contact:
                                    www.sim.org/index.php/office/list

▪Unveiling Glory   www.unveilinglory.com
    Trans-denominational and trans-cultural ministry of seminars, literature,
    videotapes, audiotapes, computer resources and formal education.

▪Vision for the Nations   www.gospelcom.net/wclbooks/
                                    visionforthenations.html
    Video series developed by the US Center for World Mission. 13-week
    curriculum designed for Sunday School and Bible Study settings, introducing
    missions from four perspectives: Biblical, historical, cultural and strategic.

▪World Evangelical Alliance   www.theimtn.org/resources
    Mission education and training resources in English, French, Spanish and
    Finnish.

▪ Drama

▪Caleb Resources   http://store.calebresources.org
    2-disc set 'Mission Skits: Dramas & Skits That Mobilize.'

▪DramaShare   www.dramashare.org
    Royalty-free Christian drama theatre resources, including full scripts of dozens
    of great missions dramas, sketches and monologues.

▪Dramatix   www.dramatix.org

▪Theatre Evangelique   www.theatreevangelique.com
    French language drama resource site.

▪World Christian Resource Directory   www.missionresources.com/drama.html

▪ DVDs, Videos and Clips, Audio

Remember to check the websites of individual missions for the excellent media
they produce to mobilise prayer and action.

▪Audiopot   www.audiopot.org
    Creative Christian audio for illustrating talks, starting discussions, etc.

- Caleb Resources   http://store.calebresources.org
'The Enemy God' film and other DVDs.

- Christian Cinema   www.christiancinema.com

- Create International   www.createinternational.com
Video people profiles, videos in unreached people group languages

- OMNItube   www.omnitube.org
Free and low-cost mission media reservoir site maintained by Operation Mobilisation's OMNIvision team.

- Operation WorldView   http://mission1.org/opwv.html/
Based partially on the life-changing course, Perspectives on the World Christian Movement, this 4 DVD set from Mission ONE introduces the Biblical, Historical, Cultural and Strategic aspects of world missions. Includes leader and participant study guides.

- Tangle (formerly Godtube)   www.tangle.com
This video library is a fraction of Youtube size, but more focused on Christian topics.

- Trinity Vision   www.trinityvision.co.uk

- Vimeo   www.vimeo.com

- Vision Video   www.visionvideo.com

- World Christian Video Directory   www.christianvideos.org/
                                            missionvideos. html
Brief descriptions of short mobilisation productions from a variety of organisations.

- YouTube   www.youtube.com
Includes thousands of excellent mission-related clips for home or church use.

■ Leader Development Ministries

- Accelerating International Mission Strategies
                                        www.aims.org
Training materials for pastors, equipping the church in Eastern Europe

- CoachNet International Ministries   www.coachnet.org
Australia-based global ministry that grows and resources leaders so they can start, grow and multiply healthy churches.

- Cor Deo (UK)   www.cordeo.org.uk
  Exists to multiply believers through mentoring small groups and combining study with outreach.

- CPAS (UK and Ireland)   www.cpas.org.uk
  Anglican agency that equips churches by developing leaders at all levels so they will be more effective in mission.

- Development Associates International www.daintl.org
  Supports and invests in national Christian leadership.

- Entrust (Eastern and Central Europe) www.entrust4.org

- Global Advance (Siberia, Ukraine)   www.globaladvance.org
  Training conferences.

- International Theological Education Ministries, Inc. (Eastern Europe)
                                www.christforrussia.org

- The Langham Partnership   www.langhampartnership.org
  Equips Majority World churches for mission and growth to maturity through the ministry of Christian leaders and pastors who believe, study, faithfully expound and relevantly apply the Word of God.

- Ministry to Educate & Equip Nationals (MTEE)
                                www.mtee.org
  The Mission Exchange, trans-denominational, in Central and Eastern Europe.

- Next Level International   www.nlieurope.com
  Exists to 'empower a whole new generation of radical leaders to equip, transform and expand the Church in Europe.' See also interactive site for women leaders: http://nliemerge.ning.com

- PreVision Partnership Inc.   www.previsionpartnership.com
  An evangelical, faith-based ministry involved in teaching, evangelism, discipleship and leadership development around the world.

■ Major Events with a Mission Emphasis*

■Antioch Network   www.antiochnetwork.org/
                                          gatherings.htm
Aimed at empowering the church and discipling the nations, this network holds
multinational gatherings twice each year in various countries.

■Balaton-Net (Hungary)   www.balaton-net.hu
4 days, for all ages.

■Destinée Impact Women's Conference (France)

                                          www.impactconference.com
Annual.

■Impact Now European Missions Conference (International)

                                          www.impactnow.eu
Pentecostal European Fellowship.

■Lausanne Congress on World Evangelisation (International)

                                          www.lausanne.org
Movement mobilising evangelical leaders to collaborate for reaching the world.

■Mission Fest (Canada)   www.missionfest.org
Missions mobilisation and support conferences held more or less annually in
key cities.

■Mission Net (International)   www.mission-net.org
Pan-European youth congress and movement to engage ages 16–30, held every
two years and commissioned by the European Evangelical Missionary Alliance
and European Evangelical Alliance.

■New Word Alive (UK)   http://newwordalive.org
Strapline of this annual conference is 'Serving the Church, Reaching the
World.' A partnership of UCCF and Keswick Ministries.

■Transform 2010 (International)   www.transform.om.org
Annual summer initiative of OM that started in 2010, gathering hundreds of
international Christians for training and service throughout the 20+ countries
in the Mediterranean region.

* Note: Many individual mission agencies also offer insightful programmes and
events throughout the year. Check their websites for details.

- New Wine (UK)   www.new-wine.org
  Summer conferences offer worship and seminars on social issues and reaching
  the community.

- Passion   www.268generation.com
  Annual conference in U. S. and several other countries that challenges college
  and university students to make their lives count for God's Kingdom.

- Urbana (USA)   www.urbana.org
  Intervarsity Christian Fellowship's international student mission conference
  held once every three years.

- RightNow Conference (USA)   www.rightnow.org
  Annual gathering for 20s and 30s, with opportunities to serve in Europe.

- Together on a Mission Conference (UK)
                                      http://newfrontierstogether.org
  Newfrontiers' annual gathering in Brighton which is really two separate
  conferences: 'Leadership International' for church leaders and 'Mobilise' for
  students and 20s.

- World Mission Conference (UK)   www.pwm-web.org.uk
  Church of England's annual 'Partnership for World Mission' conference.

■ Magazines

Most mission organisations offer periodicals that can keep you updated and allow
you and your church's mission programme to be more effective. In addition to
these, consider the following resources which are mostly online and free of charge:

- Evangelical Missions Quarterly   http://bgc.gospelcom.net/emis/
                                      emqpg.htm
  Subscription-only, a professional journal from the (U. S.) Evangelism and
  Missions Information Service. Includes insightful articles on the status of
  missions and mobilisation.

■ Global Prayer Digest *See 'Prayer'*

- Lausanne World Pulse   www.lausanneworldpulse.com
  Evangelism and missions news, information and analysis.

▪Missions Catalyst E-Magazine   missionscatalyst@takeitglobal.org
Free weekly email digest of news, ministry ideas and resources from Caleb
Resources.

▪Mission Frontiers   www.missionfrontiers.org
Bi-monthly, laypersons'-level missiology magazine.

▪Mission Network News   www.mnnonline.org
Current news from around the world

▪Brigada Today   www.brigada.org
Mission-related resources and events.

▪Momentum   www.strategicnetwork.org
Focused on the least-reached 27% of the world.

▪Retirement with a Purpose   www. retirementwithapurpose.com
Online magazine with Campus Crusade for Christ roots, providing resources
and opportunities to help communicate God's message of love and forgiveness
worldwide.

■ Miscellaneous Useful Resources

▪Nazarene Missions International   http://home.snu.edu/~HCULBERT/
                                        nmi.htm

■ Mission education resources

▪New Christians   www.newchristian.org.uk/church
                                        resources.html
Site for churches and Christians with many media resources and a teen page.

▪Wycliffe Idea Bank   www.wycliffe.org.uk/resources_
                                        ideabank.html
Collection of free, downloadable simulation games, stories, discussion materials,
a prayer DVD and more.

▪Stuff CD.   www.davidmays.org/Resources/
                                        resmays.html
Lists, outlines, handouts, forms and processes for doing missions in your
church. 4 volumes; download the first without charge.

- '*Witnessing to the Disaster Stricken*,' downloadable advice by Keith Cook, On the
  Go Ministries   www.onthego.org/tools/Witnessing%20
                                         to%20Disaster%20St.htm

Free 'Short-Term Mission Starter Kit' for your church from Delta Ministries
International; CD includes printable materials, DVD's and links that provide
resources for all phases. http://deltaministries.com

■ Prayer—Guides and Information

- Caleb Resources, Prayer Guides   http://store.calebresources.org

- Christian Renewal Ministries   www.crmin.org/prayerguide/prayer_
                                        guides.htm

Lists a variety of useful ideas and helps.

- Etnopedia   http://en.etnopedia.org/wiki/index.php/
                                        Main_Page

Ethnic people profiles in a number of languages.

- European Evangelical Alliance [EEA]   www.europeanea.org
Offers an annual 'Week of Prayer Guide,' usually in several languages.

- Global Day of Prayer   www.globaldayofprayer.com/10days_
                                        guide.html

- Global Prayer Digest   www.global-prayer-digest.org
Monthly day-by-day prayer guide focusing on unreached people groups, by
Adopt-a-People movement. Free online or subscribe through U. S. Center for
World Missions.

- '*Mobilising Churches as Houses of Prayer*' (paper). See:
                                        www.globaldayofprayer.com/down
                                        loads/10days/additional/Mobilising%20
                                        churches%20as%20houses%20of%20
                                        prayer.pdf

- International Prayer Council   www.ipcprayer.org
Connecting prayer leaders in every region, promoting national movements and
equipping local churches.

- National Prayer Center (AOG)   http://prayer.ag.org/ways_to_pray
'Ways to Pray' guides for specific ministries, special events, areas and issues.

- Prayercentral   http://prayercentral.net
  Resources to equip, engage and inspire people to pray.

- The 30-days Prayer Network   www.30-days.net
  Christian prayer guide for Muslims that coincides with Ramadan each year.

- Waymakers   www.waymakers.org
  Ministry to impart vision and practical training for leaders of local prayer
  movements,

■ Prayer for Europe—Websites

- 24-7 Prayer   www.24-7prayer.com

- Awaken the Watchmen 24-7 Prayer   www.global24-7.org

- EUReview & Call to Prayer (European Union)
                                         www.euprayer.com

- Global Prayer Community   www.prayway.com

- Harvest Prayer Ministries   www.harvestprayer.com

- Houses of Prayer   www.housesofprayer.net

- Intercessors Arise International   www.intercessorsarise.org

- International Prayer Council   www.ipcprayer.org

- InterPrayer International Partnership   www.interprayer.com

- Jericho Walls International Prayer Network
                                         www.jwipn.com

- London Prayer (London, England)   www.londonprayer.net

- Lydia Fellowship International (see Europe pages)
                                         http://lydiafellowshipinternational.org

- Open Heaven   www.openheaven.com

- Operation World   http://operationworld.24-7prayer.com

- Peoples Around the World   www.imb.org/main/aroundtheworld.asp

- Pray for Denmark   http://prayfordenmarkblog.blogspot.com

- Pray for Europe   www.prayeurope.com

- Pray for Spain   www.prayforspain.com/home

- Prayer Alert (British Isles and Ireland) www.prayer-alert.net

- Prayer for the Nations   www.prayerforthenations.com

- Prayer Forum   www.prayerforum.org

- Prayercast   www.prayercast.com

- Transformations Ireland   www.transformations-ireland.org

- TransMed (Mediterranean)   www.ffald-y-brenin.org/caleb-
                                         transmed.php

- World Prayer Centre   http://worldprayer.org.uk

■ A Few Top Websites for Awareness-Raising and Information

- Adopt-A-People   www.adoptapeople.com

- Agape Europe   www.agapeeurope.com
  Western Europe ministry news.

- Brigada   www.brigada.org
  Resources, trends, and motivation to fulfill the Great Commission

- Global Mapping International   www.gmi.org
  Research and information providers to stimulate mission interest

- Joel News International   www.joelnews.org

- Kingdom Site Ministries   www.kingdomsite.com
  Uses technology to solve ministry problems, such as providing Christian web
  page translations in 50 languages.

- Mis-Links   www.mislinks.org
  A web-based mission directory

- Peoplegroups.org   www.peoplegroups.org/
  Quick and easy website for info on the status of unreached peoples in various
  continents and countries, including Europe.

- The Joshua Project   www.joshuaproject.net/
  Another great source for data on ethnic groups in Europe as well as the rest of
  the world.

■ Trips and Opportunities

Most missions offer a range of short-term exposure and longer trips that invite participants to use or expand their skills. Check out their websites along with the more general directories below.

▪Adventures in Mission.   www.adventures.org

▪Christian Volunteering.org   www.christianvolunteering.org
General volunteering opportunities worldwide and sponsoring organisations.

▪Global Aid Network (GAiN)   www.gainusa.org
Short-term mission teams to Russia, Ukraine and Belarus. Volunteers share Christ and deliver aid to orphans, street kids, the elderly and others in need. GAiN is a division of Campus Crusade for Christ.

▪Mission Finder   www.missionfinder.org
Classified directories of mission opportunities, with search engine

▪Mission Trips   www.missions-trip.com
Online missions database of short and long term missions opportunities and directory of missions agencies.

▪Senior Volunteer Network (SVN)   http://svnet.org
Links experienced teachers with agencies needing short-term help.

▪Short Term Mission Starter Kit   http://deltaministries.com/component/
                                         ckforms/?view=ckforms&id=1
Free CD from Delta Ministries offering over 40 resources to churches.

▪Short Term Missions Arsenal   http://missionsresources.com
Practical tools and resources to prepare your group for a mission trip, equip them for ministry, and empower them to bring the experience back home.

▪Shorttermmissions.com   www.shorttermmissions.com

▪Trailblazers   www.trailblazers.org.uk
Sponsored challenges to raise money for relief and development projects.

Appendix

Missions in Europe

This list includes many of the major evangelical agencies and networks actually working within Europe, rather than those serving only as offices for sending or recruiting. It is not exhaustive, particularly in regard to denominational, specialty and national missions. Individual church or institution-based ministries are not included. The immediate section below, 'International Missions with a Variety of Ministries,' lists agencies with a broader spectrum of ministries *in at least three* European countries. Following this are key 'Pan-European Networks' and then lists by category of Christian agencies which concentrate either on a particular ministry or a certain country/region. Also see resource pages at the end of each of this book's five focus areas.

Please pray for the work of each of these missions, and explore the excellent resources and opportunities available through their online websites!

International Missions that Have a Variety of Ministries within Europe

Action International Ministries	www.actioninternational.org
Agape	www.agape.org.uk
Aglow International	www.aglow.org
Alliance International Ministries	http://aimteam.org
Allianz Mission (Covenant Church)	www.allianz-mission.de
Ambassadors for Christ International	www.afciworld.org
Assemblies of God World Ministries	http://worldmissions.ag.org/regions/europe
Association of Baptists for World Evangelism	
	www.abwe.org
Baptist International Missions, Inc.	www.bimi.org
Baptist Mid-Missions	www.bmm.org/bmm
Baptist Missions	www.ibaptistmissions.org
Baptist World Mission	www.baptistworldmission.org

Bible Centered Ministries International   www.bcmintl.org

Bethany International Ministries   www.bethanyim.org

Bible-Centered Ministries International   http://bcmintl.org

BMS World Mission   www.bmsworldmission.org

Canadian Baptist Ministries   http://cbmin.org

Christian & Missionary Alliance   www.cmalliance.org

Christian Missions in Many Lands   www.cmmlusa.org

Christian Missions International   www.cmiworld.org

Christian Reformed World Missions   www.crcna.org

Christians in Action   www.christiansinaction.org

Church Mission Society   www.cms-uk.org

Church of God World Missions   www.cog-europe.de

Church of Scotland World Mission Council
                                          www.churchofscotland.org.uk

Church of the Nazarene   www.nazarene.org

CMF International   www.cmfi.org

Commission to Every Nation   www.cten.org

Cooperative Baptist Fellowship   www.thefellowship.info

Crosslinks   www.crosslinks.org

CrossWorld   www.crossworld.org

Damascus Trust   www.damascustrust.org

Eleos International Ministries   http://eleosinternational.org

Elim Fellowship   www.elimfellowship.org

Elim International Missions   www.elimmissions.co.uk

Ellel Ministries International   www.ellelministries.org

Eurasia Now (Pentecostal Assemblies of Canada)
                                          www.eurasia-now.org

Fellowship International Mission   http://fim.org

European Evangelistic Society   www.eesatlanta.org

European Missionary Fellowship   www.emf-welwyn.org

Eurovangelism   www.eurovangelism.org.uk

Evangelical Lutheran Church in America www.elca.org

Evangelism Explosion   www.eeinternational.org

Every Home for Christ   www.ehc.org

Faith2Share   www.faith2share.net

FEG Vision Europe (Free Evangelical Church)
                                               www.feg.ch

Fellowship International Mission   http://fim.org/ministries.php#europe

Finnish Evangelical Lutheran Mission   www.mission.fi

Forum Wiedenest   www.wiedenest.de

Foursquare Missions International   http://fmi.foursquare.org

Free Methodist Church in Europe   www.fmc-europe.org

Free Presbyterian Mission Board   http://fpcmission.org

Free Will Baptist International Missions www.fwbgo.com

German Missionary Fellowship (DMG) www.dmgint.de

Global Action   www.global-act.org

Global Ministries (Disciples of Christ, United Church of Christ)
                                               http://globalministries.org

Global Mission Society (Presbyterian Church, Korea)
                                               www.gms.kr

Global Missionary Ministries   www.gmmeuro.org

Global Outreach   www.wegoglobal.com

Global Outreach Mission   www.missiongo.org

Global Partners (Wesleyan Church)   www.wesleyan.org

Got to the Nations   www.missiongo.org

Grace Baptist Mission   www.gbm.org.uk

Greater Europe Mission   www.gemission.org

Heaven Sent Ministries   www.hsminc.org

InterAct (Sweden, *Evangeliska Frikyrkan*)
                                               www.efk.se

Intercontinental Church Society (Church of England)
                                www.ics-uk.org

International Messengers   www.internationalmessengers.org

International Mission Board (Southern Baptist Convention)
                                http://imbeurope.org

International Mission Project   www.impcharity.org.uk

International Teams Europe   www.iteams.org

Interserve   www.interserve.org.uk

Korea Baptist Convention   www.fmb.or.kr

Kontaktmission (Germany)   www.kontaktmission.de

Langham Partnership International www.langhampartnership.org

Liebenzell Mission (Germany)   www.liebenzell.org

Mennonite Brethren Mission & Service International
                                www.mbmsi.org

Methodist Church: World Church Relationships
                                www.methodist.org.uk

Ministry to Unreached Peoples   www.mup.org

Mission for South-East Europe   www.msoe.org

Mission to the World (PCA)   www2.mtw.org/home

Mission Without Borders   www.mwbi.org

Missionary Ventures   www.mvi.org

NavMissions   www.navigators.org

Newfrontiers International   http://newfrontierstogether.org

Next Level International   www.nlieurope.com

OC Europe   www.ocieurope.org

Operation Mobilisation [OM International]
                                www.om.org

OMS International   www.omsinternational.org/europe

OneHope   www.onehope.net

Open Door Baptist Mission   www.odbm.org

Ora International   www.stichtingora.nl

Our Daily Bread Missions	www.ourdailybreadmissions.org
Open Air Campaigners International	www.oaci.org/europe
Partners International	www.partnersintl.org
Pentecostal European Mission	www.pemeurope.com
Pioneers International	www.pioneers-europe.org
Presbyterian Church in Ireland—Mission Overseas	
	www.pcimissionoverseas.org
Protestant Mission Service	www.missionsdienst.ch
Radstock Ministries	www.radstock.org
Ravi Zacharias International Ministries	www.rzim.org
Salt & Light Ministries	www.saltlight.org/europe
Salvation Army International	www.salvationarmy.org
SEND International	www.send.org
Serving Missions Globally	www.smgworld.ch
Swedish Pentecostal Church Missions	www.pingst.se
The Evangelical Alliance Mission (TEAM)	
	www.teamworld.org
The Mission Society	www.themissionsociety.org
Time for God	www.timeforgod.org/
Torchbearers International	www.torchbearers.org
Touch the World Ministries	www.touchtheworlduk.org
United Beach Missions	www.ubm.org.uk
UFM Worldwide	www.ufm.org.uk
United German Aid Mission (VDM)	www.vdm.org
United Methodist Church, Global Ministries	
	http://new.gbgm-umc.org
United World Mission	www.uwm.org/
WEC International	www.wec-int.org
Word of Life International Ministries	http://im.wol.org
World Gospel Mission	www.wgm.org
World Harvest Mission	www.whm.org

World Horizons	www.worldhorizons.org
World Outreach International	www.wointl.com
World Team	www.worldteam.org
WorldVenture (formerly CB International)	
	www.worldventure.com
Worldwide New Testament Baptist Missions	
	www.wwntbm.com
Youth With A Mission (YWAM)	www.ywam.org, www.ywam.eu

Key Pan-European and World Networks

Connect Europe   www.connecteurope.org
   Friendship-based community of visionaries and pioneers aiming to start and
   shape movements of prayer, justice, fellowship and missions in the continent.

Converge Worldwide   www.convergeworldwide.org
   Churches working together to start and strengthen more churches.

Council for World Mission Europe   www.cwmeurope.org
   Partnership of churches in mission.

CrossGlobalLink   www.crossgloballink.org
   Formerly the Interdenominational Foreign Mission Association.

DAWN European Network   www.dawneurope.net
   A network of European leaders, based on friendship and a common vision, to
   see a living church in easy reach of every European.

EU-CORD   www.eu-cord.org
   Pan-European network of Christian organisations in relief and development.

Europa (Youngstars Network)   www.juropa.ch
   Youth group consultancy, training and empowerment.

European Baptist Federation   www.ebf.org

Eurochurch.net   www.eurochurch.net
   A platform for dialogue and sharing to facilitate unity and strength in the
   Church in Europe.

European Evangelical Alliance [EEA]   www.europeanea.org
and European Evangelical Missionary Alliance [EEMA]
Information site bringing together both the national Evangelical Alliances of
Europe and a large number of pan-European mission agencies.

European Missions Research Group   www.emrgnet.eu
Network of missions researchers focusing on practical information for church
multiplication in Europe.

Faith2Share (F2S)   www.faith2share.net
International network of Christian mission movements.

Global Missions Network   www.globalmissionsnetwork.info/

Great Commission Roundtable   www.icta.net/gcr/

Hope for Europe   http://hfe.org
Pan-evangelical network of networks across national borders.

Micah Network   www.micahnetwork.org
Over 330 Christian relief, development and justice organisations in 81
countries.

Mission Agencies Partnership (MAP)   www.mapmission.org
Partnership of 45 mission agencies to help churches and individuals develop a
missionary vision.

Missional International Churches Network
                                     www.micn.org
Facilitating the worldwide movement of mission-minded international
churches.

Network for Strategic Missions   www.strategicnetwork.org
Helping believers strategically and effectively reach the least-reached 27% of the
world.

Partnership for World Mission (Church of England)
                                     www.pwm-web.org.uk

Pentecostal European Fellowship (PEF) www.pef.eu

World Council of Churches   www.oikoumene.org

World Evangelical Alliance   www.worldevangelicals.org

Specialty Missions

The following agencies focus primarily if not exclusively on a specific ministry, people group or geographical area.

Arts

Ad Deum Dance Company	www.danceaddeum.com
Artists in Christian Testimony International	www.actinternational.org
Arts With A Mission (Part of Youth With A Mission)	www.artswithamission.org
ArtsLink (Part of OM International)	http://omartslink.org
Ballet Magnificat!	www.balletmagnificat.com
Bill Drake Band	www.billdrake.com
BugNog Music (Jon Simpson)	www.bugnogmusic.com
Celebrant Singers International	www.celebrants.org
Christian European Visual Media Association	www.cevma.net
Christian Fellowship of Art Music Composers	http://www.cfamc.org
Christians in Entertainment	www.cieweb.org.uk
Christians in the Visual Arts	www.civa.org
Christians in Theatre Arts	http://cita.org/site
Covenant Players	www.covenantplayers.org
Creative Arts Europe	www.creativeartseurope.org
CTI Music Ministries (Part of Youth for Christ)	www.ctimusic.org
Dancelink (Part of OM International)	www.omdancelink.org
Drama Ministry Network (Germany)	www.dramaministry.de
Ethnic Worship & Arts Focus (network)	http://disciplethenations.org
Fellowship of Christian Magicians (Germany, UK)	www.fcm.org

Fellowship of Christian Puppeteers   www.fcpfellowship.org

Global Outreach—Performing Arts   http://wegoglobalcom.web20.winsvr.
                                           net/DotNetNuke/LookingtoGO/
                                           GOMinistries/PerformingArts/tabid/83/
                                           Default.aspx

Hearts Sounds International   www.heart-sounds.org

International Christian Dance Fellowship
                                           www.icdf.com

International Society of Christian Artists
                                           www.s-i-a-c.org

OM Arts International   www.arts.om.org

Riding Lights Theatre Company (UK)   www.ridinglights.org

Steiger International   www.steiger.org

UniShow   http://unishow.org

Bible and Other Christian Literature or Media Ministries

AvainMedia (Finland)   www.avainmedia.org

Bibel TV (Germany)   www.bibeltv.de

Bible Mission International   www.biblemission.org

Bible Reading Fellowship (UK)   www.brf.org.uk

Bible Society   www.biblesociety.org.uk

Biblica (formerly IBS-STL)   www.biblica.com/ministry/europe/
index.php

Biblical Literature Fellowship (Belgium, France)
                                           www.blfusa.org

Christian Broadcasting Network International
                                           www.cbn.com

Christian Media Services   www.chms.ro

Christian Vision (Ukraine)   www.christianvision.com

CLC International   www.clcinternational.org

Christian Resources International   www.cribooks.org

Christian Radio Norway   www.p7.no/infoenglish.htm

CNL New Life Channel   www.cnl.info

Compass Braille (Braille literature in 42 languages)
                                                www.compassbraille.org

Cross TV   www.cross.tv

ERF Media   www.erf.de

Evangelische Omroep (Evangelical Broadcasting Association, Netherlands)
                                                www.eo.nl

French Christian Media Website   http://e-radiotv.org

Galcom International   www.galcom.org

GCM Ministries (Russia)   www.gcmediaministries.org

Gideons International   www.gideons.org

Global Media Outreach (Ministry of Campus Crusade for Christ International)
                                                www.globalmediaoutreach.com

Global Recordings Network   http://globalrecordings.net

Good News Broadcasting   www.gnba.net

Gospel Channel   http://gospel-channel.com

Gospel Literature Outreach   www.glo-europe.org

Gospel Literature International (Russia) www.glint.org

Gospel Printing Mission   www.gpmgb.org.uk

Grace to You Europe   www.gty.org.uk

Great Commission Media Ministries   www.gcmediaministries.org

Harvest Fields Commissioning International
                                                www.hfcinternational.org

HCJB Global   www.hcjb.org

Hristiyanskoradio (Bulgaria)   www.hristiyanskoradio.net

Hungarian Evangelical Radio Foundation (MERA)
                                                www.mera.hu

International Broadcasting Association www.ibra.org

Institute for Bible Translation   www.ibtnet.org

In Touch Ministries (Radio, Dr. Charles Stanley)
                                 www.intouch.org

International Bible Society Europe   www.eurobible.net

International Broadcasting Association   www.ibra.org

Josh McDowell Ministries   www.josh.org

Language Recordings UK   http://languagerecordingsuk.co.uk

Latvia Christian Radio & TV Guide   http://latviansonline.com/links/radio

Life TV (Estonia)   www.lifetv.ee

Linden Radio (Iceland)   www.lindin.is

LINKS ('Literature in New Kontexts,' *Network connecting Christian publishers in Central and Eastern Europe with their counterparts around the world, provides training and encourages indigenous writers.*)
                                 www.inter-links.org

Media Associates International (*Encouraging writers and publishers*)
                                 www.littworld.org

Media Distribution Services ·   www.msd-online.ch

Message on the Move (UK, *Scripture posters on public transport*)
                                 www.me-mo.org

Mission Emmanuel (CBN Ukraine)   www.emmanuil.tv/english/radio-emmanuel.htm

Network 211   www.network211.com

New Life Radio-Moscow   www.crfr.org

Nucleo (Portugal)   www.nucleo.com.pt

PAX TV (Hungary)   www.pax-tv.hu

Pocket Testament League   www.pocketpower.org

Radio Radiolähetysjärjestö (Finland) www.sansa.fi

Russian Christian Radio   www.rcr.ru/eng

SCM Bundes-Verlag (Germany)   www.bundes-verlag.de

Scripture Union   www.su-international.org

S. E. A. N. International (*Writing Bible courses for Theological Education by Extension*)
                                 www.seaninternational.com

SGM Lifewords (*Formerly Scripture Gift Mission*)
                                        www.sgmlifewords.com

Source of Light Ministries International www.sourcelight.org

Tallin Family Radio (Estonia)   www.estpak.ee/~ekm/english/english.
htm

The Bible League   www.bibleleague.org

The Word for the World (*Training nationals for Bible translation*)
                                        www.thewordfortheworld.org

Trans World Radio   www.twreurope.org

United Bible Societies   www.biblesociety.org

United Christian Broadcasters   www.ucb.co.uk

Word to Russia   www.wordtorussia.org

World Harvest Radio   www.whri.com

Wycliffe Bible Translators   www.wycliffe.org

Children or Youth

(See also 'Children—Orphans' and 'Students')

Abernethy Trust (UK)   www.abernethy.org.uk

Adventure Plus (A+, UK)   www.adventureplus.org.uk

ASSIST Europe (Russia, Ukraine)   www.assisteurope.net

Atlantic Bridge International   www.atlanticbridge.org

Awana International   www.awanainternational.org

Barnabas   www.barnabas.nu

Bethel Faith Mission (Latvia, Russia, Ukraine)
                                        www.trosgnistan.se

Bright Hope International (Russia)   www.brighthope.org

Bringing Good News (Ukraine)   http://bringinggoodnews.org

Building Hope in Ukraine   www.buildinghopeinukraine.org

Care and Relief for the Young   www.cry.org.uk

Caring for Life (UK, *Housing support for vulnerable young people*)
www.caringforlife.co.uk

ChildAid (*Formerly Aid to Russia and the Republics*)
www.childaidrr.org.uk

Child Evangelism Fellowship   www.cefeurope.com

Children in Distress (Eastern Europe) www.childrenindistress.org

Children's Hunger Fund   www.chfus.org

Children's Ministries International   www.cmikids.com

Christian Endeavour   www.ce-online.org

Christian Youth International (Russia) www.forerunner.com/forerunner/
X0655_CYI_update_1292.htm

CoMission for Children at Risk (Network, Eastern Europe)
www.comission.org

CrossRoads Foundation (Ukraine)   www.crossrdsfoundation.org

East West Ministries (Russia, *Post-orphanage transition*)
www.fuqua.eastwest.org

ErikshjÄlpen (Eastern Europe, *Empowering children and their families*)
www.erikshjalpen.se

Europe Teen Challenge (International) www.teenchallenge.info

Europe2Europe (Romania)   www.europe2europe.co.uk

Every Generation Ministries   www.egmworld.org

Exodus   www.exodusonline.org.uk

Family Aid International (Ukraine)   http://familyaidinternational.com

Father's House International   www.otchiy-dim.org/en

Feed the Children   www.feedthechildren.org

Fundatia Crestina Elims (Romania)   http://fce.ro

GivenGain (Russia)   www.givengain.com/cgi-bin/giga.
cgi?c=1364

Innovista—Training & Resourcing young leaders
www.innovista.org

International Christian Youthworks   www.icy.org.uk

Jesus Revolution   www.jesusrevolution.com

Kids Alive International (Romania)   www.kidsalive.org

Kids Around the World   www.kidsaroundtheworld.com

Kindernothilfe (Eastern Europe)   http://en.kindernothilfe.org

Kingscare (Albania, Caucasus)   www.kingscare.org

King's Kids International   www.kkint.net

Last Bell Ministries (Ukraine)   www.eecoministry.org/lastbell/
                                          index.php

LifeLine Missions International (Belarus, Russia, Ukraine)
                                          www.lifelinemissions.org

Lighthouse Children's Center (Estonia)   www.lastekeskus.ee

Living Hope (Russia)   www.livinghope.org.nz

Love Russia   www.loverussia.org

Manna Worldwide   www.mannaworldwide.com

Mercy Ministries (Russia)   www.mercyrussia.com/go/eng

Mission to Children (Lithuania, Romania)
                                          www.missiontochildren.org

Normisjon (Norway)   www.normisjon.no

Oaza (Romania)   www.oaza.com

OneHope   www.bookofhope.net

Pais Project (*School and youth work*)   www.paisproject.com

PECAN (UK, *Training youth for employment*)
                                          www.pecan.org.uk

Rainbows of Hope (*Ministry of WEC International*)
                                          http://rainbowsofhope.org

Reformed Youth Federation (Hungary) www.refisz.hu

Religious Society of Friends/Quaker Service (Russia, *Autistic children in
St. Petersburg*)   www.kvakare.se/engelska.shtml

Rema (Hungary)   www.remaalapitvany.hu

River of Joy (Crimea)   www.riverofjoy-crimea.org

Road of Hope (Russia)   www.connectedbyheaven.com/th/en/
                                          th_en_index.html

Royal Rangers Online (Hungary)   www.royalrangers.hu

R.U.4 Children Ministries (Ukraine)   www.ru4children.org

Russia Inland   http://russiainland.org

Scandinavian Children's Mission (Moldova, Ukraine)
    www.childrensmission.com

Scripture Union   www.su-international.org

Seedling Mission (Hungary)   www.palantamisszio.hu

Shepherd's Purse (Ukraine)   www.shepherdspurse.org

Slavic International Assoc. of Ministries Good Samaritan (Russia, Ukraine)
    www.siags.com

Smile International   www.smileinternational.org

SOAR International Ministries (Russia)   www.soarinternational.org

Spinnaker Trust (UK)   http://spinnakertrust.org.uk

Spoken For—International Youth Ministries (Russia)
    http://www.spokenfor.org

Stoneworks International (Belarus, Montenegro, Russia)
    www.stoneworksinternational.com

StreetCry Ministries (Russia)   www.streetcry.org

The Evangelistic Association of Russia   www.tear.org

Teen Missions International   www.teenmissions.org

The Least of These (Russia, Ukraine)   www.theleastofthese.org

Urban Saints (UK and Abroad)   www.urbansaints.org

Viva Network Europe (Russia, Slovakia)   www.viva.org

Voice of the Children (Armenia, Russia)   www.votc.org

YMCA International &   www.internationalymca.org

World YWCA   www.worldywca.org

YouthReach International (Russia, Ukraine)
    www.youthreach.org

Young Life   www.younglife.org

Youth for Christ International   www.yfci.org

Youth on Mission (Scotland)   www.yom.org

Children—Orphans

Note: The agencies below concentrate primarily on orphan ministry. However, some of the organisations listed above in 'Children/Youth' also work with orphans as one facet of their ministries.

Behind the Walls*	www.russianorphanoutreach.org
Big Family Mission*	www.bigfamilyministry.org
Agape Orphan Ministries (Romania)	http://agapeorphanministries.com
Ambassadors of Love (Eastern Europe)	http://ambassadorsoflove.net
Boaz Project, Inc.*	www.boazproject.org
Brenna Engle Foundation+	www.brennaenglefoundation.org
Buckner International	http://www.buckner.org/
Charitable Children's Fund*	http://deti.ufacom.ru/
Children's HopeChest*+	www.hopechest.org
Children's Resources International (Eastern Europe)	
	www.feedorphans.org/
Comfort Foundation*	http://comfortfoundationusa.org
Friends of Russian Orphans*	www.fororphans.org
Global Care	www.globalcare.org.uk
Heart to Heart International Ministries (Romania)	
	www.h2hint.org
Hearts for Ukraine*+	www.hearts4ukraine.org
His Kids Too!+	http://hiskidstoo.org
Hope for Orphans	www.hopefororphans.org
Jeremiah's Hope+	www.jeremiahshope.org
Let's Love Charity Foundation+	http://uamissions.do.am
Life2Orphans+	www.life2orphans.org
Lifeline of Hope*	www.orphanslifeline.org
Lifesong for Orphans+	www.lifesongfororphans.org
Little Lambs Ministry (Moldova)*+	http://littlelambs.com
Mission of Tears*	http://missionoftears.org

Mountain Movers International+   http://mountainmovers.org

New Horizons for Children (Eastern Europe)

         www.newhorizonsforchildren.org

Open Arms Ukraine+   www.openarmsukraine.org

Orphan Cry*   http://orphancry.org

Orphan Outreach*   www.orphanoutreach.org

Orphan's Future+   www.orphansfuture.org

Orphan's Hope+   www.orphanshope.org/

Orphans Ministry International+   http://orphansmi.org

Orphan's Tree*   http://orphanstree.org

Project Sunshine (International)   www.project-sunshine.com

Reflections of Hope*   www.reflectionsrussia.org

Romanian Orphan Ministries, Inc.   www.romanianorphanministries.com

Russian Orphan Opportunity Fund*   www.roofnet.org

Seeds for the Harvest*   www.seedsfortheharvest.org

Strategic Angel Care*   http://www.sacorphans.org

SunErgos International*   http://sunergosinternational.org

World Orphans (Eastern Europe)   http://worldorphans.org

* Russia   + Ukraine

Chinese

Chinese Alliance Churches Union (UK) www.cacuuk.org

Chinese Alliance World Fellowship   www.chineseawf.org

Chinese Biblical Seminary in Europe   www.cbsie.org

Chinese Christian Counselling Ministries (UK)

         www.chinese-christian-counselling.
co.uk

Chinese Christian Herald Crusades   www.cchc.org

Chinese Coordination Centre of World Evangelism

         www.cccowe.org/eng

Chinese Lending Library (Germany)   www.chinese-library.de/english/
                                    english.htm

Chinese Overseas Christian Mission [COCM]
                                    www.cocm.org.uk

Christian Centre for Gambling Rehabilitation (UK)
                                    www.ccgr.org.uk

New Leaf Counselling Service (UK)   www.newleafcounselling.org.uk

Overseas Radio and Television   www.ortv.org.uk

Church-Planting

Note: For the missions below church-planting is the main ministry, as opposed to the many other groups that start churches as one aspect of their ministry.

Avant Ministries	www.avantministries.org
Baptist Bible Fellowship International	www.bbfi.org
Biblical Ministries Worldwide	www.biblicalministries.org
Centre for European Church Planting	www.cecp.eu
Christian Associates International	www.christianassociates.org.uk
Dawn Ministries International	www.dawnministries.org
Europe Advance	www.europeadvance.org
European Christian Mission	www.ecmi.org
European Church Planting Network	www.ecpn.org
International Christian Fellowship	www.icf-movement.org
Salt & Light Ministries Europe	www.saltlight.org/europe
Team Expansion	www.teamexpansion.org
World Wide Church Planters	www.wwcp.org

Disabled

(See also 'Healthcare')

Child Development International (Russia)
http://childdevelopmentintl.org

Churches for All (UK, *Partnership of disability organisations*)
www.churchesforall.org.uk

Go! Sign (UK, *Resources for deaf people, raising awareness and reaching deaf community*)
www.gosign.org.uk

Joni and Friends (International)   www.joniandfriends.org

KABB (Norway, *Christian Association for the Visually Impaired*)
www.kabb.no

Prospects International (*Assisting learning disabled and equipping churches*)
www.prospects.org.uk

Signs of God (UK, *Promoting and enabling faith for hearing impaired who use British sign language*)
www.signsofgod.org.uk

Through the Roof (*Making the Christian message accessible to all disabled people. Programmes include Churches inc., Wheels for the World and Integr8 youth programme*)
www.throughtheroof.org,
http://youth.throughtheroof.org

Torch Trust (*Christian resources for blind and visually impaired*)
www.torchtrust.org

Education

Feed the Minds (Eastern Europe)   www.feedtheminds.org

TeachBeyond (*Formerly Janz Team*)   www.teachbeyond.org

TeachOverseas.org   www.teachoverseas.org

Healthcare and Awareness

(See also 'Disabled')

AIDS Care, Education & Training (ACET)
www.acet-international.org

AIDSLink International   www.aidslinkinternational.org

Albanian Health Fund (Albania)   www.albanianhealthfund.org

Arts for Life International (*Helping the traumatised and disabled through the arts*)
                                                          http://artsforlifeinternational.com

Betel International (*Restoring substance-dependent and marginalised people to productive lifestyles*)   www.betel.org

Christian Blind Mission   www.cbmuk.org.uk

Christian Medical & Dental Associations
                                                          www.cmda.org

Christian Medical Fellowship   www.cmf.org.uk

Christian Therapists Network   www.ctn.org.uk

CrossLink International   www.crosslinkinternational.net

Evangelical Medical Aid Society (Eastern Europe)
                                                          www.emascanada.org

Fellowship of Associates of Medical Evangelism
                                                          www.fameworld.org

German Institute for Medical Mission   www.difaem.de

Global AIDS Partnership   www.globalaidspartnership.org

Global Teen Challenge (*Helping victims of substance abuse*)
                                                          www.globaltc.org

Healthcare Ministries (*International medical outreach of Assemblies of God world mission*)   http://healthcareministries.org

Humedica International   www.humedica.org

Life for the World (*Drug/alcohol-related ministry partnering with local churches*)
                                                          www.lftw.org

Life International (*Evangelical agency saving pre-born lives from abortion and bringing new life to others*)   http://www.lifeinternational.com

Medical Teams International (Moldova, Romania)
                                                          www.medicalteams.org

Remar (International, *Rehabilitation of socially rejected people*)
                                                          www.remar.org

Reto a la Esperanza (Challenge to Hope, International, *Helping victims of substance abuse*)   www.asociacionreto.org

Samaritan Medical Missions (*Division of Heaven Sent Ministries*)
www.hsminc.org/Samaritan-Medical-Missions.html

The Luke Society (Eastern Europe, *Supports indigenous health workers*)
www.lukesociety.org

Ukraine Medical Outreach				www.ukrainemedicaloutreach.org

Vision Aid Overseas					www.vao.org.uk

World Medical Mission (*Division of Samaritan's Purse*)
www.samaritanspurse.org/index.php/WMM/index

Humanitarian

Note: Some agencies may be listed under individual countries.

Action by Churches Together Alliance	www.actalliance.org

Adventist Development and Relief Agency
www.adra.org

AGRelief (Assemblies of God)			www.agrelief.ag.org

Blythswood Care					www.blythswood.org

Christian Relief Emergency Teams (Romania)
www.certinternational.org

Christian Hope International			www.christianhope.org.uk

Christian Relief Fund				www.christianrelieffund.org

Dorcas Aid International				www.dorcas.net

Family Care Foundation				www.familycare.org

Feed the Children					www.feedthechildren.org

Feeding the Nations					www.feedingthenations.org

Gift of Hope (Germany)				www.geschenke-der-hoffnung.org/

Global Aid Network					www.gainusa.org

Habitat for Humanity				www.habitatforhumanity.org.uk

Hands for Humanity (Romania)			http://handsforhumanity.org

Healing Hands International			www.hhi.org

HOPE Worldwide	www.hopeww.org
Humanitarian Aid Response Teams	www.hart.ca
Hungarian Baptist Aid	www.baptistasegely.hu
IM	www.manniskohjalp.se
Impact Ministries	www.impactministries.org.uk
International Needs	www.ineeds.org.uk
Kingscare	www.kingscare.org
NetWorks (Romania)	www.networks.org.ro
Operation Blessing	www.ob.org
Operation WellFound (Romania)	www.operationwellfound.org
Opportunity International	www.opportunity.org.uk
Orphan Grain Train	www.ogt.org
Relief for Oppressed People Everywhere (ROPE)	
	www.rope.org.uk
Romania Care	www.romaniacare.com
Samaritan's Purse	www.samaritanspurse.org
Siloam Christian Ministries (Eastern Europe, Portugal)	
	www.siloam.org.uk
SoapBox Trust (Romania, Kosovo)	www.soapboxtrust.com
Tearfund (Eastern Europe)	www.tearfund.org
Trussell Trust (Bulgaria, UK)	www.trusselltrust.org
United Methodist Committee on Relief (Armenia, Georgia)	
	http://new.gbgm-umc.org
World Emergency Relief (Eastern Europe)	
	www.wer-uk.org
World Partners	www.wpartners.org
WorldShare (Albania, Macedonia)	www.worldshare.org.uk
World Vision International	www.wvi.org
Zion World Wide Mission Inc. (France)	www.zwworldmission.org

Immigrants/Refugees

(See also 'Muslims')

Athens Refugee Centre (Greece)	http://refmin.iteams.org/index.php?option=com_content&task=view&id=19&Itemid=35
Christian Intercultural Association (Norway)	www.kianorge.no
Enabling Christians in Serving Refugees (UK)	www.ecsr.org.uk/cm/
Gave (Netherlands)	www.gave.nl
Hagen-InterAktiv (Germany)	www.hagen-interaktiv.de
Helping Hands (Athens, Greece, *Part of International Teams*)	www.helpinghands.gr
Intercultural Christian Centre (*Network of Danish Lutheran Churches*)	www.tvaerkulturelt-center.dk
International Evangelical Church in Finland	www.church.fi
KEGY: *Kelenföldi Evangéliumi Gyülekezet* (Hungary)	http://www.kegy.hu
KIA: *Kristent Interkulturelt Arbeid* (Norway)	www.kianorge.no
KIT: *Kirkernes Integrations Tjeneste* (Denmark)	www.kit-danmark.dk/dk
MEOS (Switzerland)	www.meos.ch
PECAN (UK)	www.pecan.org.uk
Refugee Highway (Network)	http://refugeehighway.net

Jewish

Christian Jew Foundation Ministries	www.cjfm.org
Christian Witness to Israel	www.cwi.org.uk
Chosen People Ministries	www.chosenpeople.com

Christian Friends of Israel   www.cfi.org.uk

Church's Ministry Among Jewish People
                                                 www.cmj-israel.org

Ezra International   http://ezrausa.org

Gateways Beyond International   www.gatewaysbeyond.org

International Board of Jewish Missions www.ibjm.org

Jews for Jesus   www.jewsforjesus.org.uk

Messianic Testimony   www.messianictestimony.com

The Norwegian Church Ministry to Israel
                                                 www.israelsmisjonen.no

Military

ALPHA for Forces (*Alpha course adapted for use in armed forces*)
                                                 http://alpha.org/forces

Arbeitskreises Soldaten (AKS—Germany) www.ak-soldaten.de

Association of Military Christian Fellowships (*Links to European Military Christian Fellowships, by country*)   www.amcf-europe.info

ECHOS International   www.echosinternational.com

Military Ministries International   www.m-m-i.org.uk

Ministry to the Military (Church of God)
                                                 www.mttm.org

Missions to Military (France, Ukraine, *Independent Baptist*)
                                                 www.mtmi.org

Mission to Military Garrisons Inc. (*British forces*)
                                                 www.mmg-online.co.uk

Naval, Military & Air Force Bible Society (*Scripture support service for forces in UK and abroad*)   www.nmafbs.org

Naval Christian Fellowship   www.navalcf.org

Royal Sailors' Rests (UK)   http://rsr.org.uk

Soldiers' and Airmen's Scripture Reading Association [SASRA—UK]
                                                 www.sasra.org.uk

Soldiers' and Airmen's Centres [SANDES—UK]
                                                 www.sandes.org.uk

Miners

International Miners' Mission (Romania, Ukraine)
www.minersmission.com

Muslims

Arab World Ministries www.awm.org

Christians Meet Muslims (Switzerland, *Network*)
www.cmnet.org

Frontiers (Balkans) http://frontiers.org

KABA: Christian Ministry Among Arabs
www.kaba.as

Orientdienst (Middle East Services, Germany)
www.orientdienst.de/english.shtml

Prisoners and Ex-Offenders

Caring for Ex-Offenders (UK) http://caringforexoffenders.org

Christian Prison Ministries—Scotland www.christianprisonministriesscotland.
co.uk

Christian Prison Resources (UK) www.christianprisonresources.org.uk

Daylight Christian Prison Trust (UK) www.daylightcpt.org

Day One Prison Ministry (UK) www.lordsday.co.uk/PrisonMinistry.htm

Kairos Prison Ministry International (UK)
www.kairosprisonministry.org

KCM Ministries Europe (Kenneth Copeland)
www.kcm.org.uk/prison-ministry

Langley House Trust (UK) www.langleyhousetrust.org

Life for the World www.lftw.org

Our Daily Bread Prison Ministries www.ourdailybreadmissions.org/
pfellowship.htm

Prison Fellowship Bulgaria (*Eastern Orthodox, independent organisation not related to PFI*) http://prisonministry.net/PFBulgaria

Prison Fellowship International   www.pfi.org

Set Free Prison Ministries   www.spiritualfreedom-setfree.org

Straight Ahead Ministries (Ukraine, *Juvenile prisons*)
                                        www.straightahead.org

Unchained Ministries Europe (Ireland) http://prisonministry.net/ume

United Prison Ministries International www.upmi.org

Refugees

(See 'Immigrants')

Roma (Gypsies)

Note: Several of the larger international missions above also have ministries among
Roma that are not included here.

Believers World Outreach (Macedonia, Greece)
                                        http://believersworld.com

Conservative Baptist Fellowship   www.gypsyministries.com

Cooperative Baptist Fellowship (European Romany Team; Hungary,
Netherlands, Slovakia, Russia)   www.romanibible.org, http://romany.
gypsyministries.com

EPF Gipsy Ministry (Hungary)   www.remenyhir.hu

Gypsies for Christ (UK, Romania, Hungary, Slovakia)
                                        www.gypsiesforchrist.org
  Gypsy and Travelers International Evangelical Fellowship
  A branch of Light and Life Mission. Branches and/or activities in 15 European
  countries

International Mission Board (Bulgaria, Czech Republic, Macedonia, Poland,
Romania)   http://romaministries.com/

Light and Life Gypsy Church   www.lightandlifegypsychurch.com

O. T. H. E. R. S. (*Outreach to Help European Roma Society; Balkans and Bulgaria,
the latter registered as 'Service to Others'*) www.others1990.com

Roma Bible Union (*Reaching out to Bayash Roma in Croatia, Serbia and Hungary*)
                                        www.romabible.com

Roma Ministry Sarajevo (*A Globe Europe ministry*)
www.romaministry.org

Roma Mission Serbia   http://roma-mission.com

Seafarers

Danish Seamen's Mission   www.dsuk.dk

Domestic Seamen's Mission (Denmark)   www.somandsmissionen.dk

Dutch Central Zeeman Foundation   www.nederlandsezeemanscentrale.nl

Finnish Seamen's Mission   www.merimieskirkko.fi/palvelut/
merenkulkija.asp

German Seamen's Mission   www.seemannsmission.org

LIFE International Seafarers Centres (Eastern Europe)
www.lifeseafarers.org

Mission to Seafarers (International)   www.missiontoseafarers.org

Norwegian Seaman's Mission   www.nettkirken.no/no/

The Norwegian Church Abroad   www.sjomannskirken.no

Queen Victoria Seamen's Rest (UK)   www.qvsr.org.uk

Royal National Mission to Deep Sea Fishermen (Fishermen's Mission, UK)
www.fishermensmission.org.uk

Sailors Society (International, *Formerly British and International Sailors Society*)
www.sailors-society.org

Seamen's Christian Friend Society (International)
www.scfs.org

The Seaman's Mission in Sweden   www.sjomanskyrkan.nu

Sports

2K Plus International Sports Media   www.2kplus.org.uk

Ambassadors (Czech Republic; *Football*) www.ambassadors.cz

Ambassadors in Sport (International; *Football*)
www.aisint.org

Association of Church Sports and Recreation Ministers
                                    www.csrm.org

Athletes in Action (International)   www.athletesinaction.org

Athletes of Christ (Italy)   www.atletidicristo.org

CampoSport (Italy)   www.camposport.it/live

CHEMPS (Netherlands)   www.chemps.org

Christian Motorcyclists Association   www.cmainternational.org

Christian Outreach International (Ukraine)
                                    www.coiusa.com/sports

Christian Skateboarders International (Network)
                                    www.christianskaters.com

Christian Surfers International   www.christiansurfers.net

Christian Team Ministries (Eastern Europe)
                                    www.christianteam.org

Christians in Football   www.christiansinfootball.org

Christians in Sport   www.christiansinsport.org.uk

Church Sports International (Network)   http://churchsports.org

Competitive Edge International—Softball
                                    www.ceisports.org

Crossover Ministries—Basketball   www.crossover.org

DjK Sports Association (Germany)   www.djk.de

European Christian Sports Union   www.veritesport.co.uk

Fellowship of Christian Athletes   www.fca.org

Global Community Games (*Umbrella for KidsGames, TeenGames, FamilyGames, EdgeGames*)
                                    www.globalcommunitygames.com

Global Outreach   http://wegoglobal-com.web20.winsvr.
                                    net/LookingtoGO/GOMinistries/Sports/
                                    tabid/82/Default.aspx

GoodSports International (Hungary, Slovakia)
                                    www.goodsportsinternational.org

Hockey Ministries International   www.hockeyministries.org

Holy Riders (International, *Multidenominational motorcycle club*)
    www.holyriders.com

Hoops of Hope Basketball Ministry   www.hoops.org

Infinity Sports   www.infinitysports.com

International Network of Christian Martial Artists (Network)
    http://incma.mmgi.org

International Christian Cycling Club   www.christiancycling.com

International Sports Coalition (Network)
    www.sportsoutreach.org

International Sports Federation   www.sportsmissions.com

Kirche und Sport (Germany)   www.ekd.de/kirche-und-sport/

KRIK (Norway)   www.krik.no/asp/index3.asp

Links Players International (*Golf*)   www.linksplayers.com

Migsport (Ukraine, *Christian basketball ministry in Kiev*)
    www.migsport.net

Missionary Athletes International (Czech Republic, Ukraine; *Soccer*)
    www.maisoccer.com/main

Nacer de novo (Spain)   www.nacerdenovo.org

Sport et Foi (France)   www.sportetfoi.org

Sport for Life (Sweden)   www.sportforlife.se

SportQuest Ministries (Belgium, Moldova)
    www.sportquest.org

SportReach   www.e3sportreach.org

Sports Across Ireland   www.sportsacrossireland.org

Sports Ambassadors (Part of OC International)
    www.onechallenge.org

SportsLink (Ministry of OM International)
    www.omsportslink.org

Sports Ministry Outreach   www.sportsoutreach.org

Sports Witnesses (Netherlands)   www.sportswitnesses.nl

SRS (Germany, Switzerland)   www.srsonline.de,
    http://srs-pro-sportler.ch

Standard (Ukraine)   http://standardua.org

Ultimate Goal Ministries (*Soccer*)   www.ultimategoal.net

Upward Global (Ukraine; *Football, basketball*)
                                            http://upwardglobal.org

Youth for Christ (International, *Widespread use of sports programmes*)
                                            www.yfci.com

Students

(See also 'Children or Youth')

Campus Crusade for Christ International
                                            www.ccci.org

European Student Mission Association   www.esma-info.net

Friends International (UK)   www.friendsinternational.org.uk

Globalscope   http://cmfi.org/serve/globalscope

International campus ministry of Christian Missionary Fellowship.
International Fellowship of Evangelical Students
                                            www.ifesworld.org

Navigators   www.navigators.org

New Generation (Norway, Sweden)   www.nygenerasjon.no,
                                       www.nygeneration.se

Universities & Colleges Christian Fellowship (UCCF; UK)
                                            www.uccf.org.uk

YouthCompass Europe (*International high school and middle school students*)
                                            www.youthcompass.org

*Individual Country or Area Focus

Note: These are mostly national missions with websites that are not already listed by specialty, above. City missions, institutions and training programmes are not included. See also national Evangelical Alliance member websites for each country: www.europeanea.org/members.html

Austria

Austrian Bible Mission   www.abiblemission.com

Balkans—Missions in More Than One Country

Aid to the Balkans   www.aidtothebalkans.com
WorldShare: Macedonian Mission to the Balkans
                                          www.worldshare.org.uk
World Vision   www.worldvision.org

Balkans—Missions by Country

Albania

Albanian Encouragement Project   www.aepfoundation.org
Albanian Evangelical Mission   www.aemission.org
CAM International   www.caminternational.org
Lightforce International   www.lightforce.org.uk

Bosnia-Herzegovina

American Friends Service Committee   http://afsc.org
Beyond Tears Worldwide   www.beyondtearsworldwide.org
Novi Most   www.novimost.org
Stiftung Mehrwert (Foundation)   www.stiftung-mehrwert.ch
World Hope International   www.worldhope.org

Kosovo

World Relief   http://worldrelief.org

Serbia

AMEN   www.amentrust.co.uk
Project Timothy   http://projekat-timotej.org

Baltics—Missions in More Than One Country

Go To Nations   www.gotonations.org
Lutheran Church Missouri Synod Board of Missions
                                           www.lcms.org/ca/worldrelief

Baltics—Missions by Country

Estonia

Baltic Mission Center   www.bmk.ee/indexenglish.html
Estonian Christian Ministries   www.estonianministries.com

Latvia

Bridge Builders International   www.bridgebuildersint.com
Christ for Latvia   http://christforlatvia.org
Latvian Christian Mission   www.70x7ministry.com/
                                           LatvianMissions.html

Lithuania

Union of Pentecostal Churches of Lithuania
                                           www.pentecost.lt

Belgium

Belgian Evangelical Mission (BEM)	www.b-e-m.org
Oasis Trust	www.oasisuk.org/world/countries/Belgium

Czech Republic

Canadian Baptist Ministries	www.cbmin.org
Brethren In Christ World Mission	www.bic-church.org/wm
Endowment Fund Nehemia	http://nehemia.cz
Trust Fund KMS	www.nfkms.cz

Denmark

Danish Missions Council (Network)	http://dmcdd.org

Eastern Europe—General; Agencies in more than one country

ActionOverseas (Apostolic Church)	www.actionoverseas.org
Action Partners (Pioneers)	www.pioneers-uk.org
Advancing Native Missions	www.adnamis.org/WorldwideMinistries.cfm?min_cont=Europe
AMEN	www.amentrust.co.uk
Baptist Union of Sweden	www.baptist.se
Breadline International breadlineinternational	www.redcliffe.org/
Christ for All	www.cfa.ch
Christ to the Nations	www.cttn.org
Christian Aid	www.christianaid.org
Christian Mission International Aid	http://cmiaid.org
Christians Abroad	www.cabroad.org.uk

Dovetales International Trust	www.users.globalnet.co.uk
Eastern Europe Mission (Hungary)	www.misszio.eu
East European Missions Network	www.eemn.org
Eastern Europe Outreach	www.easterneuropeoutreach.org
Eastern European Outreach	www.eeo.org
Eurovangelism/EuroAid	www.eurovangelism.org.uk
Free Church of Scotland International Missions Board	www.freechurch.org/missions/imb.htm
Frontline Missions International	www.frontlinemissions.info
Global Opportunities for Christ	www.goforchrist.org
God Will Make A Way	www.forgottenchildren.org
HeartCry Missionary Society	www.heartcrymissionary.com
Hope for the World	www.hftwministries.org
Hope International	www.hopeinternational.org
Hope International Missions (*FEA Ministries*)	http://feaministries.org/him/regions/europe.php
International Missions Alliance	www.missionalliance.org
Josiah Venture	www.josiahventure.com
LÄkarmissionen	www.lakarmissionen.se
Light in the East (*Licht im Osten*)	www.lio.org
Lightforce International	www.lightforce.org.uk
Mission Covenant Church of Sweden	www.missionskyrkan.se
Mission East	www.miseast.org
Mission Possible	www.mpusa.org
New Hope International	www.newhopeinternational.org
Oasis International Missions	http://oasisinternationalmissions.org
Open Bible International Ministries	www.openbible.org
Operation Blessing	www.ob.org
Partners in Mission	www.partnersinmission.org
Slavic Gospel Association	www.sga.org

Eastern Europe—Agencies Working Only in Specific Countries

Armenia

Armenian Gospel Mission   www.armeniangospelmission.org

Lithuania

Christian Relief Services   www.christianrelief.org
United Methodist Church in Sweden   www.metodistkyrkan.se

Moldova

Mission Direct   www.missiondirect.org

Romania

Christian Community Ministries   www.ccm-international.org
Christian Aid to Romania and Elsewhere
                                           www.care-online.org.uk
Cleaford Christian Trust   www.cleafordchristiantrust.org.uk
Eastern Europe Aid Association   www.genovieva.org
Heart of Hope Ministries International www.heartofhope.org
Life to Romania   www.life2romania.org
Link Romania   www.linkromania.co.uk
Operation Timothy   www.operationtimothy.net
Outstretched Hands of Romania   www.handsofromania.org
Robin Hood Ministries   www.robinhoodministries.org
Romanian Aid Fund   www.romaf.org
Romanian Missionary Society   www.rmsonline.org
Smile Alliance International   www.smilealliance.org
Star of Hope International   www.starofhope.org
Vision Beyond Borders   http://vbbonline.org

Russia

Christian World Missions	www.christianworldmissions.org
InterAct Ministries	www.interactministries.org
International Aid	www.internationalaid.org
Love Russia	www.loverussia.org
Micaiah Ministries	www.micaiah.org
MIR	http://mir-russia.com/en
Mission Russia	www.missionrussia.info
Mission2Russia	www.mission2russia.org
Odessa Mission	www.odessamission.com
Peter Deyneka Russian Ministries	www.russian-ministries.org
Relational Bridges International	http://relationalbridgesinternational.org
Russia Ministry Network	www.russiaministrynetwork.com
Russia4Christ Ministry	www.russia4christ.org
Russian Ministries	www.russian-ministries.org
World Missionary Evangelism	www.wme.org
World Outreach for Widows and Orphans	
	www.widowsoutreach.org

Slovakia

Breakthrough Global Missions	www.breakthroughgm.com

Ukraine

Christian Outreach International	www.coiusa.com
Guidelines International	www.guidelines.org
Hope Now	www.hopenow.org.uk
Lifeline Network International	www.lifelinenetwork.org
Mercy Trucks Ukraine	www.mercytrucksua.org
Mission To Ukraine	www.missiontoukraine.org

Ukraine Christian Ministries   www.ucm.org.uk

World Hope International—Canada   www.worldhope.ca

Finland

Evangelical Free Church of Finland   www.svk.fi

Fida International   www.fida.info/fi

Finnish Evangelical Alliance [SEA]   www.mesk.net

Finnish Evangelical Lutheran [SEKL]   www.sekl.fi

Finnish Evangelical Lutheran Mission(FELM)
                                      www.mission.fi

Finnish Lutheran Overseas Mission [FLOM]
                                      www.flom.fi

Finnish Mission Council (FMC)—Network
                                      www.lahetysneuvosto.fi/in_english

Lutheran Evangelical Assoc. of Finland (LEAF)
                                      http://vanhatsivut.sley.fi

Missionskyrkan (Georgia)   www.missionskyrkan.fi

Nokia Missio   www.nokiamissio.com

One Way Mission   www.onewaymission.fi

Patmos Lähetyssäätiö   www.patmos.fi/

Swedish Lutheran Evangelical Association of Finland (SLEF)
                                      www.slef.fi

France

Christian Brethren Assemblies   www.echoes.org.uk

France Mission   www.france-mission.org

Normandy Vision   www.normandyvision.org

SIM International   www.sim.org

Germany

Association of Evangelical Missions (AEM, Network)
                                        www.aem.de
Association of Pentecostal Charismatic Missions (APCM, Network)
                                        www.apcm.de
Association of German Protestant Churches
                                        www.mission.de, www.emv-d.de
German Missionary Fellowship   www.dmgint.de

Greece

AMG International   www.amginternational.org, www.amg.gr
Hellenic Ministries   www.hellenicministries.com
Torchbearers   www.kingfisherproject.org

Hungary

Christ is the Answer   www.citatoday.com
Christian Businessmen & Executive Society (KEVE)
                                        www.keve.org
NMJ Foundation   www.nmja.org
Refuge Foundation in Hungary   www.menedekalapitvany.hu
Sonflower Ministries (*Affiliate of Mustard Seed International*)
                                        www.sonflower.org

Iceland

Icelandic Mission Society   www.sik.is

Ireland

Calvary Mission, County Mayo   www.calvarymission.ie
Dublin Christian Mission   www.dcmlive.ie

Elim Ministries in Ireland — www.elim.ie

Irish Church Missions — www.icm-online.ie

Plumbline Ministries Ireland — http://plumbline.org.uk

The Haven, Cork — www.thehaven-cork.ie/index.html

Italy

Christ is the Answer — www.citaitaly.com

Netherlands

Evangelische Zendingsalliantie (Network, Evangelical Alliance Netherlands)
http://eza.nl

New Testament Missionary Union — www.ntmu.net

Norway

Areopagos — www.areopagos.org

Christian Network — www.kristent-nettverk.no

Norwegian Inner Mission Federation — www.imf.no

Norwegian Council for Mission and Evangelism (Network)
www.norme.no

Norwegian Lapp Mission — www.samemisjonen.no

Norwegian Lutheran Mission Association
www.nlm.no

Norwegian Mission Society — www.nms.no

Poland

Bible Mission Association—Wycliffe — www.bsm.org.pl

Euromission Poland — www.polska.euromission.org

Mission to the East — www.mnaw.org

Pilgrim Mission — www.pielgrzym.org

Polish Christian Ministries — www.pcmusa.org

Portugal

Abla Portugal   http://abla.org
Mevic   www.mevic.pt

Spain

Brethren In Christ World Mission   www.bic-church.org/wm
CAM International   www.caminternational.org
Free Presbyterian Mission Board UK   www.fpcmission.org
New Testament Missionary Union   http://www.ntmu.net/
South American Mission Society (SAMS)
                                       www.samsgb.org
Spanish Gospel Mission   www.spanish-gospel-mission.org.uk

Sweden

Agape Sweden [CCFC]   www.agapesverige.se
Evangelical Free Church   www.efk.se
Swedish Alliance Mission   www.alliansmissionen.se
Swedish Evangelical Mission   www.efs.nu
Swedish Mission Council (Network)   www.missioncouncil.se

Switzerland

Arbeitsgemeinschaft Evangelischer Missionen (Network, Association of the German
Protestant Missions, Switzerland)   www.aem.ch
Swiss Evangelical Alliance (Network)   www.each.ch
Swiss Portal for World Mission   www.mission.ch

United Kingdom

Amethyst (*Addicted women, children at risk, families*)
www.amethyst-inc.org

Brethren in Christ World Mission   www.bic-church.org/wm

Careforce   www.careforce.co.uk

Care for the Family   www.careforthefamily.org.uk

Church Action on Poverty   www.church-poverty.org.uk

Church Army   www.churcharmy.org.uk

Churches Together in Britain & Ireland (Network, *Assisting churches and agencies to participate in mission*)
www.ctbi.org.uk/CA/13

Congregational Federation   www.congregational.org.uk

Eden Network (*Urban ministry*)   www.eden-network.org

Evangelical Alliance   www.eauk.org

Free Presbyterian Mission Board UK   www.fpcmission.org

Full Gospel Business Men's Fellowship International
www.fgbmfi.org.uk

Global Connections (Network)   www.globalconnections.co.uk

Global Outreach Mission UK   www.missiongo.org

Latin Partners (*Supporting Latin Americans working in UK*)
www.latinpartners.org

Manna Society (*Homeless ministry*)   www.mannasociety.org.uk

Ministries Without Borders   www.ministrieswithoutborders.com

Mission Care (SE London, *Care homes*)   www.missioncare.org.uk

Mission for Christ (*Rural evangelism*)   www.missionforchrist.org.uk

Neighbours Worldwide (*WEC ministry to UK ethnic minorities*)
www.wec-int.org.uk/cms/neighbours

Oasis Trust   www.oasisuk.org/world/countries/
Belgium

On the Move UK (*Free barbeque ministry*)
www.onthemove.org.uk

Open Air Mission   www.oamission.com

Rural Ministries   www.ruralministries.org.uk
Share Jesus International   www.sharejesusinternational.com
Signpost International   www.signpost-international.org
Siloam Christian Ministries   www.siloam.org.uk
The Evangelization Society (TES)   www.tes.org.uk
Quest for Life (*Cruises*)   www.questforlife.co.uk
Urban Expression   www.urbanexpression.org.uk
Viz-a-Viz Ministries (*Helping churches communicate the gospel*)
                                   www.vizaviz.org.uk

Notes

1 Sergio Carrera and Sergio and Massimo Merlino, 'Undocumented Immigrants and Rights in the EU,' December 2009, 18 November 2010 <http://www.ceps.eu/ceps/download/2741>.

2 Martin Kreickenbaum, 'Who is Responsible for the Libyan Refugee Boat Tragedy?' 8 April 2009, 18 November 2010 <http://www.wsws.org/articles/2009/apr2009/liby-a08.shtml>.

3 'Britain's Secret Slaves,' Dispatches, Channel 4, London, England, 30 Aug. 2010.

4 Amnesty International, 'State of the World's Human Rights 2009,' 18 Nov. 2010 <http://report2009.amnesty.org/en/aggregator/sources/1>.

5 European Union Minorities and Discrimination Survey (EU-MIDIS), Data in Focus Report 1, Key Findings on the Roma by the European Union Agency for Fundamental Rights, 2009, 18 Nov. 2010 <http://fra.europa.eu/fraWebsite/attachments/EU-MIDIS_ROMA_EN.pdf>.

6 World Health Organization, 'HIV/AIDS,' 2010. 6 December 2010 <http://www.euro.who.int/en/what-we-do/health-topics/diseases-and-conditions/hivaids>

7 UNICEF, 'Blame and Banishment: The Underground HIV Epidemic Affecting Children in Eastern Europe and Central Asia,' 2010. <http://www.unicef.org/media/files/UNICEF_Blame_and_Banishment.pdf>; Mara Kardas-Nelson, 'HIV infections soar amongst Eastern European street youth,' 20 July 2010. 19 November 2010 <http://www.aidsmap.com/page/1492732>.

8 Ibid, p.7

9 Web4Health, 'Youth and Teen Suicide Statistics,' 31 July 2008, 22 Sept. 2010 <http://web4health.info/en/answers/bipolar-suicide-statistics.htm>.

10 The Camelot Foundation and Mental Health Foundation, 'Truth Hurts: Report of the National Inquiry into Self Harm among Young People,' 2006, 18 Nov. 2010 <http://www.mentalhealth.org.uk/campaigns/self-harm-inquiry>.

11 BBC Radio1 Newsbeat, 'Young People Self Harming With Sharp Objects Up 50%,' 12 March 2010, 18 Nov. 2010 <http://news.bbc.co.uk/newsbeat/hi/health/newsid_8563000/8563670.stm>.

12 Peter Anderson, Institute of Alcohol Studies, London, at the request of the European Commission, German Centre for Addiction Issues (DHS), Hamm: DH. Binge Drinking and Europe, 2008, 18 Nov. 2010 <http://www.dhs.de/makeit/cms/cms_upload/dhs/binge_drinking_report.pdf>.

13 The Telegraph, 'Britain is the "binge drinking capital of Europe," ' 22 April 2010, 18 Nov. 2010 <http://www.telegraph.co.uk/health/healthnews/7616405/Britain-is-the-binge-drinking-capital-of-Europe.html>.

14 TheSite.org, 'Binge Drinking,' 22 September 2010 <http://www.thesite.org/drinkanddrugs/drinking/problems/bingedrinking >.

15   European Monitoring Centre for Drugs and Drug Addiction, 18 Nov. 2010 < http://
      www.emcdda.europa.eu>.

16   Kids Alive International, 18 Nov.2010 <http://www.kidsalive.org/around-the-world/
      eastern-europe/romania>.

17   Cooper, Glenda (2004). "Romania's Blighted Street Children." BBC. http://news.
      bbc.co.uk/1/hi/world/europe/3665646.stm

18   Global Action for Children, Consortium for Street Children, 'Street Children Statis-
      tics,' January 2009, 18 Nov. 2010 <http://www.globalactionforchildren.org/page/-/
      Street%20Children%20Stats%20Jan%2009.doc>.

19   Ibid.

20   Wikipedia, 'Street Children,' 18 Nov. 2010 <http://en.wikipedia.org/wiki/Street_
      children>.

21   NSPCC, 'Young Runaways,' 18 Nov. 2010 <http://www.nspcc.org.uk/Inform/re
      search/statistics/young_runaways_statistics_wda48741.html>.

22   Global Action for Children, Consortium for Street Children, 'Street Children Statis-
      tics,' January 2009, 18 Nov. 2010 <http://www.globalactionforchildren.org/page/-/
      Street%20Children%20Stats%20Jan%2009.doc>.

23   Ibid, Spiegel Online, Aug. 14, 2008.

24   Ibid, Eastern European Outreach.

25   Ibid, WHO, Europe.

26   UNSCEAR Report, 'The Chernobyl Accident,' 2008, 18 Nov. 2010 <http://www.
      unscear.org/unscear/en/chernobyl.html>.

27   Sunday Times, 'Exposing Europe's guilty secret: the incarcerated children of Bul-
      garia,' 13 Feb. 2009, 18 Nov. 2010 <http://www.tbact.org>.

28   BBC News, 'Filming reveals Czech children still caged,' 15 Jan. 2008, 18 Nov. 2010
      <http://news.bbc.co.uk/1/hi/world/europe/7189556.stm>.

29   UNICEF, 'Child Trafficking,' 18 Nov. 2010 <http://www.unicef.org/protection/in
      dex_exploitation.html>.

30   Ibid.

31   European Union@United Nations, 'EU Commission cracks down on modern slav-
      ery and child sexual abuse,' 25 March 2009, 18 Nov. 2010 <http://www.europa-eu-
      un.org/articles/en/article_8600_en.htm>.

32   BBC Newsnight, 'Invisible Children,' 11 Sept. 2010, 18 Nov. 2010 <http://news.bbc.
      co.uk/1/hi/programmes/newsnight/8985967.stm>.

33   NSPCC, 'What About Us? Children's Rights in the European Union,' 2005, 18 Nov.
      2010   <http://www.nspcc.org.uk/Inform/policyandpublicaffairs/europe/whatabout
      us_wda48495.html>.

34   Save the Children, 2009/10, 18 Nov. 2010 <http://www.savethechildren.org.uk/en/
      docs/South_East_Europe_CB_2009.pdf>.

35   John Micklethwait and Adrian Wooldridge, God is Back, (Penguin Press), 2009

36   See <http://www.alpha.org>.